EXPLORING TŌHOKU

Jan Brown

EXPLORING TŌHOKU

A Guide to Japan's Back Country

with Yoko Sakakibara Kmetz

New York · WEATHERHILL · *Tokyo*

Grateful acknowledgment is made to Kodansha International Ltd. for permission to reprint excerpts from the following previously published materials:

A Haiku Journey: Basho's Narrow Road to a Far Province, translated by Dorothy Britton.

Chieko's Sky, by Kōtarō Takamura, translated by Soichi Furuta.

First edition, 1982

Published by John Weatherhill, Inc., of New York and Tokyo, with editorial offices at 7-6-13 Roppongi, Minato-ku, Tokyo 106, Japan. Protected by copyright under terms of the International Copyright Union; all rights reserved. Printed in Japan.

Library of Congress Cataloging in Publication Data: Jan Brown. / Exploring Tōhoku. / Includes index. / I. Tōhoku Region (Japan)—Description and travel —Guide-books. I. Kmetz, Yoko Sakakibara. II. Title. / DS'894.32.B76 1983 915.2'11 / 82-17467   ISBN 0-8348-0177-9

Table of Contents

Illustrations appear following page 22

Preface

THIS BOOK IS A TOOL. Through the research and experiences of other foreign visitors in the back country, your journey will hopefully be made easier and more rewarding. This guide is intended for the newcomer to Japan as well as for the experienced Japanophile. If you're new to traveling in Japan, you will be pleasantly surprised to see how far you can get and how much you can experience by substituting a bit of predeparture planning for language skills.

Since this guide is a tool for extracting the most from a back-country visit, be it for a few days or a few years, I have added brief bursts of historical background and other information to the place descriptions. The Japanese scholar will probably resent the brevity of these explanations, but I hope the majority of readers will find them useful in helping them to understand their back-country experiences.

Perhaps the greatest tool this book provides is the kanji (Chinese character) finding list, which Yoko and I thought essential to ease traveling woes for those English speakers who come to the back country in a sense deaf, dumb, and illiterate. The finding list includes every place name mentioned in the book from train lines to bus stops and museums. Use it to read maps, signs, and schedules, and when asking directions.

Where Japanese words have no precise equivalent in English, such as onsen, minshuku, kokuminshukusha, and ryokan, I have stuck with the Japanese. The four examples given here are discussed in detail in "Traveling in the Back Country." When you come to other such unfamiliar words or names in the text, you can find a definition in the glossary-index. The index will also help you locate such things as ski resorts and campgrounds. The appendices provide the dates of Japanese historical periods and a list of the principal Tōhoku festivals.

The names of historical figures who lived before the start of the Meiji era (1868) when Japan began its present course of Westernization are listed in the traditional order, family name first; others are given in Western order, family name last. Those readers who are familiar with Japanese may find such redundancies as Chūson-ji temple irritating (ji means temple), but these repetitions were intended to ease the journeys of newcomers.

On the other hand, newcomers may find strange such sentences as "The onsen are along Highway 112" and "The onsen has a large outdoor bath." Japanese nouns in their plural forms are, like our deer and sheep, identical with their singular forms.

Japanese vowels are pronounced much as they are in Italian. The a is pronounced as in father; e as in egg; i as in kin; o as in over; and u as in rude. Thus, for example, the Date clan's name does not rhyme with mate but with maté. Reminders (in the form of an accent grave) have been added to Datè and sakè for the sake of clarity.

A project such as this guide cannot be a solitary effort, especially when one begins not only deaf, dumb, and illiterate, but also ignorant in a new territory. Many people have lent a helping hand over the past four years.

At various times, travel companions Dave, Kazuyo, and Freddie Hatsuno; Renee Hill; Claire and Al Langevin; Henry, Elaine, and Rebecca Nathan; and Joe and Peggy Wall have eased the way and added insight and enjoyment to my explorations. Of course, my number one travel companion was my husband, John Brown. He has my love and gratitude for his countless good-natured kilometers spent on the road (far outnumbering the not-so-good-natured ones); his trudges up 2,000 stone steps to mountaintop temples on too many occasions; his viewing "one more" Jōmon pottery exhibit again and again; his moral support as I tried to get directions at police boxes for places the police officers didn't even realize were in their cities; his nights in business hotels with no fresh air and in tents with an overabundance of fresh air; and for his willingness to pioneer with me, knowing we'd hit some losers so that we could pick out the winners for other English-speaking travelers. And besides allowing me the luxury of writing a book in lieu of more lucrative endeavors, he also "volunteered" to draw the maps for the book.

Yoko and I also want to thank those who helped us on the home front. Aiko and Masaya Sakakibara must be first on the list. Yoko's parents were our walking encyclopedias of Japanese history and local pronunciations of place names. They opened doors to invaluable contacts when our curiosity led us in search of more and more information. We called them so often during our weekday morning maps-pamphlets-and-tea sessions that I feared they would change their phone number before we were through. We owe additional local thanks to Misawa Air Base's Mr. Fujimoto and JNR Misawa Station's Mr. Morita and Mr. Suzuki, who so patiently helped with travel arrangements over the years, and to Renee Hill for her photo contributions. And to John Brown and Louis and Kevin Kmetz, who put up with the scattered pieces of this project and demands on family time for so long. I'm sure the Kmetz family is thrilled to get their kitchen table back to normal, although I will really miss our snowbound research sessions around it.

We also are grateful to Weatherhill, who provided us two skilled and knowledgeable editors, fellow travelers, and Japanophiles in Ruth Stevens and Stephen Comee. And a special thanks to my parents, Marcia and Joe Cohn, for their encouragement to write, to Jean Pearce for the initial impetus for a "Footloose in Tōhoku," and to Elaine Nathan for her bilingual help in the initial stages.

And, of course, there is Yoko. A more sensitive, intelligent, patient, and good-natured bilingual partner can't be imagined. (Her knowledge of English is extraordinary. Towards the end of our three years together on this project, I finally ran across one word in English she didn't know—it was geyser.) What began as a haphazard, desperate gleaning of information for my own personal travels became a much more organized, complete, and professional effort than I had ever hoped for thanks to Yoko, whose friendship I will treasure always.

Without all these good people and others I have unintentionally overlooked, we could not have made this first effort in taking Tōhoku out of the black hole most travel guides have dumped it into and putting it closer to the position in the English-speaking traveler's itinerary it deserves. As John and I prepare now to leave our Tōhoku home to set up a new one in Hawaii, we envy your opportunity to explore Japan's back country. Enjoy!

JAN BROWN

Misawa City
July 1982

EXPLORING
TŌHOKU

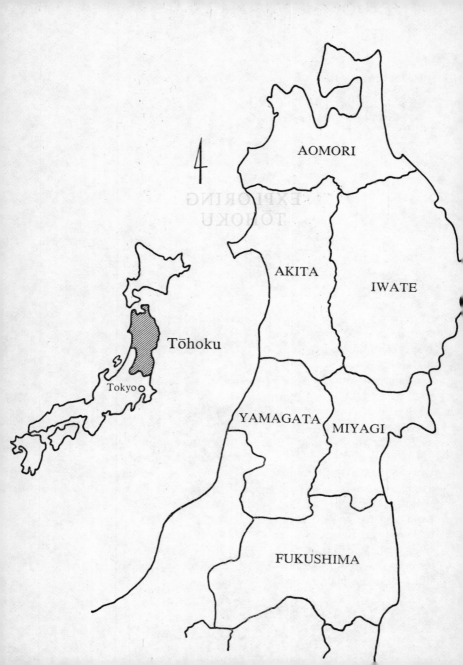

AOMORI

AKITA

IWATE

Tōhoku

Tokyo

YAMAGATA MIYAGI

FUKUSHIMA

4

EXPLORING
TŌHOKU

Introducing Tōhoku

> "Here am I, in the Second Year of Genroku (1689), suddenly taking it into my head to make a long journey to far, northern provinces. I might as well be going to the ends of the earth."
>
> *Matsuo Bashō*

SUCH WERE THE THOUGHTS of Japan's most famous haiku poet, Matsuo Bashō, as he began his five-month-long pilgrimage to what was then—and often still is—considered the back country of Japan.

Michinoku, meaning back roads, was what the northernmost part of Honshu, Japan's main island, was then called. Today, the six prefectures of northern Honshu—Fukushima, Miyagi, Iwate, Aomori, Akita, and Yamagata—are collectively known as Tōhoku, the Northeast, but the district's reputation as Japan's poor, struggling, rural back country persists. Three hundred years after Bashō's journey north, many people still think of Tōhoku as somewhere near the ends of the earth.

When I learned that the U.S. Air Force was sending my husband and me to northern Japan for several years, all I wanted to know was how far our new home was from Tokyo and how often we could afford to get there. Now, after five years as a resident of Aomori Prefecture, as far north as you can get and still be on the main island, my stomach flips when I remember

3

that I had left Japan once before, after five busy years of exploring the country, thinking I pretty well knew Japan, both old and new. Of course, I had never considered visiting Tōhoku, because apparently there was nothing there to see. No Japanese ever suggested that I look upon Japan's back country otherwise, and I could find next to nothing in English to tell me otherwise.

So I am now telling you, the English-speaking visitor to Japan, that Tōhoku is most definitely otherwise.

Exploring the six prefectures of northern Honshu is a delightful immersion into old rural and feudal Japan. You can discover the district's traditional life style lying sometimes out in clear view and at other times just beneath a translucent varnish of Westernization. Coming to Tōhoku is also a journey into the beautifully varied geography of an unspoiled and unpolluted Japan.

You'll see rustic fishing villages precariously sandwiched between steep mountainsides and the sea and thatched-roof farming communities nestled into narrow, winding valleys. You'll see lakes, mountains, gorges, spectacular coastlines, and outdoor hot-spring baths along forested river banks. You'll visit pleasant, medium-sized, modern cities with winding streets, stone foundations, and moats left over from their feudal castle-town days. In these cities you'll visit folk museums filled with items from a traditional, un-Westernized Japan, and then you'll pass through neighboring rural communities where many of the same items are still in use. You'll see the elegant homes of feudal-era samurai and the thick-walled mud storehouses of the old merchant class. In short, the back country may be the Japan you had imagined you'd see before you arrived in Tokyo, a Japan you had since given up hope of ever finding.

You'll find the people of Tōhoku different from those in the more Westernized areas of Japan. Most people here live in multi-generational homes rather than in tiny three-room apartments. Many wear traditional work clothes that are seen elsewhere only in folk museums. These country people gawk at a Tokyo-style fashion plate walking down their streets just as Tokyoites stare at the occasional visiting farmer in ballooned pants, billowy sleeved work coat, and rubber boots. Women in Tōhoku have wardrobes of kimono for all occasions just like Tokyo women have closets full of Western-style dresses.

And you'll hear a variety of local dialects as you travel in the back country, quirks of speech developed from generations spent in isolated mountain valleys or by a local daimyo's edict as a defense against infiltration by neighboring clans' spies. These Tōhoku dialects are nearly as baffling to native speakers from outside the district as they are to you.

Bashō came only as far north as the southwest corner of Akita; he missed the entire top half of Tōhoku. But, for his time, entering even that far into the wilds of Japan's northern frontier was quite an extraordinary adventure. Today, you can easily visit all six of Tōhoku's prefectures by modern roads and railways; yet, due to prevailing prejudices about the back country, you may get the impression that you're still planning quite an extraordinary adventure. Tōhoku is not yet considered a "normal" tourist destination.

When the Japanese tourists do come, they usually make quick bus tours through Tōhoku's national parks, lingering perhaps in one or two of its wonderfully relaxing hot-spring resorts, and then they leave the back country—awed by its mountains, coastlines, lakes, rivers, and forests, and amused by the strong accents, traditional grab, and lack of worldly sophistication of the local residents.

And because this snobbish disregard for the rural back country has been carried over into English-language guides, the foreign visitor to Japan has had a tough time finding out much about Tōhoku. The guides tend to give the impression that some sort of large, black void separates the city of Sendai, the last point of civilization on Honshu, and the shores of Hokkaido, Japan's northern frontier, where civilization once again resumes. One writer, forced to admit that the Hokkaido-bound traveler must get off the train from Tokyo to board a ferry in a place called Aomori City, said something like, "You'll probably have to rush from the train to catch the next ferry, but that's fine since there isn't much of interest here anyway."

On the contrary, the fact is that Tōhoku, Japan's back country, is one of the few places left where the visitor can actually explore refreshing remnants of a pre-Westernized, rural Japanese life style. Tōhoku is indeed a worthwhile and unique destination.

The first-time visitor to Japan is usually surprised upon arrival in Tokyo to find an urban giant, an international, cosmopolitan, and fantastically diverse city, but a city having difficulty holding onto its Japaneseness. Then the traveler goes to Kyoto to discover "old Japan." There he or she finds a magic oasis of twelve centuries of preserved villas of emperors and shoguns and a fabulous storehouse of Japanese high culture. And the visitor goes home, satisfied that he or she has seen Japan, old and new.

But old Japan was more than royal estates and grand temples. The backbone of the country has always been its hardworking farmers, fishers, merchants, and craftspeople in small settlements that developed anywhere the island nation's mountainous terrain permitted. These common people in Japan's past were ruled by daimyo, local feudal lords, who, backed by a skilled samurai warrior class, governed their clans' holdings as more or less independent units. Localized religions, legends, and life styles were slow to be influenced by the southern cultural and political centers. This is the back country's "old Japan."

Bashō came north in 1689 to capture a sense of continuity with the poets and pilgrims of previous generations who had had the curiosity and the courage to venture into Japan's exotic back country. He kept a journal of his travels in which he wrote haiku, succinct seventeen-syllable verses, about the places he saw;

some of these are now Japan's best known poems. You may want to take along Dorothy Britton's paperback translation of this jounal, *A Haiku Journey: Bashō's Narrow Road to a Far Province,* to add perspective to your own twentieth-century journey north.

Although most of the narrow roads Bashō covered on foot and at times by horse or mule have now been replaced by highways and train lines, some modern Japanese travelers continue to follow Bashō's now not-so-narrow roads north for the same reason he did—to experience a sense of continuity with their rural past, a past harder and harder to recall in the southern urban centers where most Japanese now live. The foreigner who has come to Japan to find out what makes it unique from anywhere else in the world will also want to come north to explore this other facet of old Japan.

But no one likes being the poor relation; the back country is struggling to catch up with the modern nation's industrial prosperity. And with each step it takes towards this new life style, more of old, rural Japan permanently fades away.

You'll find traveling in Tōhoku a different sort of experience. There is no Tokyo-style shoving in the small of the back here since the district has relatively small populations of both residents and tourists. The main tourist attractions do get crowded by Tōhoku standards during the first week in May (Golden Week, when there are three national holidays just as the northern cherry trees bloom) and in July, August, and October, but they will be nearly deserted any other time of the year. Unless you ski, though, the snowy north may hold little appeal between December and March.

Yet even in the peak tourist season, you can easily find solitude along the unpolluted beaches of the rugged Pacific Coast, quiet Mutsu Bay, and the placid Sea of Japan, and in out-of-the-way places in the back country's beautiful mountain forests.

The fact that public transportation in this sparsely populated region doesn't need to run every few minutes—and in fact may run as infrequently as once a day—may be a real irritant to someone used to Tokyo's Yamanote loop, but, if you plan ahead, you can reach all of Tōhoku except for the most remote mountain onsen by train or bus.

And Tōhoku is one of the best places in Japan to see by car. Driving here is a real pleasure compared with the Tokyo-style ordeals requiring patience and strong nerves you may be used to. The back-country driving pace is leisurely, and the roads are generally good, well-marked (but in kanji only), and, best of all, nearly empty except in Tōhoku's handful of "big" cities.

Tōhoku and the other rare pockets of traditional, rural Japan are what the rest of the country used to be, while the metropolitan centers of southern Honshu are what these "backward" regions will someday become. When you come to Tōhoku, you leave behind many of the conveniences of travel in Westernized Japan. You'll have to give up such luxuries as international-class hotels, English-speaking aid, bacon and eggs just the way you like them, and rapid public transportation.

But you'll gain so much more than you'll give up. Your efforts to discover the historical and scenic attractions of Honshu's unfairly ignored northern district will be rewarded many, many times over. You will be glad you came north to explore Japan's back country.

Traveling in the Back Country

THE BACK COUNTRY is much more Japanese than the Japan most foreign visitors see, and you'll have to compensate for the lack of familiar language and amenities. But with good pre-trip planning, you'll have a wonderful time.

The people of the back country will be flattered that you thought enough of their of the world to come by and will help you all they can; yet that help is not likely to come in English. Tokyo's mania to learn English has not penetrated very deeply in the north. You won't find well-dressed businessmen and enthusiastic college students eager to practice their English with the lost foreigner around every corner. In fact, in some places, you'll be the first foreigner to wander through in a long, long time. It's exciting to be so special, but it puts the responsibility for adapting on you rather than on your hosts.

Unless you speak some Japanese and are willing to tackle the local dialects (talk to the TV generation, not the older folks), you'll need, first of all, to adapt to your lack of communication skills. The key to a pleasant and fulfilling trip to the back country, the key to seeing what you want with a minimum of complications, is to make thorough plans where you can still do so in English. In other words, you need to gather information for your trip before you come north.

9

If you're coming from Tokyo, get all your maps, bus, boat, and train schedules, and reservations there. Even if you balk at the structure of a set itinerary, collect the information you'll need in Tokyo so you can be "spontaneous" up north without spending four hours sitting in a country train station because you didn't know only three trains come through a day. You'll find no schedules (or prices) in this guide because change comes even in the back country, and thus no outdated schedules from this source will ruin your plans.

In Tokyo the best source of travel information in English is the Japan National Tourist Organization's (JNTO) Tourist Information Center (TIC). You can get all sorts of free travel aid including maps and brochures at their office near Yurakucho Station (tel. 502-1461). Then you can make your reservations and order the current schedules you'll need at a Tokyo Japan Travel Bureau (JTB) office. The Tokyo TIC also has a Travel Phone service if you need assistance while you're on the road. Dial 106 on a yellow or blue public telephone and say, "collect call, TIC." If you call between 9 a.m. and 5 p.m. any weekday, the operator can put you through to the TIC's helpful English-speaking staff.

You'll find the people of Tōhoku curious about and surprised at seeing a foreign face in their midsts, but they will be friendly in a shy, hesitant sort of way. Every foreigner in Tōhoku has his or her collection of personal experiences to demonstrate the kindness of the back country. They tell of people pressing small gifts upon them to express a languageless welcome, of people going far out of their way to take the lost traveler to his or her destination when directions weren't understood, of farm women cautiously touching the soft blond or curly black hair of a foreign child, and of rural school children's curious stares and nervous giggles turning into friendly smiles and a textbook "Hello, how are you?" once eye contact was made. You, too, will return from the back country with your own special memories of the people you'll meet.

PLANNING YOUR ITINERARY is essential. Read this guide before you come north, select what you want most to see, and then obtain the schedules and reservations you'll need to complete your plans.

I have not suggested a set itinerary since, besides sharing a language, English-speaking back-country visitors are a diverse lot. Some are visiting Japan for only a short time and can stay in the back country just long enough for a brief introduction. They come seeking its historical sites, local crafts, and traditional, rural scenes. Others are long-term residents of Japan who come north to escape the summer heat of the crowded cities. They come to enjoy Tōhoku's unspoiled and uncrowded mountains, lakes, and beaches.

And then there is Tōhoku's foreign community. These people are often here for years rather than days or weeks. They have many, many weekends and vacations ahead to spend either wishing they were somewhere else or getting acquainted with their temporary home. Tōhoku's greatest concentration of foreign residents is U.S.-military-connected population—numbering in the thousands—living in Aomori Prefecture's Misawa City. Because so many of them own cars and have a lot of enthusiasm for but not much information on their new surroundings, the Aomori section is the most detailed of the book. Out-of-the way places throughout the district are also covered for Tōhoku's other scattered foreign residents.

Your itinerary is your own decision based on your interests and time limitations, but maybe the following information will help you to make some tough choices: Japanese tourists come north mostly to visit Fukushima's Bandai–Asahi National Park; Miyagi's Matsushima Bay; Iwate's seaside Rikuchū Kaigan National Park; Lake Towada on the Aomori–Akita border; and Akita's Oga Peninsula. They come to sample Tōhoku's fantastic natural scenery and to relax in its famous hot-spring resorts. They also flock to the back country in early August for Tōhoku's Big

Three summer festivals held in the cities of Sendai, Aomori, and Akita.

The places that have a lot to share with the foreign visitor trying to discover Japan's rural and feudal past are Fukushima's Aizu-Wakamatsu and Kitakata; Iwate's Tōno, Morioka, and Hiraizumi; Aomori's Hakkōdas and Osore-zan; Akita's Kakunodate and Hanawa; and Yamagata's Tsuruoka and Yamadera.

If you're vacationing in Japan and have had little travel experience here, the easiest way to explore the back country is to take the Tōhoku Shinkansen (Bullet Train) to Kōriyama and a connecting train to Aizu-Wakamatsu; then take the Shinkansen again to Sendai to see Matsushima Bay, and then once more to Morioka. In all of these cities, you can easily find Western-style hotels and food and can take efficient Japanese-language bus tours for an whirlwind but hassle-free glimpse of the back country. With more time, include do-it-yourself side trips to Iwate's Hiraizumi and Yamagata's Yamadera and a trip to the top of the island on the Tōhoku Main Line from Morioka to see Aomori City and its nearby Hakkōda Mountains and Lake Towada.

With detours and alternatives here and there, the book generally follows the Tōhoku Main Line and Highway 4, the main transportation arteries connecting the back country and the rest of the island via Tokyo, as they head north to Aomori City. At Aomori City, the Tōhoku Main Line connects with the Ōu Main Line, a second major artery, which covers Tōhoku's west side. The book then more or less follows the Ōu Main Line as it heads south from Aomori City until it rejoins the Tōhoku Main Line at Fukushima City in the center of Tōhoku's southernmost prefecture. The speedy Tōhoku Expressway and Tōhoku Shinkansen follow the Tōhoku Main Line and Highway 4 part of the way up, and other train lines and highways cover almost every other part of the district.

A final word of advice in planning your itinerary concerns those who are coming any time other than July through Octbeor.

Tōhoku's tourist season is short. Since visitors aren't that numerous, many tourist services can't afford to remain in operation throughout the year. Therefore, you need to check dates of operation when you get your schedules, especially for tour buses and boats. Many campgrounds and some inns on less-traveled routes close during the off-season.

GETTING AROUND is part of the adventure. When you get your bus, train, and boat schedules from JTB, they will, of course, be in kanji. Buy a highlighter pen and highlight and romanize (using this book's kanji finding list) the information you'll need on the trip.

If you're coming by public transportation, buy a few inexpensive "mini-mini guides" at a Japanese bookstore. These tiny paperback travel guides are in Japanese, but they contain a good set of local maps that make them a worthwhile investment for your trip. Romanize and highlight the page headings and map locations you'll be visiting. You'll be surprised at how familiar the strange-looking Chinese characters become as you work with them in preparing for your trip. For a quick trip, you'll need only mini-mini guide number 18, on Tōhoku. Other useful volumes are number 17, on Fukushima; 54, Miyagi; 56, Iwate; 13, Aomori; 49, Akita; and 34, Yamagata.

Tōhoku drivers need to get the Buyōdō Company's Tōhoku map, number D-8, also available in Japanese bookstores. Mercifully, Buyōdō has romanized the major cities and provided a legend in English. It is by far the best map of the district and opens in convenient sections. When you get into a city, it is also a good idea to stop at its travel information center, usually in or near the train station, to ask for a free city tourist map (kankō mappu).

A mistaken notion English-speaking people have is that they must find a map in English since they can't read kanji. You don't have to "read" kanji to read a Japanese map, but you will have to recognize place names on road signs, buildings, ticket windows, and schedules—and they will all be in kanji. This is one reason we considered it essential to include a detailed kanji finding list with this guide. The other reason is that asking directions is much easier when you can point to the written place name, because our foreign accents tend to massacre the language and some older people in the back country either can't read or feel uncomfortable reading roman letters. Contrary to what some might think, there's no shame in standing under a sign matching the legs and hats of its Chinese characters with those on your map or finding list.

If you do get turned around or just need reassurance that you're on the right trail, stop at a small neighborhood grocery store or police box for directions. Don't feel shy; the Japanese travelers regularly do the same. In a crime-free country like Japan, the neighborhood police spend a good deal of their time on duty acting as helpful guides for lost visitors. They have detailed listings and street maps for their areas and are usually very willing to help out. The police boxes near train stations are particularly well prepared to handle out-of-towners' requests for directions to their city's tourist attractions. If they don't know, they will often call your destination for you to get directions.

Of course, your directions will be in Japanese, so watch the hands for clues on which way to go and stay alert for such words as: migi (right), hidari (left), massugu (straight), and shingō (traffic signals). Ask "nampun?" (how many minutes) or "nan kilo?" (how many kilometers) it is from here. With your kanji finding list in hand, you should also be able to pick out the signs for tourist spots as you get close. And don't despair—they haven't lost a foreigner in Tōhoku yet.

STAYING OVER can be one of the best parts of your adventure, for Tōhoku is a wonderful place to experience the traditional Japanese food and bedding that comes with staying "Japanese-style." In some places in the back country, this will be your only alternative.

When you stay Japanese style, you'll get a charming tatami-matted room, almost always without private toilet or bath. At night, the futon, or comfortable cotton and nowadays polyester-filled mattresses, are laid on the mats. You may also get a buckwheat-hull-filled pillow for which you can substitute a folded zabuton, or cushion, if your neck hurts just to look at it.

You will sometimes need your own towel and soap, but you will always be issued a crisp, clean yukata, a lightweight cotton kimono, to use for both lounging and sleeping. Except in city hotels, you can wear your yukata throughout the building, and in some resort areas you can even walk around town in it.

You'll be served two Japanese-style meals—a multidish dinner based on fish, vegetables, pickles, any local specialties, and, naturally, rice and soup, and a similar, but much more modest breakfast. If you tend to have withdrawl symptoms without it, bring along instant coffee, since all Japanese-style and many Western-style accommodations provide pots of hot water and cups for green tea. It would be a shame to leave Japan without spending at least one night in this traditional manner, with or without teacups of instant coffee.

If you're coming north during Golden Week in early May, between mid-July and mid-August when the Japanese schools are out, or in October when the Tōhoku forests turn into postcards of brilliant colors, come with reservations. You'll need to book especially far in advance if you'll be here during the eight-day period beginning on August 1st. This is when three of the nation's biggest festivals join with Tōhoku's cool summer to lure several million visitors north for one crowd-filled week. At other times, if you have your heart set on staying at a certain inn or hotel or don't like to start searching for a room at the end of a full day of sightseeing, make reservations. Most Tōhoku accommodations are on the small side, and it may take only one busload of tourists to fill up an entire hotel.

If you want to stay strictly Western-style, both major hot-spring resorts and the big cities have tourist hotels (kankō hoteru), Tokyo-priced modern hotels with Western beds, private baths, and usually a Western dining room. The cities also have what the Japanese call business hotels. These inexpensive, Western-style establishments cater to traveling businessmen and tourists who want only a clean, reasonably priced, and comfortable night's rest without the frills of a tourist hotel. You'll get an extremely compact room and a fascinatingly engineered private bathroom just a bit larger than a normal-sized bathtub.

Japan's youth hostels, affiliated with the international youth hostel network, are also Western style and very inexpensive. Although you don't have to be a youth to use them, you do have to be a member of a youth hostel association to stay in some and you'll probably have to stay in barracks-style rooms segregated by sex, not a lot of fun for traveling couples. The Tokyo TIC has free youth hostel brochures in English, and this guide also notes youth hostel locations. In Tokyo, Japan Youth Hostels, Inc. can be reached by phone at (03) 269–5831.

Tōhoku has campgrounds in some fantastically beautiful spots for those travelers who are on a real budget or who just love being outdoors; they, too, are mentioned in the text. Facilities offered by Tōhoku campgrounds vary widely; some rent bungalows and futon, and others, tents and sleeping bags. Some offer only a cleared piece of ground and running water. If you're going to need rental equipment as you go along, check which camps you can use and their dates of operation with the Tokyo TIC. Off-season, you can usually still set up a tent in a closed campground, but you won't have any running water or electricity.

Japanese-style accommodations come in several options. You can stay in luxury at tourist hotels with Japanese-style rooms and in ryokan, traditional Japanese inns. Or you can experience a night of Japanese-style living at more reasonable prices in min-shuku, family-run bed and board operations, and at the government-sponsored lodges known as kokuminshukusha in the national parks and other scenic areas.

When you are making your reservations, note that distinctions can get confusing because some "hotels" have all or some Japanese-style rooms, usually at higher prices than their Western rooms, and some ryokan are multistoried modern structures with Japanese-style rooms, not the charming, old-fashioned, small inns the term conjures up. The kokuminshukusha are not uniform either. Some are run by prefectural governments, some by local governments, and others by private firms who have met certain standards. Although they range from peeling-paint-and-dusty-corners basic to absolutely terrific, I have tried to footnote them all so you can take advantage of their very reasonable rates, just over half that of the lowest-priced rooms at a ryokan or tourist hotel. I have also footnoted a few more expensive ryokan and hotels that have qualities that make them worth the additional expense.

In spite of exceptions you might run across, ryokan are usually small inns with the special atmosphere and service of old Japan. Many have rooms overlooking tiny, Japanese-style gardens and all have refreshing hot baths (in some locations with natural onsen water) and gourmet dinners and breakfasts served in your room. Meals in ryokan are much more elaborate than those in other types of Japanese-style accommodations. You'll get an array of tiny, odd-shaped dishes filled with strange-looking and great-tasting concoctions and crowded onto one or two lacquer trays. Sometime you'll even recognize an oval "Western plate" among the delicacies on your tray such as fried chicken with salad and spaghetti. Ryokan are really very special places, and, for an occasional treat, they are worth their high prices.

Minshuku are like no-frills mini-ryokan run by families who often live in adjoining quarters. In some cases, the minshuku is no more than a spare room in someone's house. Meals, atmosphere, and other amentities are much more humble than a ryokan's, but prices are much lower and you'll feel more like you're staying in a Japanese home than in a commercial establishment. You'll share the family's bath and toilet facilities and sometimes even the family dinner table. Minshuku can be found in almost any community, large or small.

As mentioned above, the best bargains for travelers who want a no-frills Japanese-style experience at a reasonable price, plus the privacy of a hotel room, are the kokuminshukusha. They look like hotels, but have the rooms and meals of a ryokan. They cut costs by asking you to take down your own futon from the room's closet and to eat your meals in a dining room during certain hours usually at a table bearing your room number.

Kokuminshukusha are located outside cities in places people come to enjoy nature. The series of kokuminshukusha along Iwate's Rikuchū Kaigan coastline are outstanding, both in the accommodations themselves and in their beautiful ocean-view locations. If you want to try this type of Japanese-style living for only one night, do it at one of Rikuchū Kaigan's lodges.

Because kokuminshukusha offer so much for a low price, they are booked solid in the peak tourist seasons. So if you want to stay in a kokuminshukusha during those times, plan ahead.

Akin to the kokuminshukusha are the kokumin kyūka mura, national vacation villages. Each Tōhoku prefecture has one of these vacation villages in a national or quasi-national park, and each of them has a lodge, a campground, and a variety of recreational facilities such as walking trails, tennis courts, and boats. The government also sponsors seishōnen ryokō mura, youth travel villages, similar to the vacation villages but on a much more modest scale. They are located in more remote natural settings and sometimes provide only camping facilities.

Mention must also be made of Tōhoku's onsen, the hot-spring resorts which dot the district's volcanic mountainsides. I have chosen to refer to such places by their Japanese term in the text, because the English-language connotations of "resort" and "spa" are misleading for most Tōhoku onsen, although a few are indeed luxury resorts.

The Japanese have been bathing in their natural hot springs for centuries. In the old days, people would hike up the mountainsides to the water sources, carrying on their backs enough rice to last them for several weeks. They would build temporary shelters out of wood and brush and spend their vacations soaking in the therapeutic waters before descending back down the mountain.

Today's onsen now occupy such sites—and the Japanese people still flock to them to cure such ailments as rheumatism and stomach problems and just to relax or socialize. Modern-day onsen range from entire towns of streets lined with one multistoried hotel after another to lonely wooden, thatched-roof inns in otherwise undisturbed mountain forests.

Some onsen have small "family baths" where your party can bathe together in privacy; others have sex-segregated, communal baths; and some remote mountain onsen still have mixed, communal bathing. If you have never tried it before, be assured that communal bathing is a very relaxing experience. The tiny Japanese towel provides an unbelievable amount of modesty, and bathing with other clean bodies (the washing is done beforehand, outside the bath) has to be much more aesthetically appealing than sitting in your own soapy scum. There are hundreds of onsen of all types all over the back country; you should experience one of the more traditional ones as part of your back-country adventure.

A FINAL NOTE on traveling in the back country has to do with my own reservations about introducing it to a diverse lot of curious foreigners. I'm torn between wanting to share this wonderful slice of old, rural Japan with the rest of the world and the desire to protect the back-country people from that world. I'd like to think that every foreign visitor will approach the back country with empathy for its people and respect for their traditional way of life.

I worry that rural people who have not traveled much might misinterpret a well-intentioned camera trying to capture them working in their traditional garb or standing before their tumble-down thatched-roof home. Similarly, people at places of worship should be able to clap their hands together in prayer without a camera in their faces. Without a telephoto lens, some scenes are better recorded only in one's memory.

It helps to keep things in perspective if you imagine yourself in your hometown, in your church, or in front of your house meeting up with camera-clicking strangers who don't speak or read English and who don't appear used to your customs. Yet they want to observe how you live, and they'll need to stay in the local motel, to eat in the local coffee shop, and to ask directions of the local people. It is asking a lot of you to accommodate them—and no matter how pleased you are that they came, you can't help but feel relieved when they go. This is what we're doing to the people of the back country. And it is amazing how well they cope and how nice they are about complying with our demands on them.

One of my favorite back-country experiencies occurred when my husband and I had to ask directions of a farm laborer at work in a rice paddy in the middle of Akita Prefecture. We were looking for the Naraoka Pottery Kiln in the tiny hamlet of Minami-Naraoka and had become completely disoriented on Akita's look-alike, narrow farm roads separating endless fields of rice.

Shocked to see two gaijin (foreigners) and a Ford Mustang on the edge of her rice paddy, the woman, only her eyes showing from under layers of light, white cotton cloths protecting her head and face from the sun, overcame her surprise enough to point in the direction from which we had come.

After a series of slow, careful maneuvers on the narrow, ditch-lined road, the car was finally pointed in the opposite direction, and we turned around to thank her.

"Oh, no," her hands and eyes told us. "On second thought, Minami-Naraoka is the other way."

The three of us broke into simultaneous laughter at the thought of getting the car turned around once more, laughter that instantaneously and completely shattered the uncomfortable language and cultural barriers between our worlds. As we started off once again, the farm woman, still holding her sickle, stood in the middle of the road waving goodbye with both hands high in the air and yelling Japanese wishes for a safe trip as loudly as she could.

We waved until we could no longer distinguish each other's arms in the distance. She then returned to weeding her Akita rice paddy and we to our travels.

It was really a small incident, but one that still comes immediately to mind when anyone asks what the back country is like. I'd like to think that the Akita farm woman, too, has not forgotten the August day in 1978 when the gaijin appeared out of nowhere and interrupted her work—nor the languageless spark of friendship that passed between us.

Traveling off Japan's usual tourist trails may seem like a difficult undertaking. Granted, it's not as easy as boarding a tour bus, but it sure increases your chances of really experiencing a different culture—and of collecting some very special memories.

FUKUSHIMA

1. A statue of Matsuo Bashō, the poet whose poems inspired the author to make her own trek through the back country, near Yamadera, in neighboring Yamagata Prefecture.

2. The Byakkotai graves on Iimoriyama, in Aizu-Wakamatsu; see pp. 43–46.

3. *A traditional kura, in Kitakata;* see pp. 50-54.

4. *A display showing how people lived in a minka, in the Minzoku-kan, near Lake Inawashiro;* see p. 57.

5. A group of kokeshi dolls from the author's collection.

MIYAGI

6. A Miyagi kokeshi maker, or kijishi, at work; see pp. 63-64.

7. *A view of Matsushima, showing the Godai-dō;* *see p. 84.*
Courtesy of the Miyagi Prefecture Tourist Office.

8. *The Tanabata Festival, in Sendai;* *see pp. 78-79.*
Courtesy of the Miyagi Prefecture Tourist Office.

9. A view of Tōno rice paddies, irrigated by a water wheel; see pp. 128-29.

10. Obaasan Kitakawa, sitting on the verandah of the family minka; see pp, 134-135.

11. Participants competing in a wanko-soba-eating contest, in Morioka; see p. 122.

12. *The Matsukaze Sekizen sakè factory, in Hanawa;* see *p. 149.*

13. *The Hara Takashi Museum, in Morioka;* see *p. 121.*

14. A Nambu-tetsubin tea kettle, decorated with a stylized wave motif; see pp. 121-22. Courtesy of the Hashimoto Art Museum, Morioka.

15. A small temple dedicated to Bishamonten, built in a cave called Takkoku-no-Iwaya, near Hiraizumi; see p. 104.

16-17. *The Japanese-style exterior and Western-style interior of the Shayōkan, in Kanagi;* see *pp. 226-29. Courtesy of the Shayōkan.*

18. The monument dedicated to Corporal Gotō, in the Hakkodas; see pp. 201-2.

19. According to local tradition, the large white crosses mark the graves of Jesus Christ and his brother, in Shingō; see pp. 162-63

20. A straw guardian-deity protecting the entrance to a small hamlet, near Towada-ko-machi.

21. Komaki Onsen, in Saigyodo Park; see pp. 174-76.

*22. A view of Osore-zan, where spirits of the departed
can be contacted through mediums;* see *pp. 179-82.*

23. The beechwood bath at Tsuta Onsen;
see *pp. 205-6. Courtesy of Tsuta Onsen.*

AKITA

25. *The Namahage Festival, in Oga; see p. 247.*
Courtesy of the Akita Prefecture Tourist Office.

26. *The Kamakura Festival, in Yokote; see p. 267. Courtesy of the Akita Prefecture Tourist Office.*

◄ 24. *The Kantō Festival, in Akita City; see pp. 257–58. Courtesy of the Akita Prefecture Tourist Office.*

27. The Chidōkan museum, in Tsuruoka; *see p. 284.*

28. The Japanese-style building housing the Sakai family possessions, part of the Chidōkan; *see p. 284.*

29. Lake Okama, a crater lake in Zaō Quasi-National Park; see p. 303.

30. The main gate (sanmon) at the foot of Yamadera; see pp. 299–301.

31. A view of the garden and teahouse at the
Homma Art Museum, in Sakata; see pp. 279–80.

32. The Yamagata City Saiseikan museum; see p. 297.

FUKUSHIMA PREFECTURE

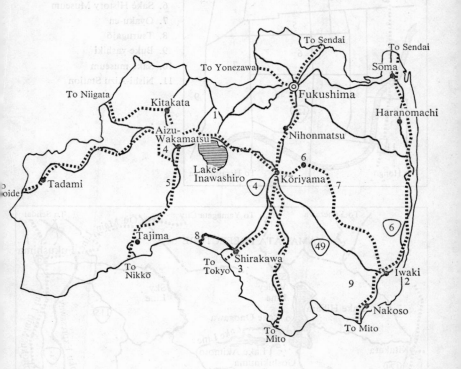

To Sendai

To Sendai

Sōma

To Yonezawa

Fukushima

To Niigata

Kitakata

Haranomachi

Aizu-
Wakamatsu

Nihonmatsu

4

6

Lake
Inawashiro

Kōriyama

7

Ōide

Tadami

5

4

6

Tajima

8

49

To
Nikkō

To
Tokyo

Shirakawa

3

Iwaki

2

9

Nakoso

To
Mito

To Mito

1. Bandai–Asahi National Park
2. Iwaki Kaigan
3. Shirakawa Barrier
4. Hongō
5. Ōuchijuku

6. Miharu
7. Abukuma and Irimizu Caverns
8. Nasukashi Toll Road
9. Jōban-Yunodake Panorama Line

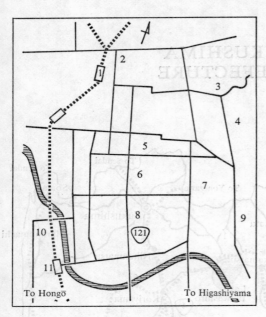

AIZU-WAKAMATSU

1. Aizu-Wakamatsu Station
2. Aizu History Museum
3. Old Takinosawa Gohonjin
4. Iimoriyama
5. Wappameshi Takino
6. Sakè History Museum
7. Oyaku-en
8. Tsurugajō
9. Buke-yashiki
10. Sakè museum
11. Nishi-Aizu Station

To Hongō   To Higashiyama

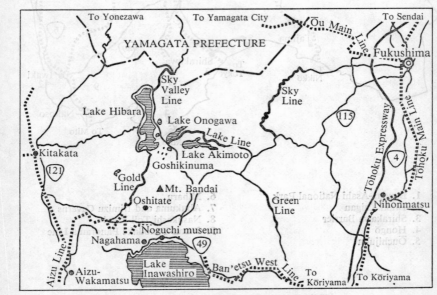

BANDAI–ASAHI NATIONAL PARK

Introducing Fukushima

IT WAS NOT UNTIL we finally reached the checkpoint at Shirakawa that we felt we were really on our way at last." Such were the thoughts of Japan's most famous haiku poet, Matsuo Bashō, as he crossed into what is now Fukushima Prefecture on his journey north in 1689. He entered the back country via one of the three main routes—each one once guarded by a fortified barrier checkpoint—used by travelers to the north since the eighth century. Nezu, the ancient barrier on the Sea of Japan, is now on the Yamagata–Niigata border. The other two barriers, Shirakawa in the eastern inland countryside and Nakoso on the Pacific Coast, now separate Tōhoku's southernmost prefecture, Fukushima, from the rest of the main island.

Although no border guards remain to check their entry papers, most present-day visitors to the back country still come through Shirakawa. They zoom past the ancient checkpoint on the Tōhoku Expressway or on the new Tōhoku Shinkansen, or they pass by at a more leisurely pace on the Tōhoku Main Line or Highway 4. Yet crossing into Fukushima Prefecture from the south— past Shirakawa, Nakoso, or on one of the newer routes—will still be a significant moment in your journey north, since you will at that point become an official visitor to Japan's back country.

Fukushima's proximity to the more cosmopolitan south has

put pressure on it to blend into an undifferentiated modern Japan. But the people of Fukushima have put much effort into preserving both their natural assets and their history and traditions. Thus, Fukushima provides a fitting introduction to the back country.

Visitors coming from the south may feel more at home in Fukushima than in the other five Tōhoku prefectures. Not only does its climate, like the rest of Honshu, lack the year-round coolness of the north, but it has lots of modern restaurants and hotels to comfortably accommodate those who have come to see its mountains, lakes, hot springs, and historical sites.

Most Japanese visitors come to see Fukushima's Bandai–Asahi National Park. They travel the park's volcanic mountainsides via a series of winding and climbing modern toll roads. Campers and hikers especially enjoy this protected natural recreation area as well as the unspoiled natural scenes of the Iwaki Kaigan beach on the southeastern coast and the lakes and forests along the Tadami Line and Highway 252 in the remote western part of the prefecture.

More appealing to foreign visitors is the former inland feudal capital of the Aizu clan, Aizu-Wakamatsu. Much of the city's castle-town past has been preserved or restored, and then proudly displayed. Here and there within the modern city, Edo-period storefronts and workshops still stand and traditional crafts still flourish. Recently, a thirty-five-room samurai-class villa, now called Buke-yashiki, was restored and opened to the public, and Tsurugajō, the Aizu clan's five-story castle, was replicated on the old castle grounds.

Across the river from Aizu-Wakamatsu in the delightful country town of Hongō a 300-year-old pottery tradition still thrives, and over two thousand kura, traditional thick-walled storehouses, remain in the town of Kitakata, just north of the feudal capital. A short ride east of Aizu-Wakamatsu is Lake Inawashiro, Japan's fourth largest lake. The boyhood farmhouse of Dr. Hideyo

Noguchi, the internationally known bacteriologist who was instrumental in developing a cure for yellow fever, shares a complex along the lake's northern shoreline with a memorial museum dedicated to the medical researcher and the Aizu Minzoku Museum, two charming old farmhouses filled with items used by the common people of rural Fukushima in times past.

Fukushima is indeed a fine introduction to what is to come on your journey through the back country—six prefectures of volcanic mountainsides, beautiful coastlines, picturesque countryside, old castle towns, traditional folk crafts, and perhaps the world's last glimpse of the fast-dying life style of old rural Japan.

The Narrow Roads North

Let's stretch our legs then
and this endlessly clear day breathe the air full of
the tree-scent of the north.
Kōtarō Takamura

FUKUSHIMA PROVIDES most back-country visitors with their first
tree-scent of the north, along one of several routes into the prefecture. If you've been sightseeing in the Nikkō National Park
in neighboring Tochigi Prefecture, you can head north via Highway 121 or the Aizu Line to the inland metropolis of Aizu-Wakamatsu or travel through the hot-spring resorts and wooded mountains around the Nasukashi Toll Road which spans the two
prefectures.

The most efficient route north is through the old barrier station
of Shirakawa along the main thoroughfares linking the back
country with the rest of the island, but you can also head north
along Fukushima's Pacific coastline on the Jōban Line or on
Highway 6. Each of these "narrow roads to a far province"
has points of interest along the way, making the location of
your first tree-scent of the north a difficult decision.

If you're coming by bus from Tochigi on Highway 121, you
can transfer to the Aizu Line at Itozawa Station, 5 kilometers
north of the prefectural border. Both train and highway go to
the former castle town of Aizu-Wakamatsu along the route of

the old Nikkō Kaidō, passing several onsen on the way—and bypassing an Edo-period daimyo's rest stop.

ALONG THIS ROUTE is the town of Tajima, 10 kilometers north of Itozawa Station. Its Oku-Aizu Folk Museum is in a wooden two-story former district government office building built in 1889. The chief government official's Meiji-period office is preserved on the first floor and the rest of the building is dedicated to southwestern Fukushima's hunting and logging traditions. A remote youth travel village is located in the deep forest along Highway 289, about 10 kilometers west of the town.

If you're interested in Edo-period architecture and are willing to make an extra effort to see some, you'll want to visit the sleepy little hamlet of Ōuchijuku. The tiny community is on a nearly deserted local road heading northwest from Highway 121 just past Yunokami Station, about 17 kilometers north of Tajima.

Ōuchijuku's quiet main street was anything but quiet a few hundred years ago when the town was an overnight rest stop along the Aizu Nishi Kaidō. The Aizu lord and his large entourage passed through the community every two years to comply with the Tokugawa government's edict that all daimyo spend part of every other year in Edo.

Today forty of the old thatched-roof inns remain standing along the road, and five are still taking in travelers for the night, even though their clients are no longer samurai but rather the curious travelers who come to admire the old buildings and their place in Fukushima's feudal-period history.

Ōuchijuku's slow death as a travelers' way station began during the Meiji period when the Nikkō Kaidō was opened, completely cutting off the town from the flow of traffic. For a brief time a few years ago, the town came to life again when NHK, Japan's national broadcasting company, chose the old inns as the site of a year-long documentary on the Edo period.

No public transportation now travels along the old Aizu

Nishi Kaidō, but you can walk from Yunokami Onsen in 90 minutes or take a 20-minute taxi ride. The onsen has sixteen inns built on a cliff overlooking a gorge; one of these inns has an outdoor hot-spring bath. The Aizu-sō kokuminshukusha[1] is about 8 kilometers north of Yunokami in the Ashinomaki Onsen.

IF YOU'RE TAKING the Nasukashi Toll Road into Fukushima, you'll be winding through another group of hot-spring resorts known collectively as Nasu Onsen. On this route you can spend the night in the mountains on the Tochigi side of the border at the Nasu Kokumin Kyūka Mura,[2] a government-sponsored vacation village with a lodge, cottages, and a campground, or in Fukushima at Kashi Onsen's Miyama-sō kokuminshukusha.[3] You can then go on to rejoin the major northbound thoroughfares at Shirakawa, about 20 kilometers west of Kashi Onsen on Highway 289.

Crossing the Shirakawa Barrier has inspired poets throughout the centuries to describe their emotions as they entered the back country. Ironically, though, the most famous Shirakawa poem, the one every Japanese can recite, was written by a man who may never have come:

> I left Kyoto in the spring mist.
> By the time I reached the Shirakawa Barrier
> The fall wind was blowing.

1. Aizu-sō, 2498–1, Yunohira, Kotani, Ōto-machi, Aizu-Wakamatsu-shi, Fukushima-ken 969–51; tel. (024292) 2427.
あいづ荘 〒969-51 福島県会津若松市大戸町小谷湯の平 2498-1
2. Nasu Kokumin Kyūka Mura, Nasu Kōgen, Yumoto, Nasu-machi, Tochigi-ken 325–04; tel. (028776) 2467.
那須国民休暇村 〒325-04 栃木県那須町湯本那須高原
3. Miyama-sō, Umadate, Mabune, Nishigō-mura, Nishi Shirakawa-gun, Fukushima-ken 961; tel. (024836) 2420.
みやま荘 〒961 福島県西白河郡西郷村真船馬立

Nōin Hōshi, a poet/monk who lived during the Heian period, was the author of this verse. However, according to a much later senryū, or humorous haiku poem, Nōin Hōshi's journey north never took place; the poet just created a clever deception to make people believe it had. He had written the poem about a far away place called Shirakawa, and he knew it was good. But he couldn't very well present his emotions about reaching a place he'd never seen, and he certainly didn't want to make the arduous journey from Kyoto to the back country just to give credence to his poem. So Nōin Hōshi simply shut his garden gate for the summer and sat inside his yard working on his traveler's suntan. When it was time for his return from the north, he reopened his gate and presented his wonderful poem to an appreciative public. But he forgot one thing which gave him away—people could not make such a long journey in those days before the bullet train and expressway without getting calluses on their feet, and Nōin Hōshi had none.

You can visit the actual site of the barrier via a local road going south from Shirakawa Station. It's about a 30-minute bus ride to the grounds of Shirakawa Shrine, where the barrier once stood to protect "civilized" Japan from the aliens of the untamed north—the indigenous and Ainu tribes collectively called the Ezo. A stone monument erected in 1800 by the Aizu lord Matsudaira Sadanobu now marks the location of the ancient barrier.

Shirakawa was a castle town of the Aizu clan, and, although the castle no longer exists, you can visit the castle site, now the wooded Shiroyama Park near the station. Nanko Park, a 10-minute bus ride south of the station is Japan's first public park. Matsudaira Sadanobu, who was also the Tokugawa shogunate's chief minister from 1787 to 1793, converted a wasteland near his Shirakawa castle into a lovely garden with an artificial lake for the enjoyment of the common people of the area. This was an unusual act at a time when such pleasures were reserved for the exclusive amusement of the samurai class.

An alternative that is not a main route into Fukushima but one that will allow you to visit one of Japan's three most celebrated gardens on your way north is the Suigun Line and Highway 118, which connect Ibaraki Prefecture's Mito with Fukushima's Kōriyama. The Kairaku-en garden is 2 kilometers west of Mito Station. It ranks along with Kanazawa's Kenroku-en and Okayama's Kōraku-en gardens as Japan's finest.

IF YOU PLAN to pass up mountains, parks, and gardens for the time being in order to get right into enjoying the freshness of the back country's unspoiled Pacific Coast, Highway 6 and the Jōban Line—which link Tokyo with Miyagi's big city, Sendai—will interest you. Both routes pass through Fukushima's other ancient barrier station at Nakoso, skirt the beautiful seaside of Iwaki Kaigan prefectural park, and then go through the Sōma area of northeastern Fukushima with its exciting wild horse roundup tradition.

The Nakoso Barrier site is 2.2 kilometers south of Nakoso Station on the Fukushima–Ibaraki border. You can spend the night near the historic site at the Nakosonoseki-sō kokuminshukusha[4] or at the Shioyazaki-sō kokuminshukusha[5] along the Iwaki Kaigan coast.

There is a campground near the latter government-sponsored inn and there are several youth hostels in the Iwaki City area.

After crossing the border, both the highway and train line head inland, bypassing the green hills and sandy beaches of Iwaki Kaigan before they go back out to the coast. There are access roads to the beach near Izumi and Taira stations.

---

4. Nakosonoseki-sō, 59 Sekiyama, Sekita, Nakoso-machi, Iwaki-shi, Fukushima-ken 979–01 ; tel. (0246) 65–5111.
   勿来の関荘　〒979-01 福島県いわき市勿来町関田関山59
5. Shioyazaki-sō, 9 Kozuka, Usuiso, Taira, Iwaki-shi, Fukushima-ken 970–02; tel. (0246) 39–3232.
   塩屋埼荘　〒970-02 福島県いわき市平薄磯小塚 9

At Taira Station in Iwaki City you have a choice of continuing up the coast on your present route or heading inland to Kōriyama on the Ban'etsu East Line, Highway 49, or the local highway that follows the train. Kōriyama is the gateway to Aizu-Waka-matsu and the Bandai-Asahi National Park. Another option if you're driving is to take the local road near Yumoto Station, which leads to the Jōban-Yunodake Panorama Line toll road that climbs Yunodake peak for an overview of the mountains and coastline of southeastern Fukushima. On the way, you'll pass Yumoto Onsen with its garish hotel complex, the Jōban Hawaiian Center. Jōban Hawaii's huge outdoor bath, its "Niagara Falls," and its foreign entertainment attract visitors from both Tokyo and Tōhoku who come to "spend the weekend in Hawaii."

IF YOU'RE STILL on the Jōban Line or Highway 6 past Iwaki and it's July 23rd or 24th, you'll want to spend some time in the coastal town of Haranomachi to see the Sōma Nomaoi (wild horse chase), one of Tōhoku's most colorful and exciting local festivals.

Northeastern Fukushima's wild horse roundup was begun by the Sōma clan's mounted warriors long ago. By the early sixteenth century, the festival had become an annual celebration, and its present form began to take shape after the Meiji Restoration.

Today several hundred riders and horses from all over Japan—both man and beast in colorful samurai-era trappings—participate in a morning parade down the town's main streets. Later at the nearby Hibarino Race Track they compete in races and mounted contests. In one competition the mounted samurai vie with one another to be the first to pluck up a sacred banner that has been shot high into the air and then deliver it to the local shrine as an offering.

The Sōma area is also known for its pottery. Sōma-yaki is a crackle-glazed pottery that sometimes has a galloping wild horse painted in the underglaze. Sōma's wild horses have been painted onto its teacups and other utensils since 1622. Several local potters, including the fifteenth generation of the Tashiro family of the Tamachi area of Sōma City, are still at it.

There is a beachfront campground north of Haranomachi near Kashima Station. The Kokuminshukusha Matsukawa Ura[6] is also on the beach; it's a 15–minute bus ride from Sōma Station, 20 kilometers north of Haranomachi.

If it's not time for the Sōma Nomaoi festival, you might want to leave the Tōhoku coastline after seeing the beaches of Iwaki Kaigan and then pick up the coastal routes later for Miyagi's famous Matsushima Bay and then again for Iwate's spectacular Rikuchū Kaigan National Park.

The Ban'etsu East Line and the local road that follows it from Iwaki's Taira Station to Kōriyama pass by one of the prefecture's natural wonders, the underground caverns of Irimizu and Abukuma. Abukuma-dō is a 30-minute walk from Kammata Station, about 50 kilometers from Iwaki. Discovered in 1967, the stalactite and stalagmite cavern is now well prepared for visitors with underground lighting that permits you to walk 500 meters into the cave past the eerie lime formations.

Irimizu Cavern is 2 kilometers east of Sugaya Station, which follows Kammata on the Ban'etsu East Line. This cavern was discovered in 1927 and has since been designated a National Natural Treasure. You can explore 900 meters of stalactites and stalagmites, underground streams and waterfalls, and resident fish and bats.

The two caverns and a third one not yet open to the public, are all part of the same underground complex. Overnight accommodations at the Kokumin Hoyō Center Senshin-sō[7] and at a campground are only a few minutes' walk from Irimizu Cavern.

6. Kokuminshukusha Matsukawa Ura, 208 Takatsuka, Ohama, Sōma-shi, Fukushima-ken 976; tel. (02443) 8–7177.
   国民宿舎松川補　〒976 福島県相馬市尾浜高塚 208
7. Kokumin Hoyō Center, Senshin-sō, Baba, Sugaya, Takine-machi, Tamura-gun, Fukushima-ken 976–36; tel. (024778) 3100.
   国民保養センター洗心荘　〒979-36 福島県田村郡滝根町菅谷馬場

About 15 kilometers before you reach Kōriyama and rejoin those travelers who entered Fukushima through Shirakawa or Mito, you'll pass the folkcraft center of Miharu, whose famous Miharu hariko ningyo, colorfully painted papier-maché dolls, are made at a few farmhouse/workshops on a local road northwest of Miharu Station. Deko-yashiki, the collective name for the five scattered workshops, can be found in the countryside about 30 minutes on foot from the station. A few buses a day come here from Kōriyama Station; the ride to Ōhira Bus Stop takes 40 minutes.

IF YOU'RE COMING from Kōriyama, Deko-yashiki may seem out-of-the-way, but if you've come to the back country to discover its folkcrafts, you will enjoy watching the artisans at work and examining their hand-carved willow and mulberry molds, locally made paper, and fine examples of the Edo-period craft.

Miharu is also known for its Miharu goma, brightly painted wooden horses, and for its "three springs" (miharu), which happen all at once when the peach, cherry, and plum trees all bloom at the same time. The area abounds with old weeping cherry trees said to have survived because the local Miharu-clan lord exempted farmers' fields from taxes if they didn't destroy their cherry trees. The 400-year-old Taki-zakura, or waterfall cherry, is 6 kilometers south of Miharu Station; it is a National Natural Treasure.

There are a few places to visit in Kōriyama itself if you have time before continuing north on the main routes or taking the Ban'etsu West Line, which begins here, to the tourist attractions in the central part of the prefecture.

The Nihō-ji temple is a 5-minute bus ride from the station. It is the city's oldest temple; a stone stupa on the temple grounds bears a date equivalent to 1208. The Kaiseizan Park, a 10-minute bus ride to Joshidai-mae Bus Stop, has a former Meiji-period meeting hall which is now the Kaiseikan Folk Museum.

If it's spring, you may also want to visit the city's two flower gardens. The Kōriyama Bara-en garden has 800 kinds of roses that bloom in June. It is a 10-minute bus ride from the station in Fukagawa-chō. The Sukagawa Botan-en garden is a 15-minute bus ride from Sukagawa Station, two local stops south of Kōriyama Station on the Tōhoku Main Line. Its 3,500 peonies bloom around the end of May.

THE CITY OF NIHONMATSU, 13 kilometers north of Kōriyama on the main routes, was the home of two well-known personalities— Chieko Takamura and the Adachigahara onibaba, or ogress.

If you take a bus from Nihonmatsu Station for 10 minutes following the course of the Abukuma River, you'll come to the Adachigahara Onibaba Park. Here a stone called the kurozuka, the black mound, marks the location of the cave where the ogress of Adachigahara once lived.

The ogresses of Japanese folklore are like the wicked old witches of Western fairy tales. Nihonmatsu's ogress got her start by killing a pregnant woman who came to the cave for shelter during a storm and eating her liver. The woman turned out to be her own long-lost daughter, and the old woman went mad from the shock of what she had done. From then on, the Adachigahara ogress always welcomed tired travelers into her cave—and then ate their flesh and sucked out their blood. Today, however, you can visit the site without fear, since a traveling priest finally killed her with the help of a divine bow and arrow.

The true story of Chieko is far more romantic, although her life came to a sad end in a mental institution. Chieko was both a frustrated artist and a frustrated big-city dweller whose heart was in the Nihonmatsu countryside. She was married to the famous poet/sculptor Kōtarō Takamura (1883–1956) who created the "Maidens by the Lake" sculpture at Aomori's Lake Towada (see that section) towards the end of his prolific career. Traveling exhibitions of his works always include the beautiful love letters and poems he wrote to Chieko, both during her lifetime and after she was gone, as well as Chieko's delicate papercuts, made while she was a schizophrenic patient.

Hundreds of sniffling romantics file ever so slowly through a Takamura exhibit, reading his tender words to Chieko, who denied herself the pursuit of an independent career in art and also the pleasure of living in her beloved back country in order to be with her husband.

Takamura's most famous poem, "Chieko's Sky," is dedicated to her homesickness. It is included in an English-language collection of his writings and her papercuts, *Chieko's Sky.*

> Chieko claims there is no sky over Tokyo
> and says she longs to see a real sky...
> gazing far away Chieko says
> the blue sky that appears each day
> over the crest of Mt. Atatara
> is Chieko's real sky.

It's hard not to think about Chieko as you travel under her sky along the mountain roads of the beautiful national park she could see from her Nihonmatsu home. There is a monument dedicated to Chieko in the city's Kasumigajō Park, a 20-minute walk from Nihonmatsu Station.

Some bus tours of the Bandai–Asahi National Park begin in Kōriyama, circle through the park, and then terminate in Fukushima City, the prefectural capital, 50 kilometers north of Kōriyama on the main routes; other buses travel the same route in reverse. You can also begin a tour of the park in Fukushima City and then end up in Aizu-Wakamatsu, or visit Aizu-Wakamatsu from Kōriyama and then go through the park to Fukushima City.

Fukushima City is the educational, industrial, and agricultural center of the prefecture as well as the capital city. It is at the junction of the Tōhoku Main Line, which covers the eastern side of

Tōhoku, and the Ōu Main Line, which covers the length of western Tōhoku. The two main back-country transportation arteries meet again in the far north, in Aomori City on Mutsu Bay.

If you're on the main routes north, you'll have to make a side trip to the west around the northern shore of Lake Inawashiro to visit the city of Aizu-Wakamatsu. It is a detour well worth the time of anyone traveling the narrow roads north in order to explore Japan's back country.

Aizu-Wakamatsu

NORTHWARD-BOUND TRAVELERS have to make a side trip around
Lake Inawashiro to reach the inland city of Aizu-Wakamatsu
and the pottery town of Hongō, but the old castle town with
so much of its past still preserved and the charming rural community just across the river are both well worth the special effort
it takes to reach them. And with enough time, you can continue
west to the mountains and forests of the Tadami area, far, far
off the tourist trail.

Aizu-Wakamatsu was the capital of the Aizu clan, second
in power only to Miyagi's Datè family among all Tōhoku daimyo. Since the out-of-the-way, nonindustrial city was fortunately
ignored by World War II bombers, much of Japan's feudal
history remains intact here, and the proud people of Fukushima
have rebuilt other reminders of their rich heritage. Highways
49 from Kōriyama and 121 from Tochigi come through the
city as do the trains of the Ban'etsu West Line, the Aizu Line,
and the Tadami Line.

The city has been thriving since its Tsuruga castle was first
erected in 1384. Today, even though it supports a population
of 110,000, the city prides itself on its history and traditions
and on the fact that it supports its citizens in a "city without
smokestacks."

Aizu-Wakamatsu at first glance appears to be just another medium-sized city done up in Japanese modern. But beneath its modern facade is the old Aizu castle town of winding streets, mud-walled storehouses, and traditional industries. There are several city bus tours leaving from the station that take you to the remains of the old city.

Only a few blocks from the station is the Aizu-Wakamatsu Green Hotel,[1] an inexpensive business hotel with a pleasant difference. "Business hotel" usually translates into a closet-sized Western-style room, but, in this case, the foreign visitor can stay Japanese style for the same price.

The city's main tourist attractions are the castle; Iimoriyama, the site where a group of young boys won the hearts of the Japanese people by dying for their defeated Aizu clan; the Oyakuen garden of the former daimyo; the Takinosawa Old Gohonjin samurai inn with reminders of past battles still scarring the walls; and Buke-yashiki, a fabulous reproduction of a samurai-class estate. Aizu-Wakamatsu's traditional crafts and sakè-brewing industry have also been carefully preserved in the city's workshops and museums.

In the city's southeastern suburbs is the busy mountain onsen resort of Higashiyama with the modern, resort-priced hotels so popular with Japanese tourists. If you want to join them, the Mukaitaki Ryokan,[2] an old-style tiled-roof building spreading into the mountainside, retains more of the feeling of old Japan than its high-rise neighbors.

What was once the most important spot in all the Aizu clan's territory is now the landmark of the city of Aizu-Wakamatsu.

1. Aizu-Wakamatsu Green Hotel, 7–23, 3-chōme, Chūō, Aizu-Wakamatsu-shi, Fukushima-ken 965; tel. (0242) 24–5181.
   会津若松グリーンホテル　〒965 福島県会津若松市中央三丁目 7-23
2. Mukaitaki Ryokan, 200, Kawamukou, Yumoto, Higashiyama-machi, Aizu-Wakamatsu-shi, Fukushima-ken 965; tel. (0242) 27–7501.
   向滝旅館　〒965 福島県会津若松市東山町湯本川向 200 番地

Tsuruga Castle has stood in the center of city for most of the past 600 years. It was rebuilt in the sixteenth century, was destroyed in 1874 during the Meiji Restoration's anti-feudalism zeal, and was rebuilt as a museum in 1965.

The present "castle" looks just like the one it replaced. It stands inside the original stone foundations and tree-lined moat. The first three floors of the five-story building are the museum and the fourth and fifth levels provide lookouts over the city. Displays covering the area's prehistory and religious history, are located on the first floor, the work of local artisans is on the second, and documents and articles from the Boshin War, the civil war leading up to the restoration, are on the third. An excellent collection of old pottery is exhibited along the exit route out of the castle replica.

If you come to Tsuruga Castle at 10 a.m. on September 22nd, 23rd, or 24th, you will be met by a parade of samurai in battle dress marching through the city's main streets for the annual Aizu Byakko Festival. The castle is a 10-minute bus ride south of the station.

Just northeast of the castle and a 15-minute bus ride from the station to Oyaku-en Iriguchi Bus Stop is Oyaku-en, the old walking and herb garden of the Aizu clan's ruling Matsudaira family. The Enshū-style garden was built with a traditional teahouse overlooking a central pond shaped like the character that means heart. Today, over 300 different kinds of herbs carry on the herb-growing tradition of the garden begun by the second Matsudaira daimyo.

Buke-yashiki, east of the castle on the bus line from the station to Higashiyama Onsen at the Buke-yashiki Bus Stop, is one of Tōhoku's best reproductions of life in its feudal past. It is a must-see for anyone interested in experiencing this part of old Japan. This lavishly rebuilt samurai manor was constructed in 1975 using the original plans of the thirty-five-room, Edo-period residence of the Aizu clan's chief retainer. Although it is a big tourist attraction with a large bus parking lot and an arcade of shops and restaurants, the reconstructed estate is so well done and filled with so much of old Fukushima that you won't even mind the "samurai" drum beater who thunderously greets each busload of visitors.

The house itself is joined by several historic buildings that have been moved here and restored, together forming a grand-scale museum complex of Fukushima's history. You can see water-wheel-powered wooden rice pounders at work inside a 150-year-old rice mill from Shirakawa; a nineteenth-century local governor's office building from southern Fukushima; an old mud-walled kura, or storehouse; the Aizu lord's sixteenth-century teahouse; and a former silkworm-raising building. Inside the open-walled rooms of the house itself and in some of these other buildings as well are displays ranging from pottery and tools of Japan's Jōmon-period stone age to the treasures and weapons of Aizu clan ruling families. The house's kitchen has an especially good collection of antique kitchenware and furnishings.

There are paths leading around the sprawling manor house, past rooms furnished with items from the days of the original samurai-class household. The family itself is depicted in a series of rooms called the Panorama Pavilion. Authentically dressed mannequins appear to be going about their daily routines, except for the room in which they are committing ritual suicide in the samurai tradition after the news that their castle had fallen to restoration forces.

Lacquerware and Buddhist altar workshops are in the kura-style buildings behind the main complex as are a small temple and shrine. Buke-yashiki's arcade offers the best selection of crafts and souvenirs in the city as well as demonstrations by local artisans and authentic local dishes in its restaurants. In spite of the crowds it attracts, Buke-yashiki is the prefecture's most comprehensive presentation of its past.

A TRUE TRAGEDY that has touched not only many Japanese over the past hundred years but a few foreigners as well took place on a hillside east of Aizu-Wakamatsu Station called Iimori-yama. It can be reached in a 15-minute bus ride from the station to Iimori Iriguchi Bus Stop. The tragedy is that of the Byakkotai, or White Tigers, a group of teenage "warriors" who died need-lessly for their lord during the Boshin War. To fully understand why nineteen young men committed mass suicide on this hill when they mistakenly thought their castle had fallen, you must know the events that led up to that day in 1868.

Although Japan always had an emperor during the 250 years the Tokugawa shogunate ruled the country from Edo, the emperor had almost no function. In fact, many Japanese during this period (1603–1868) were not even aware that they still had an emperor. The Matsudaira family, rulers of the Aizu clan during this period, were very strong supporters of the Tokugawas. They were given the use of the Tokugawa crest, and their ninth lord, Matsudaira Katamori, was a son of the shogun, and had been adopted into the Matsudaira family when he was twelve.

Katamori became the Aizu daimyo when he was eighteen, just when two southern daimyo were trying to take power from the Tokugawas by restoring the ruling authority of the royal house-hold in Kyoto. Katamori, wanting to make his adopted clan proud of their new leader, took 1,000 Aizu samurai to Kyoto on a successful mission to quiet anti-Tokugawa uprisings there. The Aizu clan was later to pay severely for siding with the losers of this domestic power struggle.

The Byakkotai was one of several groups of young people of both sexes who formed a sort of civil defense guard for their territory. During a battle with pro-restoration forces just outside the city, the Byakkotai troops, which consisted of 16- or 17-year-old boys well-versed in the samurai code of ethics, were soundly defeated. The 20 Byakkotai members who survived the battle dejectedly crawled through an irrigation tunnel connecting Takinosawa near the battle site and Iimoriyama. From their hillside perch, the devastated teenagers looked down towards their castle and saw smoke rising from it. Thinking the enemy had taken the castle, they began a mass suicide ritual in the best samurai tradition.

Only one boy was saved before he bled to death. He spent the rest of his life hiding the sword scar on his neck, deeply ashamed that he had failed to live up to the samurai code. The nineteen graves of the boys who died are lined up near the top of the hill close to the spot where they died together.

The story of the Byakkotai has affected people in different ways over the past century. Some people are moved by the tragedy of the wasted young lives, but others admire their unswerving obedience to their cause. Two foreign monuments honoring the boys' loyalty to their code stand on Iimoriyama near the graves. One was donated by a German military attaché to Japan and its inscription reads, "To Aizu's young samurai from one German man." During the occupation, the surface of the stone was smoothed out, but it was recarved in 1953 when the wartime antagonism had lessened.

Fascist Italy, too, was intrigued by the Byakkotai story. The city of Rome's contribution to the hill was a spread-winged eagle on top of a marble column from a Pompeian palace preserved by Mount Vesuvius's ashes. Its inscription reads, "To express our respect to those courageous young Byakkotai men, the city of the birthplace of civilization sends this Fascist Party symbol with a 1,000-year-old stone column, the symbol of eternal greatness, to honor the Byakkotai."

The quiet hill where the Byakkotai survivors sought refuge is now alive with visitors who come to honor their memory. There is even a moving sidewalk climbing the hill (for a fee) alongside the old stone steps. Besides the graves and monuments, the hill has several other reminders of the tragedy that took place here. Next to a small shrine is the water-filled tunnel from which the boys fled from the battlefield to the hill. And there is also the strange-looking Buddhist religious building, the Sazae-dō. The hexagonal, 60-meter-high wooden building predates the Byakkotai incident by a hundred years, but inside is a memorial to the nineteen dead boys with small images of them in battle dress. The hall's name comes from its unusual exterior shape and the spiral staircase inside, both of which tend to remind one of a sazae, the spiny-shelled marine snail that the Japanese consider a delicacy.

From one lookout point on the hill, you may be able to see in the brush below the grave of another victim of the Boshin War. This one will catch your eye because the gravestone is carved with the English-language inscription, "In memory of Okei, died 1871, aged 19 years (A Japanese Girl)."

The Takinosawa Old Gohonjin, built as a rest stop for traveling daimyo in 1595, still stands today just north of Iimoriyama. Towards the end of the Edo period, the old inn became Matsudaira Katamori's military headquarters. It is now a small museum, but you can still see bullet holes and sword slashes in the walls leftover from an attack by restoration forces.

You may wonder what happened to the defeated Aizu samurai when the emperor was restored to power. They were given the choice of staying on the land they once ruled to become farmers or starting anew on the sparsely settled poor lands of northeastern Honshu, in what is now Aomori Prefecture. Over 4,000 Aizu samurai and their families, three-quarters of the clan's former warrior class, took what they could carry and went off by boat and on foot to their new homes. Those traveling on foot faced a shortage of food along the way due to the famine of 1870 as well as other hardships. Some brought only one set of clothing since much of the weight they could carry was taken up by family altars and records rather than practical items.

When the former warriors of Tōhoku's second strongest clan arrived in Aomori, they settled mostly around Misawa City and on the Shimokita Peninsula, although some went as far as Hokkaido to begin their new lives. Those who settled in the harsh climate and on the marginal farmland of Aomori, between 14,000 and 17,000 people, became even poorer than the impoverished local Nambu clan farmers. They became known as *hato-zamurai,* or pigeon samurai, who ate the poor quality soybeans the local farmers grew for horse fodder. Today many of northern Tōhoku's government, business, and political leaders are descendants of these Aizu samurai refugees. They are as proud of their ancestors' accomplishments in settling the far north as they are of their samurai heritage.

THE SKILLS OF AIZU-WAKAMATSU'S Edo-period artisans and sakè brewers are also still in evidence in the modern city. Pre-Meiji arts and crafts of the area are displayed in the Aizu History Museum, a 10-minute walk south of the station. Nearby is the Yamada Lacquerware Museum, with its workshop and showroom, where you can view the past and present of Aizu's still popular lacquerware industry. Two old sakè factories have also become museums, displaying not only the city's old sakè-brewing tradition, but also the family treasures of rich sakè merchants. The Aizu Sakè-Brewing Museum is across the river from the main part of the city near Nishi Wakamatsu Station on the Aizu Line. The Kōno family has been brewing sakè here for twelve generations. Besides a display of the old sakè-making process, the museum exhibits the family's Edo-period furnishings and art and the old company executive office—and offers samples of their present-day output.

The Aizu Sakè-Brewing History Museum, near Tsurugajō, displays a collection of antique armor, tea utensils, screens, art, Chinese ceramics, and other treasures. Mannequins show how the old-fashioned sakè-brewing process was done, and, of course, sakè samples are available.

Other traditional crafts that the city still produces are painted picture candles; bamboo crafts; akabeko, red papier-maché cows with bobbing heads; and Aizu momen, heavy indigo-dyed striped cotton cloth now made into souvenir purses, wallets, and the like. Another local craft, the fine pottery called Aizu-Hongō-yaki, is made in the nearby village of Hongō. There are many places in this tradition-oriented city where you can purchase these crafts, including the major tourist attractions.

You can continue your encounter with old Aizu-Wakamatsu with lunch or dinner at the Wappameshi Takino,[3] an old-style country restaurant in the middle of the city. The small, modest eatery has a table-level irori, or sunken hearth, around which you can sit and grill small fish over the coals, and tatami areas where you can order their specialty, wappameshi, or rice dishes covered with your choice of toppings and served in a wappako, or old-fashioned bentwood lunch box. The menu is in Japanese, but you can order zenmai wappako, if you want to try rice topped with wild vegetables from the mountains of Fukushima; kinoko wappako, with a variety of mushrooms; ayu wappako, with fresh-water fish; gyū wappako, with beef; or yamadori wappako, with the meat of wild mountain birds.

IF YOU'RE THIS FAR into exploring Fukushima's past, you can't leave without a visit to the pottery town of Hongō, just across the river. Hongō is southwest of the city, a station along the Tadami Line. A 15-minute walk down the small country town's main street, Setomachi Dōri, will get you to the Aizu Hongō Yaki-mono Kaikan where representative pottery from all twelve local kilns is on display. Here you can pick up a map of the town's potters and then set out on foot through the country lanes to the individual potters' workshops.

Some city bus tours from Aizu-Wakamatsu cross the river to

3. Wappameshi Takino, 5–31, Sakae-machi, Aizu-Wakamatsu-shi, Fukushima-ken 965; tel. (0242) 25–0808.
わっぱめし田季野　〒965 福島県会津若松市栄町 5-31 番地

Hongō, but they stop only at the town's most modern factory-like kiln for a tour of its interesting mass-production operation. But the best part of Hongō is its country pottery town atmosphere, which you can absorb only by spending at least a few hours walking from potter to potter, seeing their hand-crafted wares, climbing around their old brick kilns, and watching them at work in their peaceful rural surroundings. Many of the potters work in specially designed kura built with low windows to let the light in while the potters work.

Hongō began its role as Aizu-Wakamatsu's pottery village 400 years ago when Gamō Ujisato became lord of Aizu and ordered Tsuruga Castle rebuilt. Clay for the tiles of the new castle roof came from a hillside near Hongō, and the tiles were made by Hongō villagers. Fifty years later, Aizu's Matsudaira lord brought in skilled potters from the famous central Japan kiln of Seto to teach the Hongō potters how to make kitchenware.

Today only one Hongō potter still handles the entire pottery-making process in a strictly traditional manner. Ryōichi Munakata is the sixth generation of his family to make hand-thrown pottery. He fires his earthenware pottery three times a year in a brick kiln using only red pine for the firewood. During the firing, the kiln is heated to temperatures of 1,300 degrees centigrade for three days and then allowed to cool for four days. His pots, vases, tea utensils, and the like are still warm when he later opens the oven.

The Munakata trademark is a rectangular, high-sided container, or nishin-bachi, once used by the inland castle town to preserve saltwater herring. Thick slabs of clay are molded with wooden frames by hand to make these well-known herring pots. A Munakata nishin-bachi won a grand prize at the Brussels World's Fair in 1958.

If you're in town on the first Sunday in August, you'll be just in time for the Seto-ichi, a one-day bargain-sale of pottery beginning at daybreak, held on the main street.

Even if pottery is not of great interest to you, the little country town is still a delightful experience (except perhaps when it is packed with bargain-hunters for the early August sale). And for those who came north to discover Tōhoku's remaining traditional crafts, an afternoon in Hongō is an absolute necessity.

TADAMI, AN ISOLATED TOWN on Fukushima's western border, is a completely different experience than you've had so far exploring the territory of the powerful Aizu clan. Tadami and the wilderness around it belonged to no daimyo, but were ruled directly by the Tokugawa central government in Edo. Therefore, the people of this remote outpost developed a culture unique from that of the Aizu territory.

The Tadami area remained relatively isolated until the very recent past when the new Tadami Line and Highway 252 linked up Fukushima's stepchild with the rest of the prefecture via Aizu-Wakamatsu.

A series of mountain onsen dot this new route. The town of Tadami itself is about 65 kilometers west of Aizu-Wakamatsu in a scenic area of unspoiled lakes, rivers, and forests. The town offers camping facilities at the Tadami Seishōnen Ryokō Mura, a youth travel village along the Tadami River on a plateau overlooking the town. It is a 5-minute bus ride and then a 20-minute walk from the bus station. You can rent bicycles here to further enjoy the uncrowded countryside of this area.

A 5-minute taxi ride from the station will take you to the Kanōzu Bansho, an old L-shaped, thatched-roof house that was once a checkpoint station along this remote route through the back country. Behind the old station is the 300-year-old farmhouse of the Igarashi family.

From Tadami you can make your way to Niigata City and then Tokyo via the Tadami and Jōetsu lines. But you really have to stay a while longer in the back country—because you have Fukushima's Bandai–Asahi National Park and five more prefectures yet to explore.

The Bandai–Asahi National Park

YOU CAN'T VERY WELL visit Fukushima Prefecture without seeing the Bandai–Asahi National Park. Japanese tourists flock here to walk along the lush green Bandai Kōgen plateau's series of lakes and ponds and to ride through the park's volcanic mountainsides. An efficient system of tour bus lines can get you through the park in half a day, or you can stay longer for some lakeside camping, boating, fishing, hiking, or just soaking up of the north's tree-scented scenes.

If you haven't really come to the back country to see mountains and lakes, you can still enjoy this north-central part of the prefecture by visiting the museums along the northern shore of Lake Inawashiro and Fukushima's kura-no-machi, or storehouse town, Kitakata, where several thousand buildings, including a temple and homes, are made in the traditional thick mudwalled style normally used for kura, or storehouses.

KITAKATA CITY is off the main tourist routes through the prefecture, 20 kilometers north of Aizu-Wakamatsu on the Ban'etsu West Line and Highway 121. You can spend the night here at

1. Kitakata Green Hotel, 4664, 2-chōme, Naka-machi, Kitakata-shi, Fukushima-ken 966; tel. (02412) 2–0011.
喜多方グリーンホテル　〒966 福島県喜多方市仲町二丁目 4664

the Kitakata Green Hotel,[1] a business hotel in the center of downtown.

Kitakata, a city of 40,000, has over 2,000 kura. It is said that you can see at least one kura from any point in the city. The city has developed a walking tour featuring its most outstanding kura, and you can take a short bus ride to the northern country-side to two rural clusters of kura, the hamlets of Mitsuya and Sugiyama. Kitakata also has two Important Cultural Treasures from the Kamakura period, the Kumano Shrine's long-floor pavil-ion, and Ganjō-ji's Daibutsu (Great Buddha).

Kitakata's unusual kura tradition started out of necessity in the city's rice, grain, sakè, miso, and soy sauce industries. The kura's thick mud walls, which even out seasonal temperature variations, combined with equally thick-walled bolted doors and tiny high windows, protected commercial products from fire, theft, and pests. Prosperous families also built kura to store and protect family treasures. You can see these warehouses and domestic storehouses all over Japan.

But Kitakata's kura are different. Somewhere along the way and for some unknown reason, the townspeople went kura-crazy. They began building kura as living quarters, as guest reception rooms, and even as outhouses. They built a temple, a city office, a police station, schools, stores, and the post office in the kura style. Kura-building became a local obsession.

There was a saying in Kitakata: "If you can't build a kura before you're forty, you're a failure as a man." Since no one wanted to be included in this category, the townspeople enthusiastically struggled to keep up with the Japanese Joneses by building the finest kura they could afford as their homes, offices, shops, and even as their storehouses. And even a few avant-garde kura in various Western styles cropped up here and there amidst the kura madness.

Kitakata's "kura-period" is over, probably to everyone's relief, and today its kura are intermingled with the mundane architecture of postwar Japan. But the visitor who appreciates traditional architecture can have a fantastic time photographing the kura, which literally cover the city and surrounding countryside. You'll see kura of all sizes, some with exterior walls of mud, others plastered in black or white, some with thatched roofs, others with tiled roofs, and a few made of brick. If you come to Kitakata, bring lots of film.

The best place to begin a tour of the city is at the Kai Shōten, the black kura storefront of an old miso and soy sauce factory near the station. You can see their kura-zashiki, a large, restored reception room, and pick up a "kura-viewing" map of the city. The city walking course has twenty buildings numbered on the map, but if you walk around the areas identified with kura pictures, you'll see many, many more. Although a few kura are still operating as retail establishments, you'll have to be content with viewing only the exterior of most.

You can rent a bike near the station and cycle from kura to kura. With only a short time between trains to devote to Kitakata, try walking around the area northeast of the station around the Kai Shōten. The city's mostly modern downtown also has some scattered kura storefronts.

The Anshō-ji temple, northeast of the station, was founded in 1422. But when a new temple building was needed in 1895, of course, the chosen style of architecture was that of a kura—complete with a temple's bell-shaped windows. A few of Kitakata's kura are odd mixtures of the thick, mud walls of old Japan and the bricks, arches, are balconies of the West. The old Wakaki Shōten, a two-story brick kura-style store with a wooden balcony extending from an upstairs window, is off the main downtown shopping street east of the station.

Another cluster of "modern" brick kura is strangely enough out in the country in the rice-growing area along Highway 121. The small hamlet of Mitsuya is 6 kilometers north of the city along a bus line connecting Kitakata and Hirasawa. The brick

kura in the country are interesting, but Mitsuya offers more.
If you haven't yet had the chance to wander through a traditional Japanese rural community, Mitsuya (and the infrequent
bus schedule that connects it with the city) provides you with
a fantastic opportunity. Unlike most other such places, Mitsuya
encourages the curious to come and to photograph its prosperous
rural homesteads. You can spend a pleasant couple of hours
quietly walking through several small clusters of farmhouses
around Mitsuya without feeling like you're intruding. You'll
see several styles of kura here, some used as barns, some as storehouses and others as homes. If you're new to the back country,
wandering around the farms of Mitsuya Hamlet will make you
feel, perhaps for the first time, that you're really in Japan.

You can catch a return bus for Kitakata at Mitsuya or at the
picturesque community just south of it, or you can go the 3
kilometers further down the highway to visit the hamlet of Sugiyama. Sugiyama is named for the sugi, or Japanese cryptomeria,
which cover a small hill between the highway and the tiny community. If you climb to the top of this hill, you'll find a typical
country shrine and a pretty view of the surrounding farms.

The nineteen families who live here used to make charcoal and
traditional straw raincapes and hats. Their white- and black-walled
kura line the community's single street. Some of these kura
were used for storage and others were reception halls for weddings,
funerals, and other community gatherings.

Back in the city, get off the bus before it turns off Highway
121 into the main part of town. From here you can walk a few
blocks further down the highway to another group of kura and
the Yamato Urushi Lacquerware History Museum and showroom,
of course, in a kura. Kitakata is known for its lacquerware and
for its furniture, and the Yamato workshop skillfully combines
the two traditions. Some foreigners have difficulty appreciating
Japanese lacquerware because it seems more like plastic than
natural woodwork to the Western eye. Yamato's lacquerware,

however, with its layers of clear lacquer which let the natural wood grain come through, may overcome this prejudice. The small museum on the second floor of the showroom displays all the tools and equipment used in the traditional production of Japanese urushi lacquerware.

One of Kitakata's two non-kura attractions is the Kumano Shrine's 700-year-old long-floor pavilion. The building, supported by rows of wooden columns, is one of the Aizu district's first non-Chinese-style shrine buildings. Kumano Shrine is 2 kilometers west of the station, across the river.

The Ganjō-ji temple, 4 kilometers northeast of the station, also not a kura, houses the 2.61-meter-high Aizu Daibutsu.

When you've reached your kura-saturation point, head back into the center of the prefecture to the northern shore of Lake Inawashiro, where you can explore two totally different aspects of Fukushima's history.

LAKE INAWASHIRO, the large, nearly round body of water in the middle of the prefecture, is Japan's fourth largest lake. Unlike Tōhoku's other two big lakes, Towada on the Aomori–Akita border and Tazawa in Akita, Inawashiro is not a caldera lake. It was formed from streams which were dammed long, long ago when the mountains to the north erupted. Thus, the terrain around the lake is rather flat and unattractive in comparison with the forested high banks of the caldera lakes.

Nevertheless, the big lake is popular with Japanese tourists who ride large swan-shaped ferries around it. The southern perimeter road offers camping and a view of the volcanic peaks of the national park across the lake. The northern perimeter road, Highway 49, is the route taken by most visitors. The Ban'etsu West Line also passes the northern shore of the big lake.

If you're coming by train, be sure to get off at Inawashiro Station for a few hours even if the lake itself doesn't interest you. Ten minutes by bus from the station is the boyhood home and memorial museum of one of the world's most notable figures in medicine, Dr. Hideyo Noguchi. It shares a tourist complex with the Aizu Minzoku-kan, one of the most interesting folk-craft museums in Tōhoku.

Accommodations in the area include a youth hostel in Inawashiro Town and several kokuminshukusha. Two, the Okinajima-sō[2] and the Minato-ya,[3] are on Nagahama Beach, a recreation area near Okinajima Station, between Aizu-Wakamatsu and Inawashiro. The Saginoyu[4] is three kilometers north of Okinajima Station, in the quiet area of Oshitate Onsen.

If you're driving along the lake, you won't be able to miss the huge parking lots and tourist facilities separating the Noguchi and folk museums. The home of Hideyo Noguchi, and example to young Japanese school children of both ambition and filial loyalty, is visited by busload upon busload of students on their school excursions. Go early in the day to avoid some of the chattering crowds, but even if the museums are crowded, don't pass up what will be one of the most worthwhile stops of your back-country tour.

The Noguchi museum and house are on the west side of the parking lots. The thatched-roof farmhouse gives evidence of Hideyo Noguchi's humble back-country beginnings, and the memorial hall, of the distance he came in fifty-two years, when the disease he was researching in Africa, yellow fever, took his life. Since the medical researcher spent most of his adult years in the West, many of the documents in the exhibition are in English.

2. Okinajima-sō, 1048 Gotenyama, Okinajimasawa, Inawashiro-machi, Yama-gun, Fukushima-ken 969–32; tel. (02426) 5–2811.
   翁島荘　〒969-32　福島県耶麻郡猪苗代町翁島沢御殿山 1048
3. Minato-ya, 870 Nagahama, Inawashiro-machi, Yama-gun, Fukushima-ken 969–32; tel. (02426) 5–2411.
   みなとや　〒969-32　福島県耶麻郡猪苗代町長浜 870
4. Saginoyu, Oshitate Onsen, Inawashiro-machi, Yama-gun, Fukushima-ken 969–32; tel. (02426) 5–2515.
   さぎの湯　〒969-32　福島県耶麻郡猪苗代町押立温泉

Dr. Noguchi (1876–1928) is a hero in Japan not only because of his international fame, but because of his touching personal saga. Although Westerners tend to admire most his driving ambition and contributions to science, the Japanese are deeply affected by his devotion to his family and undying gratitude to his early mentors. He is viewed as the epitome of the dutiful son and protégé who carried out his obligations in spite of his pressing workload abroad and his international reknown.

Noguchi was born into a poor farming family headed by an alcoholic father. At the age of two, he fell into the irori, or Japanese-style sunken fireplace, and severely burned his left hand, leaving it deformed and useless. With the help of several teachers and doctors who noticed the brilliant mind of the penniless and disabled young boy, Noguchi escaped his fate through hard work and the tenacity to grasp any opportunity that came his way. He maneuvered his way out of the tiny country town to the nearby city of Aizu-Wakamatsu where he had his fused left fingers surgically separated to regain partial use of the hand and where he could study medicine and Western languages.

His next strategic move was to Tokyo to study and practice medicine. Because of his language ability, he acted as a translator/guide during the Tokyo visit of an important American doctor. He seized this opportunity to make a prestigious foreign contact, which eventually led to a long-sought-after invitation to continue his studies in America. His years as a bacteriologist in the West culminated in his famous—and fatal—yellow fever research.

Noguchi wrote extensively in English and presented his papers at medical symposiums all over the Western world. He was a member of the Rockefeller Institute and was awarded numerous honorary degrees and other honors. He was decorated by several nations, including his own, for his contributions to mankind; Ecuador even named a town after him to honor his work in that country.

His American wife, Mary, donated many of his belongings and

papers to the Hideyo Noguchi Memorial Museum. Viewing the museum's documentation of his accomplishments, it's easy to understand what kind of pride Inawashiro takes in its only international citizen and why Dr. Noguchi is held up as an inspiration to the youth of Japan.

On the east side of the parking lots, behind the tourist facilities, is the Aizu Minzoku-kan, a complex representing another part of the Aizu district's history. A wonderfully realistic display of over 6,000 items once used by the local citizens is housed in two minka, old traditional farmhouses. The farmhouse rooms are packed with old furnishings, clothing, tools, and other elements of a pre-Westernized rural Japan. Walking through the rooms, touching, photographing, and absorbing, you can get a vivid picture of life in the days when the Sasaki and Baba families actually lived in these two lovely old houes.

The museum grounds also feature a phallic rock garden representing the role of the ancient fertility symbol in the local religion and a gift shop with a good selection of local folkcraft pieces. Unlike many museums, this one is unusually fun and realistic because of its natural farmhouse setting and hands-on displays.

Most bus tours only allow time to see the Noguchi Museum, so you may want to come to Inawashiro on your own and then pick up a bus tour of the national park from Inawashiro Station.

BANDAI–ASAHI NATIONAL PARK, Fukushima's biggest tourist attraction, is crisscrossed by five toll roads that connect the prefecture's major transportation centers with the park's volcanic peaks, lakes, lodges, campgrounds, rest stops, and lookouts. Tour buses serving the park begin at Aizu-Wakamatsu, Inawashiro, Kōriyama, and Fukushima stations. Most make quick one-way trips through the mountains and lakes with stops at strategic lookouts and tourist centers before depositing you at the next transportation center. From Aizu-Wakamatsu, you can take a local bus in the morning to the Noguchi–folk museum complex by the lake, another local bus or taxi to Inawashiro Station, and then take a tour bus through the park to Fukushima Station to continue your northward journey. The park's very efficient and fairly inexpensive bus system is designed so that you can get off at any one stop for a few hours or overnight and then catch another bus for the rest of your tour. Bus schedules and options are confusing, so this is one part of your itinerary you need to work out before you arrive.

Most of the overnight accommodations and recreational facilities are in the newest part of the local volcanic topography, the Bandai Kōgen, a lush green plateau formed less than 100 years ago by a violent eruption of the ancient volcano, Mount Bandai. Over 100 bodies of water, from the big Lake Hibara, the long narrow lake on the plateau's western edge, to the tiny, multi-colored ponds known as Goshikinuma (five-colored ponds), were formed when the mountainside was resculpted on July 15, 1888.

In less than 15 minutes on that day over forty local villages were left in ruins and 477 people were killed. Although there was no lava flow, a series of ten explosions of volcanic gases, preceded by a loud, thunderlike rumble and a sharp earthquake, propelled cascades of boulders down the mountainside. The landscape was drastically readjusted when the debris dammed rivers and streams, burying forests under a haphazard arrangement of new lakes and ponds. On the nights of July 25th and 26th each year, a ceremony is held on the shores of Lake Inawashiro to give peace to the souls of the victims of Mount Bandai's most recent eruption.

Bandai Kōgen Bus Station, at the southeast corner of Lake Hibara, is the gateway to the 3.7-kilometer-long walking path past the five-colored ponds of Goshikinuma. The highly developed tourist center is connected to Aizu-Wakamatsu via the Bandai Gold Line toll road. The toll road's name comes from the well-known folk song lines, "Bandai-san is a treasure mountain; even the sasa (bamboo grass) is crowned in gold."

The Goshikinuma path comes out on the east at Goshikinuma

Iriguchi Bus Stop. You can also reach this section of the park via a 30-minute bus ride from Inawashiro Station. The Ura Bandai Kokuminshukusha[5] is a short walk from the bus stop, and there is a small museum featuring the plateau's flora and fauna also nearby.

The popular Bandai–Azuma Lake Line toll road begins here. It heads east through the mountains past Lake Akimoto before it runs into the Bandai–Azuma Sky Line toll road, which terminates in the onsen area just outside of Fukushima City.

Another tourist center is located near Lake Onogawa. Of interest here is the Ura Bandai Mingei-kan, near Tsurugamine Bus Stop. Three old farmhouses were combined to make one minka-style folk museum filled with pottery, furniture, tools, and the like.

If you continue north on this local highway between Lakes Onogawa and Hibara, you'll run into the Nishi Azuma Sky Valley Line, the toll road linking the national park with Yonezawa, Yamagata Prefecture's southern castle town.

Campgrounds are plentiful around Lake Hibara and the smaller lakes between it and Lake Onogawa. There are many lodges located in this area between Goshikinuma and the Nishi Azuma Sky Valley Line, including the Ura Bandai Kokumin Kyūka Mura, a government-sponsored vacation village with camping facilities for 3,000, and the Hibara-sō lodge[6] for another 230 visitors.

Whether you came through Fukushima to get acquainted with its colorful history, or to sample the tree-scent of its mountains and lakes, or were lucky enough to have time to do both, you can't deny that this "first" of Tōhoku's six prefectures was a worthwhile stop on your trek north to explore Japan's back country.

5. Ura Bandai Kokuminshukusha, Goshikinuma Iriguchi, Azuma Kyoku kunai, Fukushima-ken 969–27; tel. (024132) 2923.
   裏磐梯国民宿舎　〒969-27　福島県吾妻局区内五色沼入口
6. Hibara-sō, 1092 Onogawahara, Hibara, Kita Shiobara-mura, Yama-gun, Fukushima-ken 969–27; tel. (024132) 2421.
   檜原荘　〒969-27　福島県耶麻郡北塩原村檜原小野川原　1092

MIYAGI
PREFECTURE

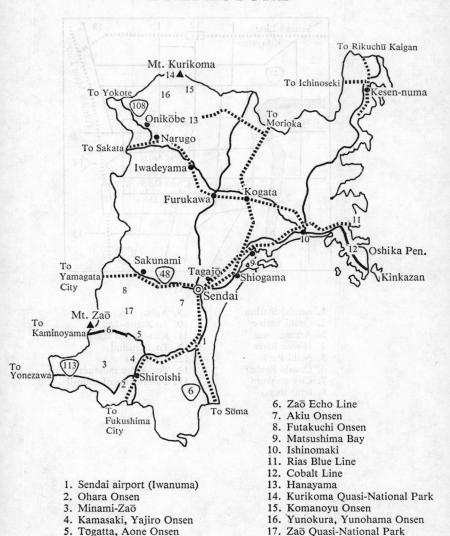

1. Sendai airport (Iwanuma)
2. Ohara Onsen
3. Minami-Zaō
4. Kamasaki, Yajiro Onsen
5. Tōgatta, Aone Onsen
6. Zaō Echo Line
7. Akiu Onsen
8. Futakuchi Onsen
9. Matsushima Bay
10. Ishinomaki
11. Rias Blue Line
12. Cobalt Line
13. Hanayama
14. Kurikoma Quasi-National Park
15. Komanoyu Onsen
16. Yunokura, Yunohama Onsen
17. Zaō Quasi-National Park

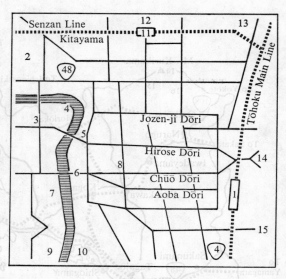

SENDAI

1. Sendai Station
2. Ōsaki Shrine
3. Art museum
4. Hirose River
5. Nishi Park
6. Ōhashi Bridge
7. City museum
8. Ichibanchō

9. Aobayama
10. To Zuihō-den
11. Kita-Sendai Station
12. To Tsutsumi
13. Tōshō-gū
14. To history museum
15. To Mutsu Kokubun-ji

Introducing Miyagi

MIYAGI IS handcrafted kokeshi dolls, a 1,200-year-old castle, and handmade paper hung out to dry in front of a thatched-roof farmhouse. It is quiet onsen situated along beautiful mountain gorges, and it is modern, big-city streets literally covered with thousands of colorful streamers to celebrate one of Tōhoku's Big Three summer festivals, Sendai's Tanabata.

Miyagi is pine-covered islets crowded into a calm bay, and it is Tōhoku's closest approximation to a cosmopolitan, modern metropolis. These two spots, Matsushima Bay and Sendai City, are two of Tōhoku's biggest attractions. Matsushima, considered one of the three most beautiful places in Japan, is a jumble of over 260 sea-eroded islands covered in varying thicknesses of wind-bent pine trees. Sendai is Tōhoku's largest city, its educational, cultural, and business center. It is a giant of a city by back-country standards, a fascinating mix of modern Japan's traffic, big stores, fine restaurants, and even high-rise "mansion" apartment complexes and the back-country life style.

Kokeshi dolls, probably the best known symbol of the Tōhoku district, are more closely identified with Miyagi than with any of the other five prefectures. The limbless, cylindrical wooden dolls developed in the forests of the back country—no one knows for sure just where, when, or why. Some say kokeshi are an offshoot of the prayer wands of a primitive native religion. Others say feudal-period kijishi, or wood artisans, who normally made bowls, trays, and other practical items, or maybe even local farmers, began making the brightly painted dolls to amuse their children over the long, bleak Tōhoku winters. A similar story tells of kokeshi originating as souvenirs for rich city dwellers who would spend weeks or even months soaking in the therapeutic hot springs of the Tōhoku mountains.

Whatever their true origin, kokeshi are an authentic folkcraft of the back country. Do not confuse them with the mass-produced wooden dolls of various shapes and sizes made in other parts of Japan. True kokeshi are always shaped on a lathe from a solid piece of unfinished wood and handpainted in the distinctive pattern of one of the ten official Tōhoku kokeshi guilds. A collector can instantly tell the origin of any kokeshi just by looking at either its shape, type of wood, or markings.

Each kokeshi guild is headquartered near a mountain forest in a usually quiet onsen where you can watch the kijishi at work. Miyagi has four of these guilds—Narugo, Tōgatta, Yajirō, and Sakunami—located at the onsen of the same names. The prefecture also hosts Tōhoku's two big kokeshi festivals, at Shiroishi in early May and at Narugo in early September. (The other six Tōhoku kokeshi guilds are Tsuchiyu in Fukushima, Hijiori and Zaō Takayu in Yamagata, Nambu in Iwate, Tsugaru in Aomori, and Kijiyama in Akita.)

A description of Miyagi Prefecture must make mention of the one figure who totally dominates its history—the Datè clan's most famous leader, Masamune (1567–1636). The nationally-known back-country lord was a compatriot of the powerful leaders Hideyoshi and Ieyasu at the height of Japan's feudal period. But Masamune was also a colorful figure in his own right—a child maimed psychologically by his mother's favoritism to a younger brother and physically by smallpox, which left him disfigured and blind in one eye, who became the "one-eyed dragon," a heroic warrior, and an enthusiastic builder of grand-scale castles, temples, and shrines. It is, in fact, impossible to spend more than a few hours sightseeing in Miyagi without running into some of the buildings, treasures, or legends that Datè Masamune left behind.

Miyagi's long history is preserved in a variety of museums and historical sites, most clustered in the Sendai area, but some in such unlikely places as along out-of-the-way mountain roads and on small islands. It's not an exaggeration to say that the foreign visitor will leave the prefecture—even after a short stay— with an excellent overview of the back country's past and a glimpse of its future.

Sendai and Southwestern Miyagi

THE CITY OF SENDAI, Miyagi's capital, is a delight for almost everyone who comes here—with the possible exception of those caught in its big-city traffic.

Foreign visitors to Tōhoku find the city an easy transition from the sophisticated southern metropolitan areas to the more traditional life style of the back country. Tōhoku's foreign residents, on the other hand, consider Sendai an exciting yet not totally unnerving plunge into the modern urban world they have, for the most part, forsaken. And Sendai residents themselves rate their city one of Japan's most desirable to live in.

With a population of over 600,000, Sendai is the unofficial capital of the entire Tōhoku district. It's the largest city between Tokyo and Sapporo (Hokkaido's capital, which has in many ways a similar appeal). A good portion of Sendai's population comes from elsewhere in Japan, attracted by the northern branch offices of many major corporations and by the city's ten colleges and universities, including the prestigious Tōhoku University.

Sendai also hosts Tōhoku's second largest foreign community; only Aomori's Misawa City has more foreign residents. Many of its foreign residents are here more or less permanently. Like many Japanese, they came to Sendai for a variety of reasons, but Sendai's special blend of traditional and modern Japan has encouraged them to stay. Luckily for the English-speaking visitor, Sendai's foreign residents have generously shared their enthusiasm for and knowledge of their city in an English-language guidebook called *In and Around Sendai*. This informative local guide is in Sendai bookstores or can be ordered by mail from co-author and long-time Sendai resident Jim Vardaman.[1]

Sendai is often referred to as the "mori no miyako," the capital of trees. Like Sapporo, its wide, tree-lined boulevards make seeking out its downtown attractions an unusually pleasant experience—if you're walking. Even the Hirose River, which winds through the city, is called "the miracle of the city of 600,000" because it remains relatively unpolluted in spite of its location.

If you're ready for a bit of big city—with a back-country flavor—plan to spend a night in one of Sendai's plentiful business and luxury class hotels, or in one of its four youth hostels. But, if you like your city in smaller doses, you can instead stay at one of Miyagi's numerous hot-spring resorts. As metropolitan as downtown Sendai may appear, the countryside is not far away.

SOUTH AND WEST of Sendai, Miyagi's terrain is composed of beautiful natural forests, scenic gorges and valleys, and, of course, more of Tōhoku's famous mountain onsen. These onsen, scattered along rivers or tucked into the forests, range from small, old country onsen to modern high-rise hotels.

Several onsen are located south of Sendai, as is the traditional paper-making center of Shiroishi. The Sendai Airport at Iwanuma is also south of the city.

Shiroishi is a stop for some trains on the Tōhoku Main Line; it is also on both the Tōhoku Expressway and Highway 4. The city itself is known for its handmade washi, traditional Japanese paper, and for its big kokeshi festival in early May. Shiroishi

1. Mr. Jim Vardaman, 305 Park Mansion, 2-1-40 Komegafukuro, Sendai-shi, Miyagi-ken 980.
ジム・バーダマン　〒980 宮城県仙台市米ケ袋 2-1-40 パークマンション 305 号

washi is made in the old way from the pulp of a kind of mulberry. The paper is extremely strong and durable. In fact, in olden times it was twisted into thread for use in clothing. Today, you can buy sheets of the sturdy paper or naturally dyed washi purses, wallets, and even noren (doorway curtains). If you can't stop in Shiroishi, you can find Shiroishi washi in some Sendai craft shops.

Every year between May 3rd and 7th, fans of another traditional craft crowd into the city for the Shiroishi Kokeshi Festival, which is highlighted by the All-Japan Kokeshi Contest. Shiroishi is near the Tōgatta and Yajirō kokeshi-making centers, but, if you attend the festival, you'll see dolls and artisans representing all ten Tōhoku kokeshi guilds.

From Shiroishi, you can explore Miyagi's beautiful countryside by heading west along either of two routes. One is Highway 113 which connects Shiroishi with Niigata Prefecture's Arakawa near the Sea of Japan. While the highway is still in Miyagi, it follows the Shiroishi River for a time, past several scenic gorges and rock formations and past the hot-spring resort of Ōhara. Highway 113 also provides the best access to Minami Zaō, a recreational community along an old daimyo thoroughfare.

Ōhara Onsen is a cluster of seven ryokan, including one with an outdoor rock bath along the river. The nearby Ōhara Gorge is particularly beautiful in fall, and the Zaimoku Iwa (Lumber Cliffs), a National Natural Treasure, is only 5 kilometers south of the onsen. The 100-meter-high, 200-meter-long group of quartzite cliffs resemble cut lumber standing on end above the river.

Another 7 kilometers west of Zaimoku Iwa is the access road heading north to Minami Zaō. There are camping facilities available at Minami Zaō's youth travel village along a river, and a youth hostel beside a small lake. But perhaps of greater interest to foreign visitors is the Yokogawa Minshuku Village, also near the lake. The thatched-roof minshuku recall the days when Minami Zaō was along the Shichigayado Kaidō, the route between Yamagata's Kaminoyama and Shiroishi that ten Tōhoku daimyo used on their regular pilgrimages to and from Edo. The road's name came from the fact that there used to be seven (shichi) groups of lodgings (yado) along this route to accommodate the large daimyo processions. Minami Zaō also offers a 3-kilometer-long walking path along the Yoko River Gorge and a short walking path around the lake. It is a 75-minute bus ride from Shiroishi Station.

On a local road heading northwest from Shiroishi are the two nearby onsen of Kamasaki and Yajirō. The former, which has a youth hostel, is a 25-minute bus ride from the station, and the latter is only 2 kilometers further up the road. Kamasaki Onsen's water is known as one of the best medicinal waters in Tōhoku; it is especially good for cuts and wounds. The Yajirō Kokeshi Guild is headquartered in this area.

Six kilometers north of Shiroishi on Highway 4 is the town of Zaō, where the access road to the Zaō Quasi-National Park begins. (See Yamagata's Zaō section.) There are two more Miyagi onsen are on this route. Tōgatta Onsen is famous as the headquarters of the kokeshi guild of the same name. It has a 2-kilometer-long walking path through the woods behind the onsen that passes several old mountain shrines. Among the many accommodations at this highly developed onsen is a youth hostel. Buses from Sendai Station stop at Tōgatta Onsen on their way to the Zaō Echo Line toll road.

Aone Onsen is about 5 kilometers west of Tōgatta. Though it now has ten ryokan where long-term visitors soak daily in its therapeutic waters, it was at one time a favorite of the Datè family. Aone's Fubō-kaku Kōgen Hotel has preserved a seventeenth-century Momoyama-style inn building, which now houses a collection of Datè-related articles.

A cluster of onsen closer to Sendai is just off the Tōhoku Expressway's Minami Sendai interchange. Akiu Onsen is a 40-

minute bus ride from Sendai Station and only 10 minutes by car from the interchange. Its fifteen ryokan are located on the Natori Rapids, the site of one of Tōhoku's oldest onsen. Several smaller old-style onsen are also located on the Natori River, as is the Tenshu-kaku Shizen Park, a new tourist center with a large Japanese-style garden and an outdoor bath. Some kokeshi artisans from the Tōgatta Guild are headquartered in Akiu.

One of Japan's most spectacular waterfalls, called Akiu-Ōtaki, is comparable to Nikko's famous Kegon Falls, and is a 35-minute bus ride west of Akiu Onsen. Next to the fifty-five-meter-high and five-meter-wide waterfall is a small religious building that was founded by the famous priest Jikaku Daishi in the early Heian period. There is a 3.3-meter-high weathered bronze statue of Fudō, one of the guardians of Buddhism, inside.

Eight kilometers further up the river is Futakuchi Onsen, a quiet mountain spa that is 2 hours from Sendai by bus. Hiking trails take off from here for Yamagata's Yamadera hillside temple complex. The 15-kilometer-long, 5-hour hike takes you past fantastic rock formations and through beautiful gorges. (See Yamagata's Yamagata City and Yamadera section for an easier access to Yamadera.)

The local road continues for a short distance beyond Futakuchi Onsen to the Banji Iwa, a beautiful cliffside of 600-meter-tall, pillar-like rocks. You can camp either near Banji Iwa at Akiu Bungalow Village or at another campground just outside Futakuchi Onsen.

If you can't spare the time to discover these out-of-the-way pieces of rural Miyagi but still want to sample a bit of the prefecture's mountain scenery and take in a hot bath, you might consider visiting Sakunami Onsen. Sakunami is directly west of Sendai on both Highway 48 and JNR's Senzan Line, the routes linking the Miyagi and Yamagata prefectural capitals. A train from Sendai Station takes only 35 minutes by express and 45 minutes by local train. A night in Sakunami is especially practical if you're combining a visit to Yamadera with your trip to Sendai.

As you might suspect by its location between the two metropolitan areas, the once quiet onsen along the Hirose Rapids has given way to several modern high-rise hotels. Even the 180-year-old Iwamatsu Ryokan[2] has added a modern four-story addition. But the old thatched-roof original ryokan is still standing next to the new wing, and the Iwamatsu's lovely outdoor rock bath along the rapids is still a delightful experience. Even if you aren't ready to splurge on a night of ryokan prices (for which you'll stay in the new building while the staff uses the charming old inn), you can buy a bath ticket to experience this traditional Tōhoku-style outdoor bath. A covered corridor of over 100 wooden steps leads down the steep river bank from the original inn to the riverside mixed-bathing hot spring.

Sakunami is a kokeshi town where, like Tōgatta and Yajirō, you can watch local wood artisans craft their distinctive dolls. From Sakunami you can also sample one of Miyagi's forested gorges by taking a local train to the next station, Yatsumori, and walking the Nikkawa Line path along the Nikkawa Rapids to Okunikkawa Station, 2.5 kilometers away.

ALTHOUGH SENDAI has the stores, office buildings, restaurants, and night life of a big city, it is a surprisingly compact, well laid out (unfortunately due more to wartime devastation than to city planning), and generally pleasant and comfortable city for the visitor sans auto to maneuver about in.

But Sendai offers more than just the amenities of modern Japan. In spite of extensive war damage, it has several reminders of its colorful past still intact, and others have been reconstructed over the years. These historical sites include Aobayama (Green

2. Iwamatsu Ryokan, Sakunami Onsen, Miyagi-machi, Miyagi-gun, Miyagi-ken 989–34; tel. (02239) 5–2211.
岩松旅館 〒989-34 宮城県宮城郡宮城町作並温泉

Leaf Hill), the site of the Datè clan castle, the Datè family mausoleum, and the old religious structures of the Ōsaki Hachiman
Shrine, the Mutsu Kokubun-ji Yakushi-dō, and the Tōshō-
gū shrine.

Both Sendai's past and its present are displayed in its many
museums, which include two devoted to the city's feudal past,
a historical and folk museum, a beautiful new prefectural art
museum, and the special interest railroad and metallurgy museums.

And for Tōhoku's foreign residents who haven't been to a
big city in a while, Sendai's department stores and its two,
long arcaded shopping streets, Ichiban-chō and Chūō Dōri,
are great entertainment in themselves. These same streets come
into the national limelight each August when Japan's most famous
Tanabata Festival celebration transforms the usually roomy
malls into magic lanes of unbelievable color and crowds.

Sendai Station itself is an impressive modern terminal that
underwent its massive facelift in the early 1970s in preparation
for the Tōhoku Shinkansen's arrival in 1982. It's hard to imagine
that not even 100 years ago the same Sendai Station was gearing
up with equal enthusiasm for another big event—the completion
of the Tōhoku Main Line, which finally linked the back country
with the rest of Japan. A small railway museum on the first
floor of S-Pal, the station department store, recaptures this
event.

If you walk a few blocks west of the station along the main
thoroughfare leading from it, Aoba Dōri, you'll run into one
of Sendai's famous green belts that give the city its "capital of
trees" title. Another concentration of trees is along Jōzen-ji
Dōri, several blocks north of Aoba Dōri. Each of these wide
boulevards is lined with over 200 large shade trees. The trees
were planted after World War II to restore some greenery to
the devastated city along its newly widened and straightened
main streets. Today, auto exhaust from Sendai's big-city traffic
is taking its toll on the green boulevards, but, for the time being,

Sendai's trees provide a restfulness that counteracts the hectic pace of the busy downtown.

Although Sendai is a particularly easy city to explore on your own, you might find it more efficient to take one of the several city bus tours which cover the most popular sights. The tours are operated by the City Bus Travel Office on Aoba Dōri next to Marumitsu Department Store, less than a block from the station. They offer varying courses, including tours to nearby Shiogama and Matsushima. (See the following chapter.)

The most famous site in Sendai is Aobayama, the hill chosen by Datè Masamune after Shogun Tokugawa Ieyasu granted him permission to build a large-scale castle from which to rule. Completed in 1602, Aoba Castle was destroyed during the Meiji Restoration. Its main gate, the Ōtemon, survived this period only to fall victim to the fires of World War II. The Gokoku Shrine now takes up most of the castle site along with a statue of a mounted Datè Masamune and the Aobajō History Exhibit. The latter is a mini-museum on the second floor of a building of souvenir and craft shops. The museum has scale models of the original castle, a mural of the large Datè clan entourage on its way to Edo, and other material connected with the hill's former residents.

The bus stop nearest Aobayama is called Hakubutsukan-mae. From there, you'll have to walk up Datè's hill to reach his castle site, but the bus stop puts you in a centralized location for visiting the other nearby historical attractions.

Just before crossing the Ōhashi Bridge, the bus will pass a statue of three men. This is the Christian Martyrs' Monument. It was donated by Portugal to honor the memories of those Sendai Christians who died here during the Tokugawa purge of Christianity in the early seventeenth century. The middle figure is the Portugese priest Carvalho; he is flanked by a samurai and a farmer to represent his Japanese converts who were also put to death. The priest himself suffered a slow, torturous drowning death near the Ōhashi Bridge.

At the intersection beyond the bus stop is a statue of another Sendai Christian of that era, Hasekura Tsunenaga. Hasekura's story is one of both great adventure and tragic disappointment. He was sent to Rome by Datè Masamune in 1613 to deliver a letter to Pope Paul V. The journey took over two years, including an overland trek through Mexico. But he did get to see the pope, and he made it safely back to Sendai in 1620, seven years after he sailed out of Miyagi's Tsukinoura bay.

However, when Hasekura reached Japan he received the heart-breaking news that his mission had been futile, since Christianity had been abolished shortly after he had set sail. The disappointed adventurer died a few years later. You can visit his grave in Sendai's Kōmyō-ji temple. The crystal candlesticks he brought to Datè as a gift from the pope are at times displayed in the Sendai City Museum and at other times in Matsushima's Zuigan-ji Museum.

Nearly 330 years after his futile journey, Hasekura was honored by the city of Sendai with this monument. Recently, on the 400th anniversary of his birth, a reproduction of this statue was presented by Sendai to its sister city of Acapulco, Mexico, to commemorate the Mexican portion of his journey.

Between the two monuments, and near the bus stop, is a road leading to the Sendai City Museum. The museum keeps a collection of several thousand artifacts concerning Sendai's history. The exhibits change monthly, with a few hundred items on display at any one time. The collection includes treasures of the Datès, old woodblock prints and maps of the area, scrolls, and items associated with Hasekura's long journey.

You can reach Aobayama, the castle site, by continuing uphill on this road past the museum. You'll go by another monument, this one dedicated to the Chinese writer and intellectual, Lu Hsün, who spent a few years early in our century in Sendai studying medicine. He is known in Japan as Rojin, the Japanese pronunciation of the characters in his name.

A 20-minute walk southeast of the Sendai City Museum or a 20-minute bus ride from Sendai Station to the Otamayabashi Bus Stop will take you to the elaborate mausoleum of Datè Masamune, the Zuihō-den. The ornate Momoyama-style building shares a wooded, gently sloping hillside along the Hirose River with the graves of other Datè clan members. The original building was destroyed during the war, and the present building was completed less than ten years ago. When the rebuilding began, Datè's tomb was opened and its contents photographed. You can see a photo display of this event in the exhibition room of the Zuihō-den. Datè's remains are now in a vault under the new building. The site of the original tomb is across the compound from the exhibition room. Fifteen of Datè's retainers who committed ritual suicide upon their master's death are also buried in the complex.

Further out of town, but perhaps of interest to some visitors, is the Metallurgy Museum. Its collection of metal artifacts from all over the world include a 3,000-year-old bronze spearhead from Ireland, sword guards from Japan's Tumulus period, iron tea kettles from Japan's Meiji-era, and metal items spanning the globe and the generations in between. Many technical aspects of metallurgy are documented and displayed here. The museum is a 30-minute bus ride from Sendai Station to the Kinzoku Hakubutsukan-mae Bus Stop.

Northwest of the Datè castle site is another museum, the recently opened Miyagi Prefectural Art Museum. Inside the modern building are displays of both Japanese and foreign art, with a special emphasis on Tōhoku artists. Three gardens, a visual center with video tapes, and an activity workshop provide additional dimensions to the static art displays. Take a bus heading for Kōtsū Kōen for 15 minutes; get off at Nikō Senshō-mae and walk for 1 minute.

Having escaped wartime damage, the 380-year-old Ōsaki Hachiman Shrine is still standing in the northern section of the city.

This National Treasure was built by Datè Masamune in 1607 in the ornate Momoyama style. But the main building, past the huge stone torii and at the top of nearly 100 stone steps, has weathered nicely over the years. Throughout the night of January 14th each year, residents from all over the city come here to add their New Year's decorations to the shrine's big bonfire during the Dondosai (Fire Festival). The shrine is a 15-minute ride from the station at the Hachiman Jinja-mae Bus Stop.

Also northwest of the station, near the Senzan Line's Kita-Sendai Station, is Kitayama, an area of many old shrines and temples. Three of the most noteworthy are Rinnō-ji, with its lovely Zen-style iris garden; Shifuku-ji, with its rock garden; and Kōmyō-ji, with Hasekura's grave.

Two other religious buildings still standing from the seventeenth century are the Tōshō-gū shrine and the Mutsu Kokubun-ji Yakushi-dō. The Tōshō-gū shrine is a 15-minute bus ride northeast of the station, at Miyamachi Go-chōme. Like Tōshō-gū shrines all over Japan, it was built to honor the first Tokugawa shogun, Ieyasu. The weathered, wooden building has been named an Important Cultural Treasure.

Southeast of the station are the ruins of the Mutsu Kokubun-ji. First built in 742 at the request of Emperor Shōmu, the temple was destroyed by Yoritomo on his way to Hiraizumi in 1189 (see Iwate's Hiraizumi section), and rebuilt by Datè Masamune in 1605 as the Yakushi-dō. You can still see some of the foundation stones of the first temple laid out 1,200 years ago. A complete model of the original temple is in a small museum to the west of the Yakushi-dō. Mutsu Kokubun-ji Yakushi-dō is a 15-minute bus ride from the station.

More Sendai history is preserved in the Sendai Museum of History and Ethnology, a stately old Meiji-era building east of the station. Both the building and its contents have historical significance. Built in 1874 as part of an infantry training center, the two-story building is the only surviving Western-style wooden barracks in Japan. The U.S. forces used it for a while during the Occupation, and later the Sendai police force used it as a police academy. It was restored as a museum in 1979 to resemble its 1910 appearance, when it was still part of the army training center.

Inside are two floors of old folk toys, pottery, art, farm tools, and some military items. The museum stands on the former training ground, which is now covered with shrubs, flowers, and grass. It's new name is Tsutsujigaoka Kōen (Azalea Hill Park); strangely enough, it is most famous for its old cherry trees, some of which are over 250 years old. The park is a 5-minute walk from Tsutsujigaoka Station on the Senseki Line or a 10-minute bus ride from Sendai Station to the Marumitsu-mae Bus Stop.

Like Tōhoku itself, Sendai's two main crafts have a simple, earthy look about them. The Sendai tansu are sturdy, keyaki (zelkova elm) chests decorated with heavy, smoked ironwork. Sendai craftsmen have been making these chests for 400 years, and a few artisans are still carrying on the tradition. Both antique chests in good condition and the new ones are very expensive, with good examples of the former becoming harder to find except in museums.

Tsutsumi-yaki pottery is also simple, yet beautiful. The craft began in Edo times in the northern Sendai suburb of Tsutsumimachi. It nearly died out in the Meiji era, was revived, and suffered a recent setback when Sendai's strong earthquake of 1978 partially destroyed its brick kiln. You can see some older pieces of the hardy pottery in Tōhoku craft museums and occasionally in antique shops.

Sendai has history for those visitors looking for the past; it has modern attractions for those seeking to enjoy the present. It offers big city to those coming from the country, and country to those coming from the big city. But most of Sendai's Japanese visitors come all at once to experience something else. They come to join the shoulder-to-shoulder crowds walking the dazzling streets of the Sendai Tanabata Festival.

THE TANABATA FESTIVAL is not unique to Sendai, but the Tōhoku capital's celebration is the most elaborate in the country. The famous festivities begin on the evening of August 5th with fireworks and folk dancing at Nishi Park. On the following three evenings attention turns to parades down Jōzen-ji Dōri. During the day, the crowds pack the lavishly decorated streets of Ichiban-chō, Hirose Dōri, and Chūō Dōri. During this period, the city's population swells with an unbelievable two million camera-clicking revelers.

The original Tanabata (Seventh Night) was celebrated on the seventh night of the seventh month of the lunar calendar; it is now celebrated on July 7th in many Japanese cities. Tanabata marks the time of year when a weaving girl and a herdsman, represented by the stars Vega and Altair, usually on opposite sides of the Milky Way, meet. An ancient Chinese legend tells of how this pair of lovers became idle due to their excessive love, and how both of them were exiled by the irate king of heaven to opposite sides of the river of heaven; he stipulated, out of compassion for them, that they could meet on one day of the year—and that day is now celebrated as Tanabata.

Thousands of bamboo, paper, and—nowadays—even vinyl decorations hang into the streets suspended from huge bamboo poles to create a mass of fluttering color for visitors to walk under, around, and through. These long streamers symbolize the threads that the girl weaves all year. You may also spot other symbols of Tanabata among the colorful decorations; these are wishes for success. A paper kimono conveys wishes for success in sewing; a crane, wishes for a long life; a purse, for wealth; a strip of paper with a poem, for skill in calligraphy; a fish net, for a large catch; and a basket, for thrift and savings over the year.

If you can take the crowds, Tanabata is an exciting time to be in town. But if you want to get to know Sendai in a more relaxed manner, a less hectic time might be better. The ideal situation, of course, would be to come twice.

Although the city itself is a great place to visit, many travelers use Sendai as a secondary point of interest on their way to one of the most beautiful spots in Japan—the pine-covered islands of Matsushima Bay, only a short train ride north of the big city.

Matsushima
and the Miyagi Coast

MATSUSHIMA BAY is Miyagi Prefecture's biggest tourist attraction
and one of the most famous spots in Japan. The 260 picturesque
islets of wind-bent pines and wave-carved rock that dot Matsushima Bay have fascinated travelers for centuries. In 1689, Bashō
called the bay the most beautiful place in all Japan.

Today, Matsushima more modestly shares its title with Ama-
nohashidate on the Sea of Japan and Miyajima in Hiroshima
Bay. Just as no traveler can go to Beijing without taking a side
trip to the Great Wall, you cannot visit Sendai without spending
at least a few hours in Matsushima.

But Matsushima is not all the northern coast of Miyagi has to
offer. If you have the time, you can also explore the ancient castle
ruin at Tagajō, the whaling center of Ayukawa, Miyagi's Golden
Flower Island, and more beautiful coastline.

WHEN THE YAMATO government sent its soldiers up north to
conquer the indigenous Ezo in the eighth century, two important
fortresses were set up. One was Akita Castle near the Sea of Japan and the other was Taga Castle near the Pacific Coast. Both
were on the tenuous border separating Japan from the land of the
Ezo. Today Akita Castle is a park surrounded by bustling Akita

City, and Taga Castle is on the outskirts of a small country town called Tagajō (jō means castle). Tagajō is just beginning to rediscover its long roots in Japanese history.

A 10-minute ride north from Sendai Station on a Tōhoku Main Line local train will take you to Sannō Station. Turn right on the highway outside the station exit to begin a pleasant 20-minute walk past rice fields, excavations of the castle's outside wall, and a small park with a very old distance marker in a tile-roofed wooden cage. Your destination is the Tōhoku Historical Museum. In this building, the scenes you have passed on your walk come together in an interesting overview of Tōhoku's prehistory and history, with special emphasis on the ancient castle site on which the museum stands.

Taga Castle was built in 724, a massive Chinese-style fortress with inner and outer walls and many buildings. Excavations of the site began only sixty years ago. On your walk you passed some excavations of the outer wall, now identified with permanent descriptive markers and rows of newly planted shrubs identifying the exact location of the old wall.

When Bashō passed this way in 1689—long after the castle was in ruins and long before modern archeologists from Tōhoku University had rediscovered it—he was deeply moved at the sight of a lone monument to that era standing at what was once the fortress's important south gate.

The Tsubo Stone, a man-sized boulder still standing on end, was used in the eighth century to declare Tagajō's place in the world in tiny etched Chinese characters. By reading the marker, travelers leaving the south gate knew how far they had to walk or ride to Nara, the seat of the government, and how far north lay the beginning the alien Ezo territory, not very far at all.

Bashō was overwhelmed at the feeling of oneness with his ancestors as he gazed at the marker on his way to Shiogama and Matsushima. "This monument was made a thousand years ago and is a very real and vivid link with the past. Seeing it is one of the things that has made my trip worthwhile and one of the happiest moments of my life. Forgetting all the trials of the journey, I wept for sheer joy."

You can peek inside the wooden lattice work of the protective building and perhaps in the dimness make out a few of the tiny characters covering the Tsubo Stone—and feel a sense of continuity not only with the residents of Taga Castle, but with the traveling poet who passed this spot on a journey much like your own.

If you stand at the Tsubo Stone and look north across the highway, you will be looking at the hillside location of the main castle, a model of which you can study in the museum, the modern building only 500 meters further down the highway. The museum, like the Tsubo Stone, stands barely within the outer wall of the castle. Bashō would no doubt have approved of its well-done displays of Tōhoku history, including a replica of the ancient distance marker he walked past on his way to the famous pine islands.

IF, LIKE BASHŌ, you stopped in Tagajō on your way to Matsushima, your Tōhoku Main Line train continues on from Sannō Station to Matsushima Station, where you can catch a taxi to Matsushima Kaigan on the shore of the beautiful bay.

But if you skipped Tagajō this trip and are coming from Sendai, head north on the Senseki Line to Matsushima Kaigan Station, located very near the famous bay. Or you might want to get off the train before you reach the bay, at Hon-Shiogama Station, for a ferry ride through the little pine islands in the bay to Matsushima Kaigan.

Bashō made a short stop in Shiogama to see the Shiogama Shrine, and you may want to do the same. The shrine is a 10-minute walk west of the station and the ferry port is also a 10-minute walk, in the opposite direction. Shiogama Shrine, an Important Cultural Treasure, was rebuilt by Datè Masamune in 1607. Bashō enthusiastically described the shrine's fine wooden pillars and brightly painted beams, which have been restored since he viewed them. You must walk up the shrine's 223 stone steps past old cryptomeria and cherry trees to view the 375-year-old building.

Ferries leave almost hourly from Shiogama Port for Matsushima Beach. You may end up on a big, gaudy "Chinese dragon" ferry, but the hour-long ride past the wind- and sea-shaped islets of Matsushima Bay is worth it. The ferry docks at Matsushima Pier from which you can easily walk to all of the beachfront attractions, both natural and historical. The Shiogama–Matsushima ferry is a good alternative to an around-the-bay cruise from Matsushima Beach, since much of the same area is covered. If you're coming into Matsushima Station on the Tōhoku Main Line, consider taking the Matsushima–Shiogama ferry and the Senseki Line back to Sendai for a memorable last glimpse of the beautiful bay.

If you're coming in by car, you have the option of getting an overview of the bay from the Matsushima Panorama Line toll road that takes you up a hill to several well-placed overlooks. The entrance to the Panorama Line is off Highway 45 before you reach the Matsushima Beach area. Some bus tours from Sendai also come this way.

From the Senseki Line's Matsushima Kaigan Station, you can see the Matsushima Aquarium just ahead. The modern building features the usual aquarium fare including seal shows several times daily.

Also near the station, to the left as you leave, is the well-known Zuigan-ji temple, established in 828 and for the past 700 years a Zen seminary. The present buildings were built in the Momoyama style by Masamune in 1605. The main temple and the priests' living quarters are National Treasures.

The grounds of the Zuigan-ji are also interesting. Stone caves and carved images surround a grove of tall cryptomeria trees in front of the temple. The caves were once used by Zen priests for prayers. A small museum displays items from Masamune's day, including, at times, the crystal candlesticks Hasekura brought back from Rome. (See Sendai chapter.) Also on the grounds are two very old plum trees, one white and the other pink, that Masamune brought back from Korea in 1592 after an unsuccessful expedition there with Tokugawa troops, and the Donjiki, a minka from the village of Kako-machi moved here as a tea house and an example of rural Miyagi architecture.

If you haven't yet gotten a close look at the famous pine islands, you may want to save the temple and the fish for last and make your way directly to the beach. Along the densely built-up shoreline are several piers offering tours of the bay in a variety of craft ranging from the dragon ferry to rowboats. The large ferries circle the bay or head through the tiny islands to Shiogama or to Ōtakamori. The latter port is on an inhabited island directly across the bay from Matsushima Beach where you can climb a hill for an overview of the bay. The boat rides are nice, in spite of the incessant commentary in Japanese on some, but the view from the shore is also lovely.

Three of the wooded islands are connected to the beach by pedestrian bridges, the longest of which charges a toll. The closest island to Matsushima Kaigan Station is Oshima. Its caves and rock carvings reveal its past as a place of Zen meditation. Today you can picnic here or just view the bay.

The picturesque and, in fact, often photographed Godai-dō is a seventeenth-century religious structure built on another land-connected pine island. You can walk across the two bridges leading to the Godai-dō, but the building is opened only once every thirty-three years. Fukurajima is at the other and of the third bridge, the one with the toll. Compared with many of the islands in the bay, it is fairly good-sized, and you can walk along paths crisscrossing the island past labeled shrubs, flowers, and trees, including a fine collection of camellias.

Back on shore near Oshima you'll see the Kanran-tei, Datè

Masamune's Wave-Viewing Pavilion. The teahouse was built in 1587 by Hideyoshi, who later gave it to Masamune. The Datè lord moved it to his Shinagawa (Tokyo) estate, but his son later had it moved to Matsushima Beach, the family's private seaside park until the Meiji Restoration. A very small museum with more Datè family articles and pictures and displays of Matsushima Bay plants and animals is behind the Kanran-tei.

The strange-shaped little islands jumbled in Matsushima Bay lend themselves perfectly to the Japanese penchant for naming such natural formations. If you take a tour boat through the bay, you'll have pointed out to you the head of a Niō, a temple guardian, on Niō-jima; the Japanese warrior's helmet of Kabuto-jima; an arched longevity island; and Sengan-jima, a rock so pretty that Masamune jokingly promised anyone who could deliver it to his garden payment of sengan (940,000) mon, a very large amount of money at the time.

As one of the Big Three scenic wonders of Japan, Matsushima Beach has been unmercifully built up to accommodate the flood of tourists who pour in daily. But you can beat the crowds by going early in the day. And it is not that difficult to block out the sounds of humanity by concentrating instead on nature's skill in sculpting such a variety of interesting rock formations, topping them with a nice touch of twisted green pines, and then surrounding them with the calm of Matsushima Bay.

IF YOU LIKED WHAT you've seen so far of Miyagi's northern coastline, you may want to continue on before turning inland. You can travel down the jagged Oshika Peninsula and then explore the well-known Kinkazan Island at its tip.

Ishinomaki, 24 kilometers north of Matsushima, is one of the gateways to this area. It is only an hour from Sendai by express train on the Senseki Line and 40 minutes from the Tōhoku Main Line station of Kogota via the Ishinomaki Line. Highway 45 from Sendai and Matsushima also goes through the port town. A daily ferry connects Ishinomaki with Kinkazan Island, and seven other daily ferries go to Ayukawa, near the tip of the Oshika Peninsula. Buses from Ishinomaki Station also go down the peninsula.

Another entrypoint to the peninsula is Onagawa, 15 kilometers northwest of Ishinomaki on a local road and the Ishinomaki Line. A 5-minute walk from Onagawa Station will take you to the 170-year-old Sanjūsan Kannon, thirty-three Kannon images carved on a hillside overlooking the port. A daily ferry connects this port with Kinkazan Island.

Near Onagawa is the entrance to the scenic Cobalt Line toll road, a 30-kilometer-long, 400-meter-high road bisecting the Oshika Peninsula. Its high perch gives the traveler a fantastic simultaneous view of the ragged coastlines of both sides of the peninsula. Near the road's end at the tip of the peninsula is the Cobalt-sō kokuminshukusha.[1]

From Onagawa you can also explore the Miyagi coastline north of the Oshika Peninsula on the Rias Blue Line, a 20-kilometer-long free seaside drive linking Onagawa and Okatsu. From Okatsu you can then make a big circle following the Kitakami River back to Highway 45 to continue your northward itinerary.

An interesting southern coastal road goes the length of the Oshika Peninsula, through a series of little fishing villages to the whaling center of Ayukawa. You can travel this route by bus from Ishinomaki Station. Fifty minutes from the station is Tsukinoura Bay, where Hasekura Tsunenaga set sail for Rome in 1613. Ten minutes further down the road is the Jūichimen Kannon at Kyūbunhama. The 11-faced, three-meter-high solid wood carving is an Important Cultural Treasure.

Near the tip of the Peninsula, both on this local road and on the Cobalt Line is the port of Ayukawa. Ayukawa Port used to

1. Cobalt-sō, Oshika-machi, Oshika-gun, Miyagi-ken 986–25, tel. (02254) 5–2281.
コバルト荘　986-25　宮城県牡鹿郡牡鹿町

be a very prosperous whaling center, but recent international pressure against whaling has put somewhat of a damper on its activities. You can, however, get a good idea of what goes on in the whaling industry and in the lives of the great sea mammals in the Oshika Town Whale Museum. The relatively new museum is near the pier where the ferries depart for Kinkazan and Shiogama.

Fifteen minutes south of the end of the Cobalt Line on a local road is the Gobansho Tenbō Park, a lookout point with a great view of the Miyagi coast in all directions. This fact was also noted by the Datè clan during the area's feudal period. A barrier guard house, or gobansho, used to be on top of this hill so that guards could monitor any activity in the Datè clan's coastal waters.

Kinkazan (Mount Golden Flower) Island is a very special place. It was referred to in the Man'yōshū, Japan's ancient anthology of poems completed in 759, and has had special religious significance since the Koganeyama Shrine was founded on the island in the eighth century. Along with Dewa Sanzan and Osorezan (see Yamagata's Dewa Sanzan and Aomori's Shimokita sections), it is one of the three spiritual spots of Tōhoku. Legend says that if you come to Kinkazan three years in a row to worship at its shrine, you'll be financially secure for the rest of your life.

The island-mountain is 24 kilometers around and its peak is nearly 450 meters above sea level. Ferries reach it from Ishinomaki in 2 hours, from Onagawa in 80 minutes, and from Ayukawa in 25 minutes. If you're planning to visit the island, check the ferry schedules beforehand, since ferries run only a few times a day. Kinkazan has a tourist hotel and a youth hostel.

The mountain forests covering the island are filled with nearly 500 deer, about 100 wild monkeys, 130 different kinds of birds, and over 600 species of plant life. This is all in addition to the beautiful seascapes you can enjoy from the top of Mount Kinkazan, a 2-kilometer hike from the shrine. It's a 2-hour hike to the east side of the island, but, if you can make it, you'll find the Senjōjiki

(1,000 Tatami Mats) Rock, a wide, "table" of white granite that gradually slopes into the sea. North of Senjōjiki is the Senjinzawa, a huge sheer rock standing on end like a giant had cut it in half.

If you're on the island on the first Sunday in October or on October 10th, you'll be able to see the annual ceremonial cutting of the deer's horns.

After getting acquainted with the northern Miyagi coast, you can get back to the main north–south thoroughfares from Ishinomaki via the Ishinomaki Line to Kogota, or Highway 108 to the expressway and Highway 4—or you can stay on Highway 45, which now and then hits some beautiful patches of coastal scenery as it heads northward.

If you're going inland and haven't yet experienced a back country onsen, consider a short visit to the Narugo/Kurikoma area on your way out of Miyagi Prefecture.

Narugo
and the Kurikoma Quasi-National Park

NORTHWESTERN MIYAGI Prefecture blends into its neighbors Iwate and Akita on the slopes of the impressive, volcanic Kurikoma-yama (Chestnut Horse Mountain), also called Sukawa-dake. The area is a fine representative of Tōhoku's beautiful mountain scenery and a good spot to sample one or two of the hundreds of typical onsen communities that dot volcanic mountainsides throughout the back country.

This part of the prefecture is more or less encompassed by the Kurikoma Quasi-National Park, which also spills over into Iwate and Akita. The center of northwestern Miyagi's tourist activity is the onsen town of Narugo, one of Tōhoku's most famous hot-spring resorts. But if Narugo's paved streets lined with hotels, hot baths, and souvenir shops are too sophisticated for your back-country itinerary, the surrounding forests hold several secluded rural onsen. The area's feudal past is kept alive in the two old gobansho, barrier guard houses, of Hanayama and Sakaida, and in the Yūbikan, once a temporary castle and later a school for the Datè clan, in the now sleepy little town of Iwadeyama.

Detouring from the main north–south transporation arteries to sample a bit of rural Tōhoku around Narugo Onsen is not difficult either by road or rail. The Tōhoku Main Line branches into the Rikuu East Line at Kogota Station, about 40 kilometers north of Sendai. However, several Narugo-bound trains leave directly from Sendai Station daily. By car you must take Highway 47 west from Furukawa, a city about 34 kilometers north of Sendai on the Tōhoku Expressway and Highway 4. Both the Rikuu East Line and Highway 47 cross Miyagi and Yamagata to terminate near Sakata, Yamagata's big seaport on the Sea of Japan. (See Yamagata's Shōnai and Dewa Sanzan sections to learn what happens to these scenic routes once they cross the Miyagi border.)

To reach the small onsen even further off the tourist trail and closer to the volcano's peak, stay on the train or highway for another 20 to 25 kilometers past Furukawa. Local roads from the towns of Wakayanagi and Tsukidate head west into the mountains as does the Kurihara Dentetsu, a tiny electric railway which begins at JNR's Ishikoshi Station.

A third thoroughfare through the area is the Senshū Line (Highway 108), linking Narugo and Akita Prefecture. This new highway follows the 200-year-old route used by northern Tōhoku daimyo to cross the Ōu Mountains on their required treks to Edo. (See Akita's Kakunodate section.)

The majority of visitors to northwestern Miyagi come to see the famous Narugo Onsen. And most of them pass through the town of Iwadeyama, about halfway between Furukawa and Narugo, with barely a glance out the window at this now ordinary-looking little town.

Only the Yūbikan is left to remind the twentieth-century traveler that, for a brief period, Iwadeyama was the most important spot in Miyagi. Iwadeyama was the headquarters of the Datè clan for only 11 years, from 1591 to 1602, before Lord Datè Masamune built his grand-scale castle at Aobayama. When the main castle was moved to Sendai in 1602, Iwadeyama became a minor castle town. And when fire destroyed the castle in 1663, the Yūbikan was built as a temporary replacement. It later became a school for samurai children, and today the 320-year-old thatched-roof building surrounded by a garden is a quiet reminder of the days when Iwadeyama was a vital part of the Datè empire. It is also the oldest surviving example of the shoin-zukuri style of architecture in Japan.

The Yūbikan, now a small museum, and the castle site, now called Shiroyama Park, are just west of Iwadeyama Station. The two are connected by a footpath. If you decide that Iwadeyama is worthy of a short stop and some reflection, also visit the town's bamboo crafts exhibition hall, one block south of the station, to see examples the works of local craftsmen.

The resort community of Narugo is known for its therapeutic hot water, plentiful accommodations, beautiful autumn colors, and kokeshi tradition. As the town that produces more of the limbless, wooden kokeshi dolls than any other single location, Narugo holds a kokeshi festival each year from September 7th through the 9th to honor the Tōhoku craft.

Although the town's popularity and resultant building boom detract somewhat from its charm, Narugo's beautiful location along the Narugo Gorge, its kokeshi, and the old-fashioned public bathhouse, the Takinoyu, make it an interesting stop, especially if you can't spare the time needed to reach some of the outlying onsen.

The only exception to the Japanese resort prices charged by its hotels and inns is its youth hostel, the Takishima Ryokan, a 6-minute walk from the station. A campground and the Onikōbe Lodge kokuminshukusha[1] are a 40-minute bus ride north of town on Highway 108.

The nicest and cheapest way to experience Narugo's potent hot water is to visit the Takinoyu Public Bath, a 5-minute

1. Onikōbe Lodge, Fukiage Kōgen, Narugo-machi, Tamazukuri-gun, Miyagi-ken 989–69; tel. (02298) 6–2331.
鬼首ロッジ 〒989-69 宮城県玉造郡鳴子町吹上高原

walk from the station. The small, traditional bathhouse uses open wooden "pipes" to bring cascades of steaming hot water (taki no yu) into its two large wooden tubs. The building is not very old, but the spot it stands on has been used for bathing since underground volcanic activity brought forth the hot water in 837. The water won't lather at all, but it is supposed to be great for health problems connected with the stomach, nerves, joints, and, especially, the skin.

KOKESHI are Narugo's second attraction. Over seventy men and women kijishi, or wood artisans, work here to produce the distinctive Narugo kokeshi. By turning right as you leave the station and going uphill, you'll be on Kokeshi Dōri, a street lined on both sides with the workshops and sales outlets of Narugo's kijishi. You can also visit the Nihon Kokeshi-kan to see its 3,000-piece collection of outstanding kokeshi from all over Tōhoku. The rustic white building is on a hillside near Narugo Gorge, a 10-minute bus ride from the station.

Although Narugo kokeshi are known for almost always dressing in painted chrysanthemums, their most distinctive feature is their bird-like squeak. Turn the head of any Narugo kokeshi and you will hear this sound. Probably not coincidently, naru, the first character of Narugo is formed by combining the characters for mouth and bird, and go means child. But Narugo also means "rumbling sounds," specifically those which accompanied the first surges of hot water and steam from beneath the ground 1,150 years ago.

The quiet little Onsen Shrine, founded at the onsen's inception and located at the water's source on a hill behind the Takinoyu, comes to life each September 7th when its festival coincides with the Narugo Kokeshi Festival. During these three busy festival days, each kijishi dedicates one of his or her best creations of the year to the shrine, and the artisans attend a memorial service for all the defective kokeshi they had to unceremoniously toss in the woodpile over the year. The kijishi add demonstrations, sales, and competitions to the otherwise typical small-town Tōhoku festival, making it a popular annual event for residents and visitors alike.

To see the festival or Narugo's equally famous fall colors, you must visit the onsen in its busiest season. But when the busloads of tourists become oppressive, you won't have to go far to return to the area's quiet forests and simple back-country onsen like Narugo once was.

If your plans are to continue west on Highway 47 or the Rikuu East Line past Narugo, in only 11 kilometers you will be crossing into Yamagata Prefecture. Today's travelers don't arouse much fanfare as they cross this border, but in feudal times you would have had to pass the scrutiny of the guards at the Hojin-no-ie barrier guard house. If you're on a local train or traveling by bus or car, you can still visit the thatched-roof guard house. It is only a 10-minute walk from the local Sakaida Station.

North of Narugo is the Onikōbe Onsen cluster, where Narugo's nearest campgrounds and kokuminshukusha are located. Onikōbe is on Fukiage Kōgen, a 500-meter-high plateau with an unusual combination of attractions—a ski slope, pastures of grazing horses and cows, a geothermal power plant, a geyser that spews hot water and steam ten meters into the air every thirty minutes, and a forest museum featuring the animals and plants of the Kurikoma Quasi-National Park. A 2-hour hike east of the onsen or a 40-minute drive from Narugo on a local road that leaves Highway 108 just above the Narugo Dam will take you to the Katayama Jigoku, a barren "hell" of bubbling ponds, steaming ground, and the rumbling sounds of thermal activity just under your feet.

IF YOU HAVE THE TIME and really want to get off the tourist trail, you might want to visit a series of out-of-the-way onsen between Narugo and Kurikoma's peak. Begin your explorations of this part of the Kurikoma park from the towns of Wakayanagi or Tsukidate if you're traveling by car or from the local Ishikoshi Station on the Tōhoku Main Line. The two stops on the Kurihara Dentetsu Line from Ishikoshi that will take you near the mountain onsen are Kurikoma and Hosokura stations.

From Kurikoma Station, you'll have to travel the mountain roads by bus for 90 minutes to reach Komanoyu Onsen, three ryokan, and a minshuku tucked deep into a forested gorge. Two kilometers north of the onsen is a government-funded campground and workers' lodge, the Kinrōsha Ikoi no Mura Kurikoma,[2] which is, in fact, open to all visitors.

The other onsen in this area are accessible from Hosokura Station, the end of the Kurihara Line. An hour's bus ride directly west of the station is the Hanayama Dam recreation area. There are campgrounds on either side of the lake, and the Hanayama Youth Travel Village is further up the road. Nearby are Nuruyu Onsen, two ryokan along the river, and the Hanayama Gobansho, Miyagi's feudal past still standing for all who manage to get far enough into the back country to find it. The National Historic Site consists of an Edo-period wooden building and its thatched-roof gate from which Datè clan guards once controlled access into their territory via this old mountain trail. The building is still in good condition, and it provides a nice excuse to explore this far-off-the-main-roads area.

If any place on a bus route is still too civilized for your back-country travels, make your way to the Yunokura Onsen, an old ryokan located across a suspension bridge 90 minutes on foot north of Nuruyu Onsen. Another half-hour's walk further up the road will get you to Yuhama Onsen, a former rest stop for nomadic mountain hunters. Drivers can eliminate the walk but must then face a bumpy, unpaved mountain road instead.

2. Kinrōsha Ikoi no Mura Kurikoma, Numakura, Kurikoma-machi, Kurihara-gun, Miyagi-ken 989–53; tel. (02284) 6–2011.
勤労者いこいの村栗駒　〒989-53 宮城県栗原郡栗駒町沼倉.

Even though you must leave behind public transportation, pavement, and even electricity to visit these inns, you will gain the feeling of what the Japanese call rampu no yado. This is the warm nostalgia of staying in an old lamp-lighted inn nestled into a beautiful natural setting—a feeling you just may have come to the back country specifically to find.

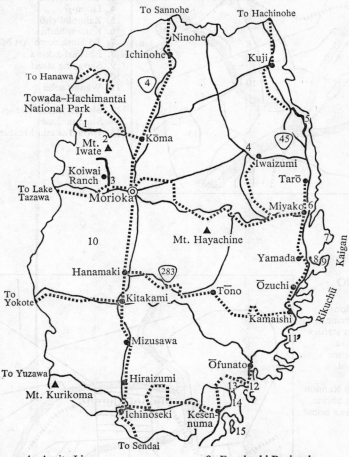

IWATE PREFECTURE

To Sannohe
To Hachinohe
Ninohe
Ichinohe
Kuji
To Hanawa
4
Towada–Hachimantai
National Park
5
1
Kōma
45
2
Mt.
Iwate
4
Iwaizumi
Koiwai
Ranch
Tarō
3
Miyako 6
To Lake
Tazawa
Morioka
7
Mt. Hayachine
Yamada 8 9
10
Hanamaki
283
Ōzuchi
To
Yokote
Kitakami
Tōno
Kamaishi
Mizusawa
11
Ōfunato
To Yuzawa
Hiraizumi
13 12
Mt. Kurikoma
14
Ichinoseki
Kesen-
numa
To Sendai
15
Rikuchū
Kaigan

1. Aspite Line
2. Matsukawa Onsen
3. Koiwai Toll Road
4. Ryūsendō cave
5. Kita-Yamazaki
6. Jōdogahama
7. Todogasaki
8. Yamada Bay
9. Funakoshi Peninsula
10. Hanamaki Onsen cluster
11. Chitose Kaigan
12. Goishi Kaigan
13. Takada Matsubara
14. Karakuwa Peninsula
15. Ōshima

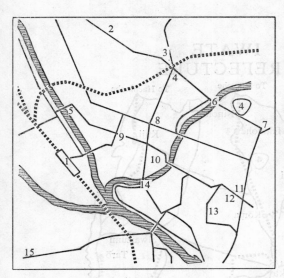

MORIOKA.

1. Morioka Station
2. To prefectural museum
3. City museum
4. Hōon-ji
5. Zaimoku-chō
6. Kaminohashi
7. To Hashimoto Art Museum
8. Ishiwari-zakura
9. Shopping street
10. Iwate Park
11. Wanko soba
12. Hachiman-gū
13. Sixteen Rakan statues
14. Shimonohashi
15. Hara Takashi Museum

TŌNO

1. Tōno station
2. Nambu Shrine
3. 500 Rakan statues
4. Chiba house
5. Tsuzuki Stone
6. Kappa Pool
7. Old torii
8. Fukusen-ji Kannon
9. Komagata Shrine
10. To Kitakawa house

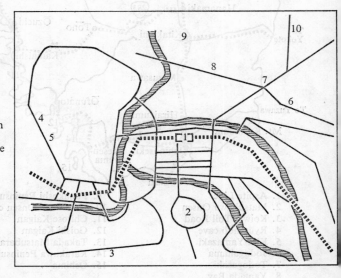

Introducing Iwate

IWATE PREFECTURE, Honshu's largest in area, is usually considered Japan's poorest prefecture. Eighty percent of the prefecture is made up of mountains that have isolated Iwate's people from the rest of the country and have severely limited their ability to earn a living in a far from ideal climate. The standard Japanese image of Iwate can be compared to the American stereotype of Appalachia—its people are often looked down upon as the hillbillies of Japan.

But the factors that made Iwate Prefecture Japan's poorest (a distinction traded back and forth with runner-up Kagoshima in southernmost Kyushu) have also made Iwate one of the richest places in Japan for the visitor seeking both glimpses of old Japan and outstanding examples of the country's natural scenery.

The latter category is represented by the two national parks within Iwate's borders: the mountainous southern portion of the Towada-Hachimantai region and the rugged cliffs and bays along the Pacific Coast's Rikuchū Kaigan. But more beautiful and perhaps better representatives of why Iwate is as it is—poor and unsophisticated but rich in natural scenery and local color—are the breathtakingly beautiful mountain passes running across the prefecture. Paved highways, train lines, and modern tunnels now allow travelers easy access through mountainous areas once steep, dangerous, and often completely impassable.

Three Iwate communities—Hiraizumi, Tōno, and Morioka—represent a good chunk of the history of Japan in microcosm. Much of this history is preserved in Hiraizumi, Tōhoku's 900-year-old former "Mirror of Kyoto." The rich, powerful, four-generation-long Fujiwara dynasty created in Hiraizumi a military capital of elaborate Buddhist temples rivaling even the opulence of Kyoto. This is where the popular Japanese folk hero Yoshitsune fled to escape the wrath of his brother, the shogun Yoritomo. Today the remains of its former glory make the otherwise humble little town of Hiraizumi the most historically significant spot in Tōhoku.

Tōno, a picturesque farming area in a basin surrounded by beautiful mountains, was for a very long time almost totally isolated from the rest of the world. In its isolation, folk beliefs and customs flourished undisturbed by the ways of the Yamato conquerors from the south. Even after roads and trains linked them with the outside world, the independent people of Tōno clung to their ways and their legends. Early in our century, folk-lore chronicler Kunio Yanagita documented the legends of Tōno for all the country to experience.

In the same tradition, the people of Tōno are not in any great hurry to abandon their old-fashioned rural life style. Today between the town and the rolling foothills around it are farms straight out of your image of what old rural Japan should be, down to water wheels still standing in the rice paddies and moss-covered wooden footbridges over winding streams. For those seeking a glimpse of this part of Japan's past, Tōno may be the highlight of a trip to the back country.

Finally, Morioka, the centrally-situated capital city, reflects a still later feudal age in Japanese history. The Nambu clan was headquartered here throughout the Edo period, a time officially preserved in Morioka's museums and castle grounds and, unofficially, in its old neighborhoods, which still retain much of their original flavor.

It's true that most of Japan laughs at the hicks of Iwate with their unsophisticated rural ways and unintelligible local dialects. Yet even though the Japanese may look down on the mountainous prefecture, you, the foreign traveler exploring the many facets of Japan, will no doubt find traveling through this poorest of prefectures one of your most enriching experiences while in Japan.

Hiraizumi

IWATE WASN'T ALWAYS looked down on as poor and backward
by the rest of the country. In fact, at one time, Hiraizumi, the
area's political and cultural center, rivaled Kyoto with its ornate
temples and the high level of its Buddhist culture, while the
wealth and power of its ruling family were considered threats
to the central government.

   That was a long time ago—in the eleventh and twelfth centuries—just as Japan's political power was shifting from the Imperial
court in Kyoto to the new military government in Kamakura.
Even the back-country town of Hiraizumi, headquarters of the
wealthy Fujiwara clan, was involved in the story of this fascinating
period of struggle for national power. The Fujiwaras were in
power for only four generations, but the remains of their brief
but glorious empire make the small town of Hiraizumi the most
historically important place in Tōhoku—a place no visitor to
the back country should miss.

   "The glory of three generations of Fujiwaras is now but a
brief-remembered dream" wrote the poet Bashō in 1689 as he
wept at the ruins of the Fujiwara's grand empire. (The poet
possibly failed to mention the fourth Fujiwara lord because
it was his greed that destroyed the dynasty.) Since Bashō's visit,
what remained of the Fujiwaras' Hiraizumi has been tastefully

restored to give modern visitors an idea of what this Mirror-of-Kyoto culture must have been like when it flourished in the far northern reaches of civilized Japan in the twelfth century.

Hiraizumi is just 9 kilometers north of Ichinoseki, a major stop on the Tōhoku Main Line. To get there you must transfer to a local train, bus, or taxi at Ichinoseki Station. Highway 4 and the Tōhoku Expressway also go through the town.

Its two main attractions, the temples of Mōtsū-ji and Chūson-ji, each offer accommodations—Mōtsū-ji, a modern youth hostel, and Chūson-ji, the Tabashine-sō,[1] a reasonably-priced Japanese-style inn behind the temple's main building. There is a campground on the road linking the two temples.

The Ichinoseki area also includes two natural attractions, the gorges of Gembikei and Geibikei (similar in name but very different from each other and in opposite directions from town) and the Takkoku no Iwaya cave temple, which was founded 1,100 years ago by the first Yamato conquerors from the south. You can enjoy all of the above, including a leisurely exploration of Hiraizumi, in a leisurely two-day stopover.

GEMBIKEI IS A PRETTY but not spectacular small gorge formed by a clear and surging river making its way through a tumble of angular rock cliffs and water-smoothed boulders. It's one of those places that makes for a nice Saturday outing but that could easily be skipped by busy travelers—except that it fits so well into an exploration of the Hiraizumi area.

Gembikei is about a 30-minute bus ride west of Ichinoseki Station along Highway 342. An interesting local road heads northeast from the gorge, beyond the cave temple and some wonderful, prosperous-looking, old-fashioned farmhouses just begging to be photographed, and right to the front gate of Hirai-

1. Tabashine-sō, Hiraizumi-machi, Nishiiwai-gun, Iwate-ken 029–41; tel. (019146) 2326.
東稲荘　〒029-41 岩手県西磐井郡平泉町

zumi's Mōtsū-ji. The short distances between the sights along this road make a taxi a reasonable alternative to the infrequent buses.

The Takkoku no Iwaya cave temple is about a 10-minute ride from the gorge. It is a miniature of Kyoto's Kiyomizu Temple built into a large natural cave. On the cliff face to one side of the cave is the outline of a Buddha's head and shoulders, all that remains visible of a once full-figured image said to have been carved in the late eleventh century.

The temple itself is dedicated to Bishamonten, the Buddhist guardian deity of warriors, and is said to have been built by Sakanoue no Tamuramaro, one of Japan's most famous warriors, who conquered the Ezo tribes of the back-country in the early ninth century. One version of the story claims that the cave was an Ezo fort which Tamuramaro dedicated to the warrior deity when he conquered it. The present building, a reconstruction built in 1961, replaces a seventeenth-century restoration that was destroyed by fire in 1946.

THE TOWN OF HIRAIZUMI lies just another 10 minutes up the road, past the lovely Iwate farmhouses. The glorious Hiraizumi culture began after years of localized struggles for power when the central government awarded formal control of the northern provinces of Dewa and Mutsu—most of present-day Tōhoku—to Fujiwara Kiyohira, a local magnate, in the eleventh century. It ended with the beheading of Kiyohira's great-grandson at the order of Shogun Minamoto no Yoritomo.

Kiyohira was an extremely rich (from local gold mines), powerful, and independent ruler. At the urging of Kyoto priests, he used his wealth to create in his domain what was to be an ideal paradise on earth. In this earthly paradise, there would be no more fighting and people could become devoted practioners of Buddhism. Thus, in 1105 he began building his Mirror of Kyoto along the classical Chinese design. His son and grandson continued this pursuit of peace and culture; his great-grandson, unfortunately, did not.

Events occurring down south at the time greatly influenced the fate of the Fujiwara empire. Minamoto no Yoritomo, on his way to becoming Japan's first shogun, distrusted the independent northern power in Hiraizumi. On the other hand, his younger brother Yoshitsune chose to spend his teenage years with the Fujiwaras to take advantage of the high level of their culture and to practice martial arts. A few years later, his military skills helped Yoshitsune to be victorious over the Taira clan, which greatly enhanced his family's influence over the Imperial Court. Yoritomo, jealous of his brother's successes in battle and fearful of the young warrior's popularity, ordered him killed.

Yoshitsune and his loyal friend Benkei, an independent warrior-priest, disguised their party as yamabushi (ascetic mountain priests) so that they could flee north through the various barrier gates to the territory of Yoshitsune's friends, the powerful Fujiwaras. Hidehira, Kiyohira's grandson, permitted the refugees to stay in Hiraizumi and offered them protection.

On his deathbed, Hidehira advised his son Yasuhira to continue protecting their friend, to ignore Yoritomo's promised rewards for his brother's demise, and to continue to kill Yoritomo's messengers so they would eventually stop coming. But tempted by Yoritomo's offers of more land and fearing that the shogun's soldiers would massacre the Fujiwaras, Yasuhira turned against Yoshitsune and ordered him killed. According to legend, Benkei, a great favorite of Japanese fans of faithful companions, protected his master to the end even with many arrows in him. It is believed that in 1189 Yoshitsune was killed in or very near Hiraizumi, although throughout Tōhoku romantic legends persist of an escape further north to Hokkaido and perhaps even to Mongolia.

Yasuhira's reward for turning on his friend was the annihilation of the Fujiwara clan by Yoritomo, which brought an end to their northern center of culture and peace forever.

When Bashō came to Hiraizumi, the battles and fires of the intervening five centuries had obliterated almost all of the once grand Fujiwara capital. He wrote:

> The summer grass—
> 'Tis all that's left
> Of ancient warriors' dreams.

Today the castle site is still covered in summer grass, but much has been done to restore the Fujiwaras' two centers of Buddhist culture.

The Heian-period garden of the once massive Mōtsū-ji temple is the visitor's first stop if coming from Gembikei. Although founded in 850, the second Fujiwara lord built it in the twelfth century into a magnificent complex of forty halls housing 500 priests. Today, except for their foundation stones, the buildings are gone, but the garden has been restored as one of Japan's few remaining good examples of a Heian-period Jōdo (Pure Land)-style garden.

The present Mōtsū-ji was built in 1909 on the opposite side of the garden's large pond from the original temple's location. Beside it is a small treasure house/museum, a youth hostel, and a stone monument with Bashō's summer grass lament. As you ponder Bashō's message, study on a display board next to the temple an artist's depiction of the huge complex of buildings which once stood across the pond.

At one time a bridge connected the temple's gate to this complex via the small island still remaining in the center of the pond. There is no longer a bridge across the pond, but you can walk around its perimeter and over the hardened earth and foundation stones which once supported the temple buildings. The original Mōtsū-ji also extended across the gravel road outside the present temple's fence. This road, by the way, leads to the temple Chūson-ji.

On January 20th each year, traditional dances from the Heian period are performed at Mōtsū-ji. The dances have been designated a National Treasure, since few from that time have been preserved. But if you prefer your temples in sun rather than snow, you can instead catch Mōtsū-ji's 30,000 irises in bloom during its annual Iris Festival between June 25th and July 15th.

While Mōtsū-ji was once the largest temple in all of northern Japan, the nearby Chūson-ji was the most beautiful—and its fabulous golden pavilion still is.

Chūson-ji is a 20-minute walk or five-minute ride from Mōtsū-ji and about the same distance from Hiraizumi Station. Its many buildings dot a low wooded hill overlooking a stretch of rice paddies and the meandering Koromo River. A wide cryptomeria-lined footpath leads to the temple buildings. The main temple is near the top of the hill, so if you're staying at the Tabeshine-sō behind it, don't carry more than you'll need for overnight. Chūson-ji, as one of Japan's most important historical sites, can get crowded when the tour buses unload, and nothing is nicer than to spend the night behind the temple and then stroll through the silent wooded complex very early the next morning.

Kiyohira began his new Kyoto with Chūson-ji in 1105. Today two of his original buildings are still standing and are joined by newer religious buildings, a treasure house/museum, an archives building, a thatched-roof open-air Noh stage, a teahouse, and other tourist accommodations.

But the main attraction has remained the same for almost 900 years. The glittering Konjiki-dō (Golden Hall), Japan's first National Treasure, is a small but spectacular monument in gold leaf, lacquer, and inlaid mother-of-pearl to the glory that once was Hiraizumi. The only other original building is the Kyōzō (Sutra Repository). Also still standing from Hiraizumi's early years is the first protective shelter for the Konjiki-dō built in 1288 at the urging of a Kamakura government official who sought to preserve what was left of Hiraizumi's faded splendor.

A new protective shelter was constructed in the 1960s when the Konjiki-dō was last restored, but Bashō paid homage to the farsighted official who 400 years earlier had taken the first steps to preserve it:

> The Hall of Light's enamel decoration would have been scattered long ago and lost—the gem-studded doors shattered by the winds, the gold leaf on the pillars decayed by frost and snow, and the hall itself reduced to a pile of rubble in an empty field of grass— had it not been encased by four new walls and covered over with roof tiles to protect the building from the elements. Thus, it will probably stand for a long time as a memorial of a thousand years.

> All June's rainy days
> Have left untouched the Hall of Light
> In beauty still ablaze.

Today this shelter stands empty but erect with the Konjiki-dō's original foundation stones still in place.

Many structures have been added to the Chūson-ji complex since Kiyohira's northern capital was gradually destroyed. The major buildings along the cryptomeria-lined path begin with the Benkei-dō, a small wooden hall to the left of the path built in 1826 to honor Yoshitsune's loyal friend. It is crammed with Yoshitsune- and Benkei-related articles including Benkei's six-sided sword guard, a main image of the bodhisattva Jizō carved in 1571, and two life-sized statues of Benkei and Yoshitsune carved by Edo-period and Meiji-era admirers respectively.

Beyond the teahouse and the first of several overlooks to the fields below is the Chūson-ji Hondō, the main hall, with the inn behind it. Dark blue fans with sutras printed in gold are sold here as beautiful souvenirs of Chūson-ji's original sutras now in the treasure house and archive buildings further up the hill.

Across from the Hondō is a new hall, the Onnaishōja, devoted to the Buddha Ichiji Kinrin, the only remaining Heian-period example of this image in Japan. The image's eyes are made of crystal, its hands are held in a pose usually associated with another image, the Dainichi Nyorai, and its back is open. This very special image has spent a good deal of the past 800 years behind locked doors and now can be viewed only from March 27th through November 10th.

Many of the temple's treasures were moved to the fireproof Sankōzō when it opened in 1955, including the coffins of the mummified first three Fujiwara lords and the jewelry taken from their bodies, images whose halls were destroyed over the years, and personal belongings of the Fujiwaras. Particularly interesting—and, in fact a symbol of Hiraizumi—are the lacy bronze ornaments which once hung in the Konjiki-dō. Gold from Hiraizumi's mines was mixed with copper to form these delicate bronzes, several of which are National Treasures. You can buy inexpensive reproductions of them to use as pendants or bookmarks. Set back into the trees beyond the Sankōzō in its modest-looking new shelter stands the 850-year-old Golden Hall of the Fujiwaras. Also called the Hikari-dō, or Hall of Light, the Konjiki-dō's ornate lacquer, gold leaf, and inlaid mother-of-pearl pillars, ceiling, and altar form a dazzling contrast to the drab simplicity of nearly everything else you'll see in the back country. It originally took 15 years to build, beginning in 1109, and there have been several attempts at restoration over the centuries. The latest such effort, a six-year project begun in 1962, involved complete regilding, relacquering and replacing of the badly deteriorated original Chinese mother-of-pearl inlays using Okinawan shells. Materials salvaged from the first building and from earlier restorations are on display in the shelter.

The Konjiki-dō's images are all from the Fujiwara period.

The mummified remains of the first three lords and the head of the misguided fourth rest beneath them. The latter item was returned to Chūson-ji after having been sent in a box to the shogun Yoritomo to admire. Allot enough time here to examine the intricate details of this sole remaining architectural representative of the wealth and craftsmanship of the Fujiwara culture.

Behind the Konjiki-dō are two other very old buildings, the original shelter and the Kyōzō sutra hall. The latter structure was built in 1108 but lost its second floor in a fire in 1337. It used to house 30,000 scrolls with sutras delicately written in tiny characters of gold and silver. Once one of the finest complete sutra collections in Japan, most of the scrolls in their inlaid lacquer boxes were removed after the Fujiwaras were destroyed. Some of the 2,700 scrolls that remain are on display in the Sankōzō and the modern archives building directly across the main path from the Kyōzō.

The archives building has a first-floor rest house, the hill's best view of the surrounding countryside, and a sutra scroll and art display on the second floor. Nearby is Chūson-ji's thatched-roof outdoor Noh theater. Performances are held here each year on January 20th, and on August 14th, two days before a daimon-ji is burned on nearby Mount Tabashine in honor of the souls of the four Fujiwara lords. Another series of performances is held from Nov. 1st through the 3rd during the Fujiwara Festival, which also features parades and folk dances. Another major event in Hiraizumi is the Azuma Kudari Gyōretsu, which recreates each May 3rd, during the May 1st through 5th Spring Fujiwara Festival, the flight of Yoshitsune and Benkei to Hiraizumi in 1172.

If, like most Japanese, you are moved by the drama of the courageous but persecuted Yoshitsune and the equally courageous and unfalteringly loyal Benkei, you may want to make one more stop before you leave Hiraizumi. The site of Yoshitsune's home-in-exile is now marked by a small wooden Buddhist hall, the Yoshitsune-dō, off the main road between Chūson-ji and the station.

GEIBIKEI GORGE, an interesting side trip from Ichinoseki, has fantastic 100-meter-high cliffs that shoot up steeply from the banks of a now unbelievably calm and shallow river. You can get there from Rikuchū-Matsukawa Station on the Ōfunato Line, a small trunk line linking Ichinoseki and the Pacific Coast. An 8-minute bus or taxi ride from the station will take you to the terminal of a fleet of wide, flat-bottomed river boats which run on frequent schedules to a sandy beach which is the most scenic spot in the gorge. The boat ride itself is as entertaining as the beautiful cliffs it slowly passes.

But you will have to be in the right mood for the boat ride. When you join a group of jovial Japanese tourists as everyone takes off shoes before stepping onto the plastic mats where you all sit for the 20-minute ride up the river. The scramble to reclaim the right pair of shoes on the swaying boat when it docks at the beach and again at the terminal is great fun. Your boatman will sing local folk songs as he skillfully uses a pole to push the boat along the nearly motionless river. At one point he'll edge close to the shore so his passengers can grab ropes set into the bank to help pull the boat up a rise in the river.

You can take along a picnic for the beach or simply walk around photographing the soaring cliffs before taking another boat back.

Although severely scarred by a huge rock quarry near Rikuchū-Matsukawa Station, the scenery along the 30-minute train ride from Ichinoseki features picturesque farm scenes in isolated mountain valleys typical of the beautiful Iwate countryside.

You may find the scenes along the Ōfunato Line so appealing that you'll want to stay on to the end of the line, which is just north of the city of Ōfunato in the southern part of the Rikuchū Kaigan National Park. But, if you do, you'll have to cross the mountainous prefecture once again so that you won't miss another interesting part of Iwate's past and of its present. Morioka, the Nambu castle town turned modern prefectural capital, lies directly north of Ichinoseki and Hiraizumi on the main train lines and highways heading north through the prefecture.

Morioka

MORIOKA IS one of those delightful Japanese cities which combine the conveniences and opportunities of modern Japan with the tranquil atmosphere and tangible reminders of old Japan. For Tōhoku's foreign population, Morioka is a great weekend adventure; for visitors to the back country it is a fine example of where Tōhoku is headed and where it has been.

Most foreign visitors have declared the city one of their favorites, although a single reason why is hard to express. Morioka is a combination of good things: many narrow roads left from the city's castle-town days and three broad rivers lazily meander through the city, encouraging the curious visitor to do the same; a large handful of interesting destinations structure one's wanderings; the city is beautifully situated against the backdrop of the majestic volcano, Mount Iwate; and a pervading atmosphere of warmth (in spite of the cool climate) makes the visitor feel comfortable and welcome.

If you're coming to the back country, do stop here for a day or two to see if you concur.

HANAMAKI IS directly north of Hiraizumi on the Tōhoku Expressway, Highway 4, and the Tōhoku Main Line. To get to Morioka, you must pass through the city of Hanamaki, gateway to the plush onsen communities in the mountains to the northwest collectively called the Hanamaki Onsen Prefectural Natural Park. And if you're flying into Tōhoku, the Hanamaki Airport may be on your itinerary.

If you have time to visit Hanamaki Onsen, about a 25-minute bus ride from the station, you can see inns ranging from the fantastic (and fantastically priced) Kashō-en,[1] a replica of a Momoyama-period teahouse, to a peacefully rustic ryokan in the woods. The Kashō-en was built in 1965 using the sukiya-zukuri style of Kyoto's Katsura and Shūgaku-in Detached Palaces.

Less elaborate and more secluded is the Namari Onsen, on a different route out of the city. A noted ryokan there is the Tōzō Ryokan,[2] with its deep indoor rock bath. If you're on a budget but still want to see Namari, there is a youth hostel nearby.

Hanamaki itself is a good-sized city where people have found interesting antiques and where potter Katsuyoshi Abe makes his Kajimachi pottery in an old-fashioned kiln next to his traditional house in the Ishigami-chō district. His house is hard to find (tel. 3-3679), but once you're there you'll find a small but high-quality selection of his green-tinged white pottery and the atmosphere of the old-time kilns which still produce such fine pots.

GETTING OFF THE TRAIN at Morioka Station or making your way through city traffic on streets originally laid out in pre-Toyota days, you may wonder what's so great about Morioka. It won't take long to find out.

Iwate's capital is the home of folkcrafts such as heavy cast-iron

---

1. Kashō-en (reservations and information), Hanamaki Onsen, Inc., Yumoto, Hanamaki-shi, Iwate-ken 025-03; tel. (01982) 7-2111.
   佳松園　〒025-03 岩手県花巻市湯本花巻温泉株式会社
2. Tōzō Ryokan, Namari Onsen, Hanamaki-shi, Iwate-ken 025-02; tel. (01982) 5-2311.
   藤三旅館　〒025-02 岩手県花巻市鉛温泉

tea kettles, or Nambu tetsubin, and cotton fabric dyed in traditional patterns; of the prefectural and city museums and a private
art museum; of several interesting old religious works; of the
largest private ranch in Japan; of the famous wanko-soba-eating
contests; and of the colorful Chagu-Chagu Horse Festival in the
late spring.

The city has the usual assortment of business hotels and the
the very nice but slightly more expensive Morioka Terminal
Hotel,[3] at the station. But a better deal for those who like Japanese-
style rooms at business hotel prices is the Sakura Kaikan,[4] a
lodging facility run by the Hachiman-gū shrine and located on
their grounds. The inn, which is run much like a kokuminshukusha,
was built to house out-of-town guests of the shrine's brides and
grooms, but when there's room other guests are welcome. The
Sakura Kaikan is just off the Highway 4 bypass, a good hike from
downtown.

If you get to the station in the morning during the tourist season
and you want to get a thorough overview of the city, you can take
the city bus tour leaving from the adjoining bus station. The
tour takes you to the city museum, the Hashimoto Art Museum,
to a restaurant for a wanko-soba-eating contest, to an iron tea
kettle factory showroom, out into the countryside to the boyhood
home of Japan's first commoner prime minister, and into the
suburbs to see the new prefectural museum. As with most bus
tours, this is not the cheapest way to go, and you spend too little
time at places you really like and too much at the others, but it's
the most efficient way of seeing the city in the shortest amount of
time with the least amount of hassle. And you'll return to the

3. Morioka Terminal Hotel, 1–44, Morioka Eki-mae, Morioka-shi, Iwate-ken
   020; tel. (0196) 25–1211.
   盛岡ターミナルホテル 〒020 岩手県盛岡市盛岡駅前 1-44
4. Sakura Kaikan, 22, 13 Hachiman-chō, Morioka-shi, Iwate-ken 020; tel.
   (0196) 51–8411.
   桜会館 〒020 岩手県盛岡市八幡町13の22

station with enough of the day left to wander through an old Morioka neighborhood or two.

One such neighborhood is only a 10-minute walk from the station. Cross the bridge and turn left for Zaimoku-cho. Here modern boutiques mingle with but don't infringe upon the charm of old-style shops. On weekends in the summer, the street becomes a colorful vegetable market when the noise of traffic is replaced by the shouts of welcome from cheerful produce vendors.

The two main drawing cards for the foreign visitor are the Kōgensha Mingei Shop and the Ebisu-ya dyed fabric shop and mini-museum. But the old-fashioned basket and rope shop, the traditional calligraphy and sumi-e (ink painting) supplies shop, and even the boutiques which feature modern creations made from old and old-style indigo kimono material are just as fascinating. Kōgensha features a large selection of crafts from all over Japan, mainly pottery, lacquerware, and fabrics. It is part of an interesting complex of buildings built around a narrow landscaped courtyard which extends back to the river.

At the end of the street at the traffic light you'll see the gold tile roof of the Kyoto-style building across the street which houses the Ebisu-ya. Here you can see Saburō Ono's dyed fabrics made into everything from purses and placemats to kimono and noren. Above the shop, the Ono family's personal collection of museum-quality old clothing and other articles is professionally displayed. You can ask in the salesroom for permission to go upstairs.

Ono-san's heavy cotton fabrics, all hand-dyed with natural dyes, go through a process of time-consuming handwork, the kind not often done today. He first creates a hand-cut stencil, borrowing from the designs of old Nambu samurai kimono. The stencil is placed on the fabric and the exposed areas of the cloth are coated with a special dye-resistant paste. The stencil is then removed and a natural dye is applied with a brush. After the dye has set, the paste is washed away. The paste used to transfer Ono-san's bold patterns onto the cloth is also handmade from an old formula: a combination of mochi powder and lime is kneaded into a taffy-like blob, steamed for three hours, and then mixed with hot water until it has the consistency of honey. Although there are obviously easier ways to produce a piece of patterned cloth today, Saburō Ono prefers to do it in the manner of Morioka's Nambu clan castle-town days, the way generations of Onos have been doing it for the past few hundred years.

Other places of interest in the city are further away from the station. Two landmarks of the city are the Shimonohashi and the Kaminohashi, the lower and upper bridges crossing the Nakatsu River. Their metal post tops have become symbols of the city, along with the iron teapot. The bridges were built by the first Nambu lord when he built his castle into the curve of the river between them. The date Keichō 14 (1609 to us) is etched into the metal of the posts.

The castle grounds, now minus the castle and known as Iwate Park, is a pleasant walk from the station either the "back way" over the Shimonohashi and along the river, or across the big bridge in front of the station and through the city's modern downtown. Downtown Morioka is not that different from any other downtown, although the Sambiru Department Store near the castle site has a good selection of local crafts and souvenirs on its first floor.

Your objective in finding the castle grounds is to cross the Nakatsu River behind it to find a delightful neighborhood of Nambu castle-town winding, narrow streets. Here you can wander past a tiny ironware workshop or two, a few antique shops, traditional sembei (rice cracker) shops and the like that are scattered among the coffee shops and modern storefronts which seem to be taking over the old streets.

If you have reservations at the Sakura Kaikan and haven't gotten too turned around on the Nambu lord's twisting streets, you're heading home, past the Meiji-era brick bank and McDonalds to the Hachiman-gū shrine complex. Also near the shrine are the Sixteen Rakan, the two-meter-high disciples of the Buddha carved in granite. The statues were the twelve-year-long project of a priest who began his work in 1837 to honor the souls of the victims of one of Iwate's frequent famines.

Back towards Iwate Park on a street lined with government buildings stands an unusual natural phenomenon. The Ishiwari-zakura, or Rock-Splitting Cherry Tree, does just that in front of the Morioka District Courthouse. The National Natural Treasure is 300 years old and has a trunk four meters around which is bulging out of a split in a large granite boulder. The tree stands in the former front yard of the Kita family, retainers of the Nambu lord. No one knows whether the rock was split by lightning, allowing the cherry seedling to sprout inside or whether pressure from the growing tree beneath it got the big rock in a vulnerable spot. Either way it is all that remains of the old samurai family residence.

Another interesting neighborhood of old Morioka is to the north of Iwate Park towards the bypass, but this one is a neighborhood of temples. A notable member of this community is the temple Hōon-ji where between 1731 and 1735 eight sculptors from Kyoto carved and lacquered 500 wooden rakan (disciples). The Japanese say they always see someone they know personally in these collections of typical Buddhist disciples, some grimacing, some gesturing, some making funny faces. Although you may not recognize a friend in this group, you may be able to pick out the non-Japanese faces of Marco Polo or Kublai Khan.

The Morioka City Kyōdo Shiryōkan, the city museum, is just across the bypass from Hōon-ji. The new building is on the site of the summer home of the Nambu lords. The old garden is still here on one side of the museum with its small teahouse intact and the Nakamura family's old house has been moved to the other side. Inside the "old-style" modern museum building are nice displays of the city's history and Nambu family treasures. Particularly interesting is a display from local festivals. From

Morioka Station the museum is a 10-minute bus ride. Get off at the Kōminkan-mae Bus Stop.

A short taxi ride south along the bypass from the Kyōdo Shiryōkan or a 20-minute bus ride from the station to Chosuichi-mae will get you to the Hashimoto Art Museum, one of the most interesting spots in town. The museum is about halfway up Iwa-yama, a forested hill from which skiing, golf, and amusement park facilities have been carved out.

Yaoji Hashimoto was a local artist who built this fascinating modern structure with his own funds to display his art and that of other local artists. The three-story concrete building was constructed without blueprints, a fact which will become evident as you walk through it. At first the museum seems to be based on a modern version of an old temple; once inside its narrow stone stairways are more like those of a European castle dungeon. The biggest surprise though is on the roof, where a complete Iwate farmhouse stands, thatched roof and all, wonderfully furnished and filled with articles from Iwate farmers' daily lives. The artist saved seven of these beautiful old houses from drowning when a new dam was scheduled to flood the land they had occupied.

Hashimoto-san, a man of eclectic taste, collected not only Iwate folkcraft in his unusual museum, but Western furnishings as well. In addition, beautiful examples of local lacquerware, ironware, and pottery are on display, as well as modern sculpture and painting, many in Western style but of Japanese subjects. Hashimoto-san's own paintings include several large canvases featuring working people in dark, dark colors, colors perhaps reflecting the gloominess of the subjects' hard lot in life.

The city bus tour unfortunately rushes through this interesting collection of arts and crafts so it can climb to the top of Iwayama for a much too long view from Iwayama Lookout of the rooftops of the suburban community below. The bus passes by the museum on the way down the hill; so, if you can swing it, try to have the bus pick you up as it descends the hill; you'll not miss a thing by skipping the lookout.

The city's third museum, the Iwate Prefectural Museum, is even further out in a newly developed area in the foothills north of the city. Take the Ueda Line bus for Matsuzono New Town; get off at Nishi-Matsuzono 2-chome.

With room to spread out in the new development, the prefectural museum was able to include a botanical garden and two relocated Iwate farmhouses on its grounds. The ultra-modern museum building is interesting in itself as a statement that Japan's poorest prefecture now views itself as a fully participating member of a prosperous modern Japan. A second-story wall of glass frames a magnificent view of Mount Iwate, the prefecture's own Fuji-like peak.

The museum follows the usual prefectural museum format and once again most foreign visitors will find the history and folkcraft sections most appealing. There is also an "experience study room" where visitors can try on old costumes and handle the tools and toys past generations used in their daily lives.

The two minka moved here are a magariya, or L-shaped house representing the typical Nambu style, and a sukoya, or straight, rectangular house from the northern reaches of the Datè clan's territory.

The L-shaped Old Sasaki Family House was built in the late nineteenth century and moved here from Iwaizumi, a small town northeast of Morioka. It is now a National Important Cultural Property. The short end of the "L" was the barn, a most practical set up during cold and snowbound Iwate winters. Driving through the prefecture, you'll probably pass many such thatched-roof magariya, some still in use by both farm families and their animals and others turned over to the animals after the family moved into a modern house next door. But if you can't get out into the countryside, the Sasaki House can help you imagine how it was and how it still is in many cases on an Iwate farm.

The Fujiya Family House was moved from the southern part of the prefecture which used to be part of Miyagi's Datè clan's holdings. It was built in the early nineteenth century.

A final old house to mention in Morioka is again on its outskirts, but this time in the opposite direction. The Hara Takashi Museum is included in the city bus tour. Although foreigners miss most of the historical significance of this memorabilia collection of Japan's first commoner prime minister, you can enjoy the country architecture and garden of his birthplace. It's not hard to imagine how proud the people of this humble village in the poorest of prefectures must have been when a local boy went on to international success.

Takashi Hara, the untitled man from back-country Japan, held the office of prime minister from 1918 to 1921; he was assassinated while still in office at the age of 66. During his time, mocking sophisticates from down south were fond of the derisive saying, "All of Japan north of Shirakawa is worth no more than 100 mon." (Shirakawa was once the site of a major barrier gate between Michinoku and the rest of Japan; the mon was Japan's smallest-denomination coin.) To survive, back-country people have to be hardy and resilient, qualities exemplified by Hara's good-natured incorporation of the key elements of this taunt into his personal seal. All of the prime minister's poems and other creative works are stamped with a seal that reads Ichizan Hyakumon, One mountain, one-hundred mon.

The Hara Takashi Museum is a 20-minute bus ride southwest of the station across the Shizukuishi River.

Unfortunately for souvenir collectors, the most notable craft of this northern castle town is both heavy and expensive. Nambu tetsubin, or Nambu ironware tea kettles, began to be made when a Nambu lord asked a Kyoto craftsman to make him a tea kettle for the tea ceremony. Today Morioka ironworks turn out many, many variations of the first Nambu tetsubin tea kettle, along with a plethora of other iron objects—from wind chimes to large cooking pots, and everything imaginable in between. If you came into town by train you may have already noted the significance of this craft to the city, either from the huge iron tea kettle on the platform or from the station's many iron wind chimes responding in clear, tinkling tones to the rush of air of an incoming train.

Morioka's dyed cotton fabric is its second most notable craft. Local mingei and omiyage shops carry the work of Ono-san and other local artists, souvenirs that are much more portable than ironware but that can also be costly.

Finally, Morioka's edible specialty needs mention. Wanko soba is thin noodles of buckwheat intended not to be savored but rather to be swallowed as quickly as possible—in noisy contests with fellow diners to see who can consume the most bowls within a given time limit. The noodles are served in small bowls, or wanko; hence the name of the contest. If you aren't in a group, you can have just as good a time enjoying your noodles and watching the slurping and gulping of the bibbed contestants. There are wanko-soba shops all over town; there is a large one on the bypass near the Sakura Kaikan.

In a wanko-soba contest, you are presented with a box of matches to be dumped out on the table and a miso-soup-sized bowl. Once the competition begins, waitresses stand by to fill your bowl as you empty it. When you down a bowl you return a match to the box; if your matchbox is full but you're not, continue counting by removing matches. You'll be surprised to find fellow contestants having to do just that. The Japanese noodle-consumption capacity is always astounding, and it's at its best during a Morioka wanko-soba-eating contest.

Horses have always been an important part of the lives of the Nambu people. They grazed on land too poor to plant and were a source of livelihood and pride as they became invaluable to both local and distant samurai. Once a year, on June 15th, Morioka honors the role of the horse in its Nambu heritage when over 100 horses are dressed in elaborate trappings for the Chagu-Chagu Umakko Festival.

In the morning the horses and their costumed owners pray together for a successful harvest of the newly planted rice crop at the Komagata Shrine, 15 kilometers west of the city. Komagata Shrine is north of Highway 46 and Ogama Station on the Tazawa-ko Line. Later that afternoon, the beautifully adorned hoses are paraded through the streets of Morioka, the many tiny bells on their trappings seeming to say "chagu-chagu."

MT. IWATE, the omnipresent conical volcano that looms over the area, can't be missed when traveling through central Iwate. Iwate-san (not to be confused with Aomori Prefecture's volcanic Iwaki-san) is the southern portion of the Towada–Hachimantai National Park's most outstanding landmark. Many visitors to the area are satisfied just to photograph the huge peak from the city or from the highway or train, but, if you're determined to get a closer look, Morioka is a good starting point for a ride up the mountain. Along the way, you can also stop in at Iwate's version of the American midwest. Head west from Morioka along Highway 46 or the Tazawa-ko Line to Koiwai Station and then up the Koiwai Toll Road.

The road goes about halfway up the 2,000-meter-high mountain to the Iwate-san Roku Kokumin Kyūka Mura,[5] which includes overnight accommodations, a campground, and a ski slope. On the way, you'll pass the rolling plains of the Koiwai Ranch, Japan's largest private ranch.

Koiwai Ranch is a real treat for Japanese travelers, particularly if they are from the very crowded cities of the south, but this Midwestern-American-style livestock and dairy farm may not be that exciting for visitors from roomier nations. The big attractions here are the wide-open spaces of its very un-Japanese-looking rolling hayfields and pastures; horseback riding, biking, archery and other sports facilities; a Genghis Khan cooked-at-your-table barbecue at the Casa de Prado Restaurant or a picnic in a mown hayfield; a night in a berth of the ranch's stationary train; and a ride in a horse-drawn carriage. During the first ten days of February each year, Koiwai Ranch's pastures are covered with snow sculptures and igloo-like kamakura for the Iwate Snow Festival.

Koiwai's own brand of dairy products including butter and cheese are on sale in the Morioka area as well as on the ranch. Their contribution to East-meets-West innovations is hakkō batā, a kind of fermented butter.

The ranch was bravely founded by three men, Ono, Iwasaki and Inoue, in 1891, long before most Japanese had developed a taste for Western dairy products, fermented or otherwise. The founders named their ranch by combining the first character of each of their names: ko (or o), iwa and i.

An alternative approach to the majestic mountain is from the north via the ski resort of Higashi Hachimantai. (See the Hachimantai section.)

After seeing Hiraizumi and Morioka, a Tōhoku traveler must make some choices unless he or she has the time to crisscross the prefecture a time or two (which, by the way, is done via beautiful although time-consuming mountain passes). Probably the best way to see Iwate on a limited time schedule is to take in Hiraizumi and Morioka, backtrack slightly to the southeast to Tōno and continue east on Highway 283 or the Kamaishi Line, and then sample the Pacific Coast's lengthly Rikuchū Kaigan National Park while heading north along the coast to Aomori's Hachinohe.

5. Iwate-sanroku Kokumin Kyūka Mura, Amibari, Shizukuishi-machi, Iwate-gun, Iwate-ken 020-07; tel. (01969) 2-2425.
岩手山麓国民休暇村　〒020-07　岩手県岩手郡雫石町網張

An alternative route includes the mountains of the Towada–Hachimantai National Park and the northeastern corner of Akita Prefecture before you end up in Aomori Prefecture either at Lake Towada or the Tsugaru clan's castle town of Hirosaki.

Whichever route north you choose, if sampling Iwate's past in Hiraizumi and Morioka sounds appealing, you won't want to miss a very different aspect of old Iwate still alive in the rural ways and preserved legends of the Tōno Basin.

The Tōno Basin

THE WORD FURUSATO means one's native place. But you can hear city people use the word when they see apples for sale in baskets woven from bamboo rather than stamped out of green plastic, when they taste homemade pickles from a country store, or when they come across a thatched-roof farmhouse tucked into a cove behind a green rice paddy.

Like bamboo baskets, homemade pickles, and thatched farmhouses, the Tōno Basin is the furusato of all Japan.

Here the modern nation's past is preserved in the natural beauty of unscarred mountains and quiet rivers and in unbelievably picturesque farms that most Japanese assume no longer exist. But, more importantly, traces of a pure Japan can still be found in Tōno. These are the reminders of the primitive Japan that existed before the Chinese brought over Buddhism in the sixth century, reminders that are preserved in the once isolated area's ancient customs, folk beliefs, and legends. There are very few places like Tōno left in Japan.

A day or two in Tōno will give you a sample of Japan's furusato and of the rural lifestyle of its more recent feudal past. The insular community is now linked to the twentieth century via the modern tunnels of Highway 283 and the Kamaishi Line from the Tōhoku Main Line's Hanamaki. These tunnels have tamed the intimidating but beautiful mountains that surround the basin.

A scenic local road links the city of Tōno with Morioka via the small village of Ōhazama, which skirts the lofty peak of Mount Hayachine. During Edo times, Ōhazama was a popular stop for traveling daimyo, but the town shriveled into obscurity when the train line bypassed it in the Meiji era. Today, besides its pretty location, the town offers visitors a taste of Edel Wein, Iwate's only grape wine. Ōhazama's vineyards were established thirty years ago and have thrived in its Bordeaux-like climate.

Plan to spend a night in Tōno at the Minshuku Magariya,[1] a converted thatched-roof, Nambu-style farmhouse located 3 kilometers southwest of Tōno Station off Highway 283. Magariya, meaning bent house, is the general term for the Nambu area's typical L-shaped farmhouses in which the family occupies the long part of the "L" and their animals the short end. In this magariya you can enjoy local country cooking featuring fish from Tōno's rivers, and later you can sit around the irori, the traditional sunken fireplace, soaking up Tōno's pervading furusato feeling. The minshuku is near the Tōno Bus Center and the best of Tōno's official attractions.

Tōno may be easy to reach these days, but finding your way around its unmarked country roads is more challenging. On the other hand, its countryside is so captivating that the time spent looking for the rural tourist attractions will be the best part of your trip. If you're really intent on finding a certain place though, you might want to consider splurging on a taxi. Buses go out into the countryside from Tōno Station, and you can rent a bike near the station to see the places close to town.

It's possible to "do" Tōno in a day, especially if you're using a taxi to avoid getting lost. But, if you've come north for this

1. Minshuku Magariya, 30–58–3 Niizato, Ayaori-machi, Tōno-shi, Iwate-ken 028–05; tel. (01986) 2–4564.
民宿曲り家　〒028-05 岩手県遠野市綾織町新里30の58の 3

type of old-rural-Japan experience, you can happily occupy yourself for a week exploring rustic country roads in search of old
temples, shrines, and farms tucked here and there along them.

Begin your trip to Tōno with a little homework. In 1910,
Kunio Yanagita, a wealthy bureaucrat with an interest in legends, interviewed Tōno native Kyōseki Sasaki at length and
then published the 118 legends he was told in his *Tono Mono-
gatari*, now a classic. Robert Morse translated the book in 1975
as the *Legends of Tono* so the English-speaking world could
also share in these tales of supernatural experiences and primitive folk beliefs.

As you exit Tōno Station, to your right is the Tōno Tourist
Information Office (Kankō Annai-jo). Stop here for maps and
directions before you take off for such historic or legendary
spots as the 500 Rakan, the Chiba Family Magariya, the Kitakawa
Family Oshira-sama House, the Kappa Pool, and the ancient
torii marking the old path up sacred Mount Hayachine. The
tourist office also stocks copies of the *Legends of Tono*, which,
unfortunately, is the extent of their English information.

A tour of the Tōno Basin can be divided into two parts—the
city and country sites southwest of the station and the rural
sites northeast of the station. But any country road you take
out of the city goes past fantastic rural scenes that soothe the
spirit and make you forget you are on a schedule or happen
to be terribly lost.

Before you begin your wanderings, a final word of advice:
Don't let the spirit of furusato overtake your perceptions. Tōno
is not an anachronism. You will see lots of quaint thatched-
roof magariya, but the eye tends to quickly pass over the modern,
styleless farmhouse next door, and the mind may refuse to accept that the old house is now just a barn. You may also stumble
across postcard scenes of rice paddies with moss-covered water
wheels and humble peasants bent over their rice seedlings. The
old water wheels are furusato for the Tōno farm family more

so than for the visitor, but, if you're savoring the feeling of having stepped back into the peaceful countryside of 100 years ago, don't get too close or you may hear the hum of the mechanical water pump now inside. And the peasants toiling in the fields are filling in the spots their gas-powered rice planters missed.

The people of the Tōno Basin most certainly have welcomed the conveniences of the modern world, which have eased their struggles with the land. But what makes this area so wonderful is that these people also cherish the reminders of their traditional life style, a life style left undisturbed for so long. And they are proud to show off their heritage to visitors seeking to share in the warmth of their furusato. If you work at it, you can still get the magariya, the wooden footbridge, and the rolling hills into the picture with maybe only a corner of the metal roof and aluminum siding of the new farmhouse.

The city of Tōno is in itself not very interesting, and you'll want to get out to the countryside as quickly as possible. On the way out, about 1 kilometer south of the station, you can see the site of Tōno's castle, built in 1573 by a branch of the Nambu clan and dismantled in the Meiji era. The Nambu Shrine now stands in the middle of the park-like, hillside castle grounds. Remnants of Tōno's samurai residental area still exist, however, in the Motomachi district, west of the castle grounds toward Highway 283.

A kilometer beyond Motomachi on Highway 283 is the Tōno Bus Center. Across the highway are the shrines of Unedori and Atago, the 500 Rakan, and the Minshuku Magariya.

The Unedori Shrine caters to the unmarried who wish to alter their status. Tie a red cloth on the tree in front with your left hand, and good luck should come your way. Atago Shrine, 100 meters further down the road, houses a deity who puts out fires. But what you've come to see is the natural tumble of moss-covered rocks on the wooded hillside 300 meters above Atago Shrine, rocks on which the faces of 500 disciples of the Buddha were painstakingly and beautifully carved over 200 years ago.

Tōno's history is one filled with tragic famines, the worst of which came in 1754 when one-fourth of the basin starved to death during two consecutive years of poor harvests. Thirty years later, a Buddhist priest spent his days in this quiet forest reading sutras to comfort the spirits of the famine victims while he carved images on scattered boulders. Today you can still see 380 of these rakan, most covered with moss that is sometimes scraped away so the faces can be seen. If you are very quiet, you can hear the spirits of the dead conversing, a sound much like an underground stream rushing downhill beneath the rock tumble. It is impossible not to linger at this peaceful spot as you climb the path through the trees discovering one barely visible image after the other.

Two other attractions, the Chiba Family Magariya and the Tsuzuki Stone, are further down the highway in the foothills north of the Sarugaishi River. Both are near the local Iwate-Futsukamachi Station on the Kamaishi Line, about a 9-kilometer bus ride from Tōno Station. In these same foothills on a road heading north from Ayaori Station (between the Tōno Bus Center and Futsukamachi Station) is a cluster of magariya, some with lilies growing on their thatched roofs. If you're driving or biking, one of the nicest things you can do for yourself is to "get lost" for a while in these beautiful hills.

The mysterious Tsuzuki Stone is a huge boulder balanced on two smaller rocks that bears a resemblance to the dolmens or stone graves built during Japan's Tumulus period, but it is believed to be much older and may be a natural formation. To confuse matters further, the local legend is that the rocks were stacked by Benkei, who was not really killed in Hiraizumi but instead escaped north, with a stop in Tōno. Yoshitsune-was-here markers also dot the basin. The Tsuzuki Stone's two base stones are each two meters wide, and the large one which rests on them is three meters wide and nine meters long.

Five-hundred meters further up this local road in the hills stands the Chiba Family Magariya, a beautiful example of how a wealthy Nambu farm family lived 200 years ago. The huge farmhouse was chosen for restoration by Tokyo University as one of the ten most important minka in Japan. The big house and its outbuildings used to house not only the Chibas, but also fifteen servants and twenty horses; today it houses an interesting collection of folk articles. Although still somewhat rustic to our eyes, the Chibas' house must have seemed like a palace to the poor farmers who built the more humble magariya nearby. A modern house stands awkwardly in the middle of the old house's complex of buildings and a small family shrine is on the hillside above it. You may not find this restored giant of a magariya as appealing as its merely preserved smaller neighbors, but it exemplifies Nambu rural architecture at its best.

If you want to explore more of this side of the basin, follow the country road going south from Futsukamachi Station to a small stream along which you'll find a working water wheel just east of the road. Then take the intersecting local road which heads west just above the stream until it meets Highway 107. You'll see a small shrine, famous for its homemade yōkan, near the intersection. It is said that Hiraizumi's Fujiwaras had a gold mine in this area that was the source of their wealth, and that there is still gold here yet to be discovered. Follow Highway 107 south for about six kilometers to find the old Araya Barrier station house, which at one time protected the southern border of the Nambu clan's holdings from unauthorized entry or exit along this route. Highway 107 also intersects with Highway 283 near Masuzawa Station. These destinations will structure your wanderings, but, once again, it will be the beautiful countryside itself that will stand out in your memory.

Many of the strange events recorded in the *Legends of Tono* took place on the other side of town in the area facing Mount Hayachine and its neighboring peaks, places where mountain gods dwell and where evil creatures attack stray humans who wander too far, especially after dark. Country roads taking off from Highway 340 take you past a pool full of kappa, or mischievous water creatures; a Buddhist household altar that enshrines the primitive deity Oshira-sama; and more of the basin's old country temples and shrines.

About 4 kilometers northeast of town along Highway 340 is the local road that heads northward to Mount Hayachine. The Nitagai Bus Stop is near this intersection. If you have time, take this road for about two kilometers to the Fukusen-ji Kannon, Japan's tallest wooden Kannon at seventeen meters high. During cherry- or maple-viewing season, make a special effort to visit Fukusen-ji's extensive wooded grounds.

Next try to find the Komagata Shrine. It is about 8 kilometers up the mountain road on a right fork which takes off from the Kami-Yanagi Bus Stop. A series of old torii lead to the decaying shrine, which has a phallic symbol lacquered in red and more than 1,000 ema, small wooden plaques with hand-painted horses on them. For campers, the Arakawa Plateau is another 10 kilometers up the road.

Back on Highway 340 just beyond this turnoff, a weathered wooden torii stands along the highway. This wonderfully photogenic old torii marks the original path leading up the holy mountain. With some maneuvering, you can get the concrete poles and power lines out of your picture.

Across the highway from the old torii is a road leading to the temple Jōken-ji and the Kappa-buchi (Water Imp Pool) behind it. Jōken-ji is the site of the strange events of Legend 88 (reference is to Morse): A seriously ill old man came to this temple and had tea with the priest. As he left the temple gate, he vanished. The priest later learned that the man had actually died that day and that his phantom visitor had surreptitiously poured his tea between the tatami.

The temple is the home of Obinzuru-sama, an image which

helps the afflicted recover from illness (although it didn't do much for the guy in the legend). Pat the image's body on the same part of the body that ails you and your pain will go away. The image has shiny places where it has been patted over and over again.

Jōken-ji's temple dog is also worth noting for its concave head, a characteristic of the mythical kappa who live in the pool behind the temple.

Approach the Kappa Pool with caution lest you should run into one of the ugly water creatures that exist in bodies of water all over Japan. Since they have been known to pull babies and small children (as well as horses) into the water, Japanese mothers make liberal use of kappa stories to keep their children away from dangerous bodies of water. Kappa can also impregnate women (see Legends 55 through 59) who later bear grotesquely deformed demi-kappa. But kappa occasionally do good deeds if it's to their advantage to do so (see Legend 58). When Jōken-ji caught fire once, it was a kappa who put out the blaze. Author Ryūnosuke Atakugawa of *Rashōmon* fame wrote a modern allegory of an underground society of kappa in 1927.

In case you don't get to see one at the Kappa-buchi, a kappa can be described as slippery-skinned and sharp-beaked with webbed hands and feet at the end of long human-like arms and legs and, of course, with a unique dish-shaped concavity at the top of its head. Although it can breathe on land, the dish must be kept filled with water or the creature will lose its power and may even die. If a kappa threatens you, just bow to it and, when it returns your bow, the dish will empty and it will have to quickly return to the water. And if you've taken a liking to the independent little creature, be sure to visit Komaki Onsen in Aomori's Misawa (see that section) to see its extensive and unusual collection of kappa-related art.

Further up Highway 340 near the Wano Bus Stop, the old Kitakawa Magariya is hidden behind its modern replacement, a few doors down a side road along a stream. Hopefully, when you go, and for many years to come, Obaasan Kitakawa will still be warmly welcoming visitors to this private farmhouse. This lovely old woman will show you around her house and then take you to see her venerated Oshira-sama in the family altar, all the while providing a running commentary in her thick Iwate country accent.

Oshira-sama is part of Tōhoku's ancient folk beliefs; you'll find the deity all over the back country but it is sometimes known by different names. Oshira-sama images are thirty-centimeter-long sticks made from mulberry branches or bamboo. They are "dressed" in brightly colored or brocade cloth, which is changed each year, and their heads are either carved like a horse's or a human's head or left uncarved. Some experts think the ancient deity is the origin of Tōhoku's kokeshi dolls.

Oshira-sama is connected with the itako, or blind mediums, whose craft also goes back to Tōhoku's very early days. (See Aomori's Shimokita Peninsula.) When the itako of old communicated with the dead, they would chant the oshira-matsuri-bumi, the story of a girl and a horse, while they danced and waved a pair of sticks. Later the sticks became Oshira-sama, and today only the Oshira-sama are moved about during the itako's chant.

Yanagita chronicled a version of the ancient chant told to Sasaki by a very old woman with supernatural powers; you can read it in Legend 69. A young girl loved her horse so much that she married him. Her enraged father then hanged the horse from a mulberry tree. As the daughter wept and clung to the dead horse's head, the father chopped off the animal's head with an axe, at which time his daughter and the horse's head flew off together to heaven. The first Oshira-sama images were made from the mulberry branch on which the horse had been hanged.

Obaasan Kitakawa's Oshira-sama's being kept in a Buddhist

altar does not pose the same problem it would in a similar circumstance involving a Western religion. The people of the back country have had no difficulties in harmoniously blending interesting new ideas with their cherished old beliefs, and the promoters of the new have usually allowed these local folk beliefs to be assimilated into their standard practices. Change comes slowly, but smoothly, to the back country.

The interior of the preserved but not restored Kitakawa House will give you a better idea of life inside the other magariya you see dotting the Tōno Basin than did the Chiba House. The difference is not only in size; the latter is elegant, sterile, and somehow artificial; the former is warm, homey, and more real.

After seeing the Kitakawa House, follow their road and/or the highway further out of town for many more great farm scenes. This is another area where it's to your advantage to "get lost" for a while; just bring lots of film.

If you can stay longer, the guide maps of Tōno are filled with more out-of-the-way temples and shrines around which you can structure your exploration of the countryside. But if you have to get on with your back-country itinerary after seeing Tōno's main tourist attractions, and if you've had a chance to read Tōno's collection of sometimes strange and sometimes spooky tales, you'll leave the basin filled with beautiful memories of a beautiful place and with a better understanding of Japan's furusato—even if you didn't get to see a kappa.

If your next stop is the Rikuchū Kaigan National Park on Iwate's Pacific Coast, you'll have to pass through the mountains via the long, curving Sennin (Hermit) Tunnel, a toll tunnel for drivers. The tunnel is a great improvement over the old Sennin Pass which goes over it, nine kilometers up and nine kilometers down. But if you want to try the old pass, do it before you read the *Legends of Tōno*. It's better to be unaware of the strange things that happen to people who cross the mountains surrounding the Tōno Basin.

The Rikuchū Coast

THE RIKUCHŪ KAIGAN NATIONAL PARK is what most Japanese tourists come to Iwate to see. The seaside park covers nearly 200 kilometers of fantastic sea-eroded cliffs, strange rock formations, and a series of weirdly shaped bays and promontories that extend from Kuji in the north to Miyagi's Kesen-numa.

You, too, will want to sample Iwate's beautiful and varied Pacific coastline. But, unless you are a real fan of seascapes, consider Rikuchū Kaigan a relaxing detour rather than the focal point of your trip.

One of the nicest features of the park, other than its scenery, is the string of modern kokuminshukusha tastefully set into some of the most beautiful spots along the coast. Most are tucked into the trees of wooded capes and have walking paths leading right to a cliff's edge for breathtaking views of the seascape below. Hotels, minshuku, youth hostels, and campgrounds also dot the popular coastline. So reserve at least one night of your vacation for listening to the waves break on Iwate's Pacific shores.

The city of Miyako is considered the dividing line between the submerged beaches of the southern half of the park and the uplifted cliffs of the north. Nearby Jōdogahama (Paradise Beach) is Rikuchū Kaigan's best-known attraction. Two other popular spots are Goishi Beach, between Kesen-numa and Ōfunato, and Kita-Yamazaki, near Fudai. But there are many lovely beaches and seascapes along this so-called "Alps of the Sea." Even if you pick a section of the park to explore based solely on available transportation and accommodations, the closer you can get to the shore (most, but not all, of the coast is accessible by land), the more delighted you'll be with your selection.

The Yamada Line runs from Morioka on the Tōhoku Main Line to Miyako. Two other trunk lines also head east from the main line—the Ōfunato Line from Ichinoseki and the Kamaishi Line from Hanamaki and Tōno. The Kesen-numa Line goes north from Sendai along the Miyagi coast, and train service continues up some sections of the Iwate coastline as well. Buses also cover the popular coastline. Even more fun are the large, modern, sightseeing boats that link the park's major ports from April to early November.

Highways crossing the prefecture at various points intersect with Highway 45, which runs along the coast from Sendai to Aomori's Pacific port of Hachinohe. The straight highway often strays from Rikuchū Kaigan's highly irregular coastline, but local roads frequently take off from the highway toward the sea.

START YOUR TOUR of Rikuchū Kaigan in Kesen-numa if you don't want to miss anything. The city is served by the Kesen-numa Line, the Ōfunato Line, and Highways 284 and 45. Nearby ocean-viewing spots are the cliffs of Iwaizaki, the big island in the bay called Ōshima (Big Island), and the Karakuwa Peninsula.

Iwaizaki is 45 minutes by bus south of Kesen-numa Station, on the southern edge of Kesen-numa Bay near Rikuzen-Hashikami Station. Its shoreline of jagged sea-etched rocks sends sprays of water shooting twenty meters into the air.

Like a jigsaw puzzle with some critical pieces missing, the strange-shaped island of Ōshima takes up most of Kesen-numa Bay but is a poor fit for the horned bay's even more irregular outline. Over 5,000 people live on the island, which is connected to the mainland by ferry from the Kisen Hatchaku-jo Pier. Ōshima's attractions include the Kesen-numa Ōshima Kokumin Kyūka Mura[1] facing the Karakuwa Peninsula; the Kaichū Kōen, Sea Life Park, with its glass-bottomed tour boat; and two bays with calm beaches for swimming.

The Karakuwa Peninsula is a 40-minute bus ride from Kesen-numa Station. Its scenic coastline between Ōgama and Hanzō has a short walking path past strange rock formations. At Ōgama the waves hitting the rocky shore look like water boiling in an ōgama, or big pot, that appears to be split in half (hanzō) by a sharp cliff.

A youth hostel is further down the peninsula, and the Karakuwa-sō kokuminshukusha[2] is located at the very tip.

If you're not planning to spend the night on the island or the peninsula, you may prefer to see the bay on a two-hour sightseeing boat ride which leaves from the Kankō-sen Hatchaku-jo Pier near the station.

The Ōfunato Line turns northward and inland at Kesen-numa but heads back toward the ocean in time to pass the 2-kilometer-long sand beach and calm waters of Takada Matsubara. Get off the train at Rikuzen-Takada Station if you want to spend the night at the youth hostel or campground along this beach. Takada Matsubara is a 10-minute bus ride from the station.

North of the sand beach near Hosoura Station is perhaps the most photographed piece of Iwate's famous coast—the Anadōshi, a triple arch of uplifted rocks standing on end in the sea off Goishi-gahama (Go-Stones Beach) named for its smooth black pebbles, which were once collected for the checker-like go, the favorite game of Miyagi's Datè lord.

1. Kesen-numa Ōshima Kokumin Kyūka Mura, Sotohata, Kesen-numa-shi, Miyagi-ken 988–06; tel. (0226) 28–2626.
   気仙沼大島国民休暇村 〒988-06 宮城県気仙沼市外畑
2. Karakuwa-sō, Karakuwa-machi, Motoyoshi-gun, Miyagi-ken 988; tel. (02263) 2–3174.
   からくわ荘 〒988 宮城県本吉郡唐桑町

The beach is a 15-minute bus ride from Hosoura Station. It has a campground and a 4-kilometer-long walking path past its fantastic rock formations. Anadōshi is a 40-minute walk or 10-minute ride from the bus stop. If you can only stop at one or two spots in the park, place Goishi Beach high on your list of sites to consider.

The last major station on the Ōfunato Line is the city of Ōfunato, where you can transfer to a bus for the 60-kilometer-long ride north to Kamaishi. Along the way, the straight-forward highway by-passes a series of pretty little capes and bays. One of these lovely spots is the Chitose Kaigan, close to Yoshihama Station, which is the terminus for the Ōfunato Line.

You'll also pass through the town of Sanriku, off whose coast warm and cold currents meet. Several major universities and scientific institutes have branches here for on-site study of the Rikuchū coast's geologic, oceanographic, and meteorological phenomena.

At Kamaishi you can pick up the Yamada Line heading north to Miyako where it turns inland for Morioka. Kamaishi is an industrial city at the mouth of the Kōshi River and the terminus for the Kamaishi Line from Hanamaki. It is the largest city around but lacks the abundance of natural scenery which pulls in the tourist trade for its smaller neighbors. In 1970 this situation was corrected when the white concrete Kamaishi Dai (Great) Kannon, Goddess of Mercy, statue was erected to hover majestically over the city and Kamaishi Bay. Near the thirteen-story walk-up deity is the East-Indian-style Sekiōzen-ji Busshari-tō, which houses a speck of the Buddha's bones sent from Sri Lanka in 1975. The Kamaishi Dai Kannon is a 15-minute bus ride from Kamaishi Station.

You can also cruise Kamishi Bay from June through October. The hour-and-a-half sightseeing boat trip leaves from the Uo-ichiba Fish Market.

Three ocean side spots to spend the night are located north of the city. The Nehama Kaigan campground faces Ōzuchi Bay near Unosumai Station; the Ōzuchi-sō kokuminshukusha[3] lies across the bay near Ōzuchi Station; and the JNR Namisaka Camp Village is on a beautiful sand beach near Nami-ita Station.

Between Ōzuchi and Yamada, both tracks and highway ride along a cliff overlooking the Pacific. Be sure to hit this stretch in the daylight for an all-too-brief bit of effortless sightseeing.

At Iwate-Funakoshi Station, south of the nearly land-locked Yamada Bay, also known as the Lake Towada of the Sea, you have another chance to bed down for the night at the Tabunoki-sō kokuminshukusha[4] and a nearby campground. Both are on the southern tip of the Funakoshi Peninsula.

The port of Tanohama is also near Iwate-Funakoshi Station. Here is your first opportunity to continue north via the sea; you can enjoy an 80-minute boat ride that leaves Tanohama for Miyako's Jōdogahama twice a day, or you can take a shorter ride around the rugged Funakoshi Peninsula and into peaceful Yamada Bay.

On the way to Jōdogahama, you'll pass the easternmost point on Honshu, the small lighthouse at the tip of Cape Todogasaki. If you're still on land, you can take a side road off Highway 45 just above Yamada Bay to see this geographically significant spot. There is a campground south of the lighthouse for those who want to see the sun rise over the land of the rising sun before anyone else does.

MIYAKO AND THE NORTHERN COASTLINE could be your next stops on this coastal tour. If you've come by land thus far, Miyako is

3. Ōzuchi-sō, 28–39–3 Kirikiri, Ōzuchi-machi, Kamihei-gun, Iwate-ken 028–11; tel. (01934) 2–2315.
大槌荘　〒028-11 岩手県上閉伊郡大槌町吉里吉里28の39の 3
4. Tabunoki-sō, Tanohama, Yamada-machi, Shimohei-gun, Iwate-ken 032–04; tel. (01938) 4–2031.
タブの木荘　〒032-04 岩手県下閉伊郡山田町田の浜

the place to put on your sea legs for a short cruise from Jōdo-gahama Pier around lovely Paradise Beach and northward past a costline of interesting rock formations that includes two National Natural Treasures—Rōsoku Iwa (Candle Rock), a 40-meter-high stone candle standing out from the green shoreline, and Shiofuki Ana (Salt-spraying Hole), where waves and the rocky coastline join forces to send a spray of water shooting forty to fifty meters into the air.

From Jōdogahama Pier you can also take sightseeing boats heading further north to the ports of Mazaki, Tarō, and Ōtanabu. The beach itself is a 17-minute bus ride from Miyako Station. The 2-kilometer-long Jōdogahama Toll Road links Highway 45 and the beach.

A visiting priest named Jōdogahama (Paradise Beach) for its resemblance to his vision of the hereafter. And indeed the beach seems to possess a sample of everything that is beautiful about Rikuchū Kaigan. Beyond its long, white-quartz sand swimming beach, sea-sculpted rock formations stand guard and wind-bent pines cover the nearby seaside cliffs. It is not only its central location that makes Jōdogahama the most popular spot in the park.

Beyond the city of Miyako on an access road leading from the highway to the sea are the Rikuchū Miyako Kokumin Kyūka Mura,[5] with its hotel, tennis courts, and swimming pool, and the nearby Nakanohama Campground. This side road also takes the land traveler past the Rōsoku Iwa and the Shiofuki Ana.

The town of Tarō is a 20-minute ride north of Miyako on the tiny Miyako Line which terminates here or a 30-minute bus ride from Miyako Station. Tarō's coastline is noted for its surplus of umineko, or noisy black-backed seagulls, whose meow-like screech has earned them the name of sea cats. They boldly follow the tour boats to snatch offerings from passengers' outstretched hands.

5. Rikuchū Miyako Kokumin Kyūka Mura, Anegasaki, Sakiyama, Miyako-shi, Iwate-ken 027; tel. (01936) 2–9911.
陸中宮古国民休假村　〒027 岩手県宮古市崎山姉ヶ崎

A 10-minute bus ride from Tarō Station goes to the park's largest kokuminshukusha, the Sanno-kaku,[6] which has an exciting cliff's-edge location and a large saltwater swimming pool. A 5-minute walk away is the Sannō Iwa, a much photographed sea-carved formation shaped like a phallus. Cape Mazaki and the sand beach of Mazaki Kaigan, which has a campground, are a 15-minute bus ride north of the station.

Before going much further north along the coast, you may want to make a jog inland to Ryūsen-dō Cave, a natural limestone cavern a few kilometers north of the town of Iwaizumi. The cave is one of the three largest in Japan; so far, 2,500 meters of it have been explored, and it is thought to be twice that size. Inside the deep cavern is the world's clearest underground lake, a truly amazing piece of nature over which you have the opportunity to climb a series of precarious metal steps for a look down extending forty-one meters below the surface of the 120-meter-deep lake. A second cave, discovered across the highway, has been turned into an underground mini-museum of Japanese prehistory. A relatively high admission fee gets you into both caverns. The Ryūsen-dō Youth Travel Village campsites and a new hotel can be found next to the caves.

Reaching Ryūsen-dō Cave from the coast involves a 30-minute bus ride from Tarō Station north to Komoto and then another 50-minute ride inland to Iwaizumi following a river valley through the mountains.

The Iwate countryside north of the Ryūsen-dō area is also interesting. A beautiful mountain stream surges past the caves and a good local road traces the stream's path through the mountains northward to the coastal city of Kuji. Besides the pretty mountain scenery along this road, you'll also see some real evidence of the hard lot of many Iwate farmers as you pass isolated clearings

6. Sannō-kaku, Otobe, Tarō-machi, Shimohei-gun, Iwate-ken 027-03; tel. (019387) 2161.
山王閣　〒027-03　岩手県下閉伊郡田老町乙部

with fields going straight up unterraced hillsides and still occupied by rundown thatched-roof magariya. If you've come to Tarō by car and have had enough ocean for a while, this alternative route north will prove both refreshing and enlightening.

On the other hand, if it's more lovely seascapes you want, you'll find them north of Tarō. A planned train link-up extending from Tarō north to Kuji is not yet completed, so you'll be on the highways from Tarō to Kita-Yamazaki, the next set of Alps-like cliffs along Rikuchū Kaigan's spectacular coastline. The main highway strays far from the water north of Tarō, but, once you reach Tanohata, an access road takes you to the 14-kilometer-long Hokubu Rikuchū Kaigan Toll Road, which in turn leads to another access road and the cliffs of Kita-Yamazaki. Kita-Yamazaki Lookout Point has restaurants and souvenir shops as well as a long series of steps leading down to the water for a close-up view of the beautiful eroded cliffs and sea-carved archways which line the popular cape.

You can also see the cliffs of Kita-Yamazaki from the sea. A 70-minute sightseeing boat ride leaves from Shimanokoshi Pier, west of Tanohata near the southern entrance to the toll road. Boats from Shimanokoshi also dock on the other side of Kita-Yamazaki at Ōtanabu Port, which is near Fudai Station, the terminus of the Kuji Line from Kuji.

Just north of the toll road in Fudai is a large seaside campground with its own pool. Three kokuminshukusha dot this northern section of the park, offering you more overnight alternatives. The Kurosaki-sō[7] is on the toll road 3 kilometers north of Kita-

7. Kurosaki-sō, Kurosaki, Fudai-mura, Shimohei-gun, Iwate-ken 032–03; tel. (019435) 2611.
　くろさき荘　〒032-03 岩手県下閉伊郡普代村黒崎
8. Eboshi-sō, 2–6 Tamagawa, Noda-mura, Kunohe-gun, Iwate-ken 032–02; tel. (019478) 2495.
　えぼし荘　〒032-02 岩手県九戸郡野田村玉川 2-6
9. Hokugen-kaku, 7–133–4 Yokonuma, Samuraihama-chō, Kuji-shi, Iwate-ken 039–14; tel. (01945) 8–2311.
　北限閣　〒039-14 岩手県久慈市侍浜町横沼

Yamazaki; the Eboshi-sō[8] is near Horinai Station in Noda; and the Hokugen-kaku[9] is north of Kuji near the Hachinohe Line's Samurai-hama Station. There is also a youth hostel near Noda-Tamagawa Station.

The women divers of Kosode Kaigan, a 20-minute bus ride from Kuji Station, are the northernmost divers for abalone and sea urchins in Japan. Their activities, of course, are limited to Tōhoku's least frosty months. North of Kosode Beach is Kuji Beach where you'll see the last of Rikuchū Kaigan's seaside cliffs and rock formations, although the Tanesashi Beach just to the north is also lovely in a quieter way.

Kuji is the home of Kokuji-yaki pottery, a hefty kitchenware in deep browns and speckled creams. The workshop and sales outlet for this simple earthenware is in the foothills west of the city. From Highway 45 turn inland at the Osanai Bridge and follow this local road until you can see gentle foothills on your right. At the large wooden sign for the pottery, follow the gravel road up the hill to the workshop and showroom. Kokuji-yaki is about a 15-minute taxi ride from Kuji Station. Limited selections of the pottery are also sold in many mingei and omiyage shops in northeastern Iwate.

Kuji is not only your last stop in the Rikuchū Kaigan National Park, but also your last in Iwate Prefecture. Highway 45, a scenic coastal road, and the Hachinohe Line, all take you north from the city into Aomori Prefecture. The train closely follows the Tanesashi Beach coastline (see Aomori's The Nohes section for details).

Few, if any, visitors to Tōhoku have the time to see every fantastic rock formation, wooded cape, and peaceful sand beach along Rikuchū Kaigan's 200-kilometer-long coastline. You may leave the park feeling cheated that you didn't get to see more of its spectacular scenes. But a day or two touring Iwate's coast is like a few days in Kyoto. In that historic environment, leisurely exploring a few of its hundreds of fantastic temples, gardens, and shrines is unquestionably wiser than racing through as many historic sites as you can physically handle during your short stay. The latter course leaves you exhausted, with blurred memories and mixed feelings about that wonderful city. Likewise, you're much better off selecting one or two of Rikuchū Kaigan's many lovely scenes to thoroughly enjoy. In this way, your memories of Iwate's Pacific Coast can't help but be as beautiful as the national park itself.

Hachimantai

HACHIMANTAI, the mountainous southern portion of the Towada–Hachimantai National Park spreads across both sides of the Akita–Iwate border about 60 kilometers south of Lake Towada, the caldera lake which dominates the northern half of the park.

Hachimantai is a nature lover's paradise—for skiers, in winter, and for those who enjoy mountain vistas, alpine flora, nature trails, and remnants of volcanic activity, in other seasons. This natural museum of volcanic activity has within its borders four different types of volcanos as well as "frozen" lava flows, bubbling mud pools, marshy caldera lakes, jets of steam gushing out of cracks in the mountainsides, unlimited supplies of natural hot water, and Japan's first geothermal power plant. Hachimantai offers scenery that, like that of Rikuchū Kaigan, may be more appealing to the big-city Japanese than to the foreign visitor; but, if you're ready for a short detour through the mountains, a ride through Hachimantai will provide a pleasant contradiction to the "crowded island of wall-to-wall-people" stereotype of Japan you may have held before coming to Tōhoku.

If you choose this northwestern route out of Iwate, you can take advantage of the Tōhoku Expressway or JNR's Hanawa Line, which take you through a corner of Akita Prefecture to the Aomori cities of Hirosaki and Aomori. Or you can change direction slightly at the town of Towada in Akita to go past Tōhoku's mini-Stonehenge at Ōyu and on to Lake Towada by bus or car on Highway 103. Either way, you'll pass through the interesting Edo-period merchant-class neighborhood of Hanawa, now a part of Akita's Kazuno City.

HACHIMANTAI IS just south of the Tōhoku Expressway, Highway 282, and the Hanawa Line from Kōma Station (north of Morioka on the Tōhoku Main Line), which cross into Akita prefecture between the two sections of the national park. Thus, to go through the scenic mountains of Hachimantai, you must leave the main routes at Ōbuke Station or the Nishine Interchange to take the 27-kilometer-long Hachimantai Aspite Line toll road through the mountains to Highway 341 south of Kazuno. Heavy snows close the toll road from November through April, but winter skiers can take advantage of the slopes at lower elevations on either side of the toll road.

If you're coming from Morioka and its skiing season, or if you're a Tōhoku resident looking for a summer place to enjoy the great outdoors, the resort of Higashi Hachimantai will be worth checking into. The resort is on the eastern side of Mount Iwate, south of the Kōtsu (Travel) Center Bus Stop on the access road to the Aspite Line. Buses run from nearby Ōbuke Station and from Morioka Station.

Higashi Hachimantai has several large modern hotels, a golf course, the ski slopes, and the vacation village of Puutaro-mura,[1] an unusual complex for back-country Japan. Puutaro means wooden house in Finnish, and the village centers around sixty imported prefab knotty pine puutaros. Each cabin in the woods has a complete kitchen, a private onsen, and a color TV. The village also has a variety of recreational facilities including a pool,

1. Puutaro-mura, Yoriki, Matsuo-mura, Iwate-ken 028–73; tel. (019578) 2276.
   プータロ・ムラ　〒028-73 岩手県岩手郡松尾村寄木

tennis courts, nature trails, a public bath, and a conference room. You can rent a cabin for part of a day or overnight or just pay admission to the village. Prices are a cut above those of kokumin-shukusha but are very reasonable for a Japanese resort, especially if you have at least four people in your cabin. Puutaro Village, if nothing else, makes a statement about where Japan's poorest prefecture is headed these days.

On the same road heading south into the mountains is the Matsukawa Onsen with its campgrounds, youth hostel, and the Kyōun-sō kokuminshukusha.[2] Nearby is the Matsukawa Geothermal Power Plant built in 1966.

Note as you travel past the "backside" of Mount Iwate the barrenness of this side of the mountain. This is due to a "recent" eruption about halfway up the slope which sent hot lava pouring down to the base of the ancient volcano 250 years ago. Along the access road to the Aspite Line the rolling alpine forests are as pretty as the views you'll later pay for once you enter the toll road. Just before the toll road begins, the Hachimantai Ski Resort offers another chance for overnight accommodations at its youth hostel and resort hotel.

Several hiking trails and side roads lead from the toll road to the sights of Hachimantai. Hachiman Numa is near the Hachi-man Mikaeri Tōge Bus Stop about 9 kilometers and lots of twists and turns past the toll road entrance. A 29–minute walk north of the bus stop will take you to this volcano-formed lake surrounded by green marshes through which the visitor can walk on narrow wooden footbridges. A 10-minute ride south of the main road from the bus stop leads to Tōshichi Onsen,

2. Kyōun-sō, Matsukawa Onsen, Kitanomata Kokuyūrin, Yoriki, Matsuo-mura, Iwate-gun, Iwate-ken 028–73; tel. (019578) 2256.
峡雲荘 〒028-73 岩手県岩手郡松尾村寄木北の又国有林松川温泉
2. Hōrai-sō, Kitanomata Kokuyūrin, Yoriki, Matsuo-mura, Iwate-ken 028–73; tel. (01956) 2–2991.
蓬莱荘 〒028-73 岩手県岩手郡松尾村寄木北の又国有林

where you can find another kokuminshukusha, the Hōrai-sō,[3] spring skiing through the first part of June, and a wooded nature trail through an area of strangely shaped trees, cliffs, and rocks.

Mikaeri Tōge is the place for your farewell to Iwate as you are standing on the Akita–Iwate line. Past another series of twists and turns through the mountains are the Akita-Hachimantai ski area and Ōnuma Onsen, where, once again, you are offered your choice of a campground, a youth hostel, or the Ōnuma Lodge kokuminshukusha.[4] Other onsen featuring the plentiful hot waters of Hachimantai dot the toll road until it intersects with Highway 341 for Kazuno, where you can rejoin either the Hanawa Line or the Tōhoku Expressway, having completed your detour through the volcanic mountains of Hachimantai.

AKITA PREFECTURE'S KAZUNO is a new city formed from four smaller towns in 1971. The center of the new city is the old castle town of Hanawa, in Edo times a prosperous political and economic center.

On the side streets around Rikuchū Hanawa Station, you can see evidence of the prosperity of Hanawa's merchant class of 200 years ago in the sturdy old wooden buildings that are still standing, some still housing their original businesses. From the station, cross the main highway and then turn right at the next street. You can't miss the large Sekizen Sakè Factory which is still in operation. If you come during a school vacation, you may get to meet their English-speaking daughter-in-law Taeko Seki; she teaches English in Tokyo while her husband helps the family to produce sakè, but she comes back whenever she can. Plan to spend about an hour strolling through this old merchant area.

Just above Kazuno on Highway 282 (which Highway 341 merged with south of the city), at the expressway's Towada

4. Ōnuma Lodge, Kumazawa Kokuyūrin, Hachimantai, Kazuno-shi, Akita-ken 018–52; tel. (01862) 3–7041.
大沼ロッジ 〒018-52 秋田県鹿角市八幡平熊沢国有林

Interchange or at Towada Minami Station on the Hanawa Line, you'll have to make a decision. The train continues on to the mountain city of Ōdate where it joins the Ōu Main Line for Hirosaki and Aomori, and the expressway heads for the same cities in a more direct route, both passing through the busy ski resorts and onsen of Ōwani and Ikarigaseki. The alternative route, Highway 103, takes you to Lake Towada via the town of Ōyu with its prehistoric stone circle.

IF YOU CHANGE TRAINS in Ōdate, you may want to spend some time in this overgrown logging town set in the middle of a thick rolling forest of sugi, or cryptomerias, one of the three most beautiful forests in Japan.

At one time these mountains were frequented by hunters looking for the bear, rabbit, deer, and fox which lived in the deep woods. Today only a few of these matagi, or mountain hunters, still make their living by selling animal hides and bear organs for medicine. But every year a wild vegetable or mushroom gatherer who has strayed too far into the thick woods reports a terrifying encounter with a Tōhoku bear.

In front of Ōdate Station you'll see a statue of a group of Akita dogs. The hunters of Ōdate are responsible for the development of this impressive breed. They bred the strong, thick-bodied, and heavy-coated dogs to accompany them when they hunted bear and deer. The dogs later became popular with farmers and samurai who trained the powerful animals to fight each other. Every May 3rd, the best of Japan's Akita dogs come home to Ōdate's Katsurajō Park for the All-Japan Akita Dog Show. Today's Akita dogs can be much gentler than their fighting ancestors, but they have retained the thick fur of their Tōhoku bear-hunting past, fur which sheds unmercifully inside a warm house. Nevertheless, no animal is more beautiful than a strong, healthy Japanese Akita dog.

A more reasonable souvenir of a short stop in Ōdate, however, is a piece of magewappa: a vase, bowl, box, or tray made from cryptomeria that has been bent into shape and then lacquered red inside. The craft began toward the end of the Edo period when hungry samurai who needed to supplement their dwindling incomes sold their magewappa lacquer as obentō-bako, or lunch boxes, to farmers and hunters. If you don't have time to stop in Ōdate, you can still buy a piece of Ōdate magewappa in many craft and souvenir shops in Akita and western Aomori.

On the way to Ōdate, some visitors may want to stop at the Haristo Sei Kyōkai, a 100-year-old Greek Orthodox church built in the Byzantine style in the wilds of northern Akita. If you go, be sure to ask to see the inside of the small wooden building. The church is in the village of Magata on Highway 103 near Ōtaki Onsen. The onsen, once the location of Akita's Satake lord's private hot springs, is about halfway beween Towada and Ōdate. The church is a 15-minute bus ride from Ōtaki Onsen Station.

Although the expressway bypasses Ōdate, if the mountain city sounds interesting to you, note that Highway 103 from Towada will get you there and that Highway 7 heads north from Ōdate to rejoin the Tōhoku Expressway at Ikarigaseki. This is a slow lumber-truck route surrounded by beautiful rolling woods which make the poking along not at all unpleasant.

ŌYU, A SMALL RESORT TOWN, lies between Hachimantai and Lake Towada. To end up at the lake rather than in Hirosaki or Aomori, you'll have to take Highway 103 heading northeast from the town of Towada. Ōyu is on the way.

Ōyu has significance to skiers because of its slopes, but out of season it becomes important to the history, or rather prehistory, buff. Once the snow is gone, the Ōyu Stone Circle becomes visible in the foothills southeast of the city, a few kilometers east of the highway. This tiny community's piece of prehistory goes back 4,000 years, long before General Sakanoue no

Tamuramaro came to northern Tōhoku to conquer the native Ezo and long, long before the town bordered on the quarreling Tsugaru, Satake, and Nambu clan territories.

The stone circle is really two large circles shaped by individual rocks and filled with other rocks and stones in various patterns including its much-photographed "sundial." There is also a small museum on the site. The stones were first discovered in 1932 by government surveyors looking for farmland, and they have been seriously studied since the forties. The site is now designated as a Special Historical Relic.

Ōyu Stone Circle is the best example of the countless sites from Japan's stone age that dot most of Tōhoku. Japan's stone age culture is known as the Jōmon (rope-pattern) culture because much of its pottery was decorated with rope designs.

The period is generally considered to have lasted from about 3,000 B.C. to 200 B.C., until the rice-growers of the Yayoi culture finally reached the back country to dominate the Jōmon hunters and fishermen. Jōmon sites are especially plentiful along the coastal areas of Aomori's Tsugaru and Shimokita peninsulas, although many inland sites have also been discovered.

Near bodies of water, Jōmon-period shell mounds have been found. These hill-sized heaps of broken pottery and discarded shells are believed to have been "public garbage dumps" outside small clusters of houses. The shell mounds are marked on some maps of Tōhoku, although not all sites are easily accessible.

Some sites, such as Ōyu, still have the foundations of some Jōmon pit houses, partially underground dwellings once covered with pole-supported straw roofs. And all over Tōhoku numerous shards of pottery and some clay images have been discovered and continue to be accidently unearthed by farmers and construction crews. Outstanding pottery and images from Tōhoku Jōmon sites are displayed at the National Museum in Ueno, in Tōhoku's prefectural museums, and at museums near the various sites such as the Kamegaoka Museum on Aomori's Tsugaru

Peninsula and the Hachinohe City Historical and Folk Museum, also in Aomori Prefecture.

What you'll see at Ōyu is the best of the thirty or so carefully laid out stone circles which have been discovered in Tōhoku and Hokkaido. Inside the two large circles, each about forty meters in diameter, are smaller circles, rectangular patterns thought by some archeologists to be graves, and the strange spoked wheels of the "sundials." The foundation of a pit house, beside one circle, is now covered by a protective roof.

Archeologists have strongly differing theories on the significance of the Ōyu remains. Some believe the "sundial" is just that and, along with the other stone arrangements within the two circles, forms a primitive calendar. Others feel that Ōyu is instead just a graveyard, with the stones' patterns having religious rather than astronomical meaning. Experts even disagree as to whether or not the Jōmon-period bones which have been found represent an Ainu race, a Japanese race, or another race that predates them both.

If you've been to Stonehenge or aren't particularly interested in prehistory, you might not find a stop at Ōyu worthwhile. But for many it is an emotional experience to stand among the stones Ōyu residents dragged from the nearby Ōyu River 4,000 yeara ago—and to wonder why. It certainly helps to put the rest of Tōhoku's history you've been exploring into a new perspective.

The boundary between Aomori and Akita goes right down the middle of Lake Towada, so by following Highway 103 from Ōyu to the lake, you will visit three of Tōhoku's six prefectures in a single busy and varied day of exploring the back country.

AOMORI
PREFECTURE

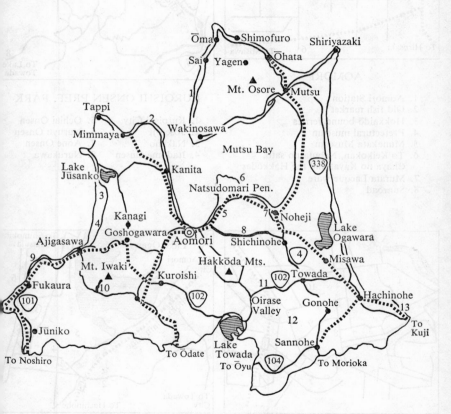

1. Hotokegaura
2. Horozuki Kaigan
3. Cheeseborough Monument
4. Kamegaoka Museum
5. Asamushi Onsen
6. Hotel Kokumin Kenkō Shukusha
7. Makado Onsen
8. Michinoku Toll Road
9. Senjojiki Rock
10. Iwaki Skyline
11. Yakeyama, Tsuta Onsen
12. Christ's tomb
13. Tanesashi Kaigan

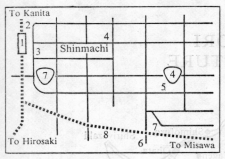

AOMORI

1. Aomori Station
2. Old fish market
3. Hokkaidō-bound ferries
4. Prefectural museum
5. Munakata Museum
6. To Keikokan, Nebuta no sato, Chaya no Kaya, and the Hakkōdas
7. Murata Lacquerware
8. Sunroad

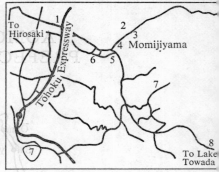

KUROISHI ONSEN PREF. PARK

1. Kuroishi City
2. Jōsen-ji
3. Nakano
4. Itadome Onsen
5. Ochiai Onsen
6. Nuruyu Onsen
7. Aone Onsen
8. Nurukawa

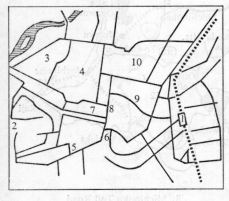

HIROSAKI

1. Hirosaki Station
2. Chōshō-ji
3. Seigan-ji
4. Hirosaki Park
5. Shin-Teramachi
6. Saishō-in
7. Old Aomori Bank
8. Folkcrafts shop
9. Shopping street
10. Tōshō-gū

MISAWA CITY AREA

1. Misawa Station
2. Komaki Onsen
3. Shopping street
4. Misawa airport
5. Misawa Air Base (U.S.)
6. Sabishiro Beach

Introducing Aomori

APPLES THAT SPEND their growing season wrapped in coated newspaper so they will come to fruit shops unblemished in the fall; giant illuminated monster floats that are raucously borne through the streets of the capital city once a year at Nebuta time; and a beautiful caldera lake that lures visitors from all over the country to admire its fall splendor—these are the images of Aomori Prefecture.

But Aomori (Green Forest) Prefecture is more. It's the beyond-this-world eeriness of the barren crater on dreadful Mount Osore; it's the Hakkōda Mountains that once held two hundred Japanese soldiers captive in a blinding blizzard until nearly all froze to death; it's a famous author's Meiji-era house, which now takes in boarders; it's a traditional Japanese garden and house with an English manor built on top; and it's the 54-kilometer-long Seikan Undersea Tunnel linking the islands of Honshu and Hokkaido by rail.

Honshu's northernmost prefecture is surrounded by the sea on three sides. Its interior was once divided into the territories of the Nambu clan on the east and the Tsugaru clan on the west. Although Aomori City is now the official capital, the Tsugaru castle town of Hirosaki still tenaciously holds onto much of its former role. The rolling hills of eastern Aomori, once used by

Nambu lords to graze their famous horses, today produce race horses in the same tradition.

Aomori, the nation's apple capital, conjures up the image of a fall apple harvest when each apple is tenderly freed of its newspaper covering and the surrounding leaves are picked to allow sunlight to reach the fruit. Farmers then lay reflectors beneath the trees so that each perfect apple will develop just the right tinge of color before it is gently picked, carefully packed in a long wooden box, and shipped to some distant prefecture.

It is a fitting coincidence that Mutsu Bay, the body of water nearly enveloped by Aomori's two northern arms, the Shimokita and Tsugaru peninsulas, is shaped somewhat like an apple as it joins the lands of former rival clans with the symbol of a unified prefecture, once backward and poor, now sharing its bountiful harvest from land and sea with the rest of the nation.

The Nohes

LOOKING AT A MAP of northeastern Tōhoku, you may wonder about the cluster of communities between Aomori City and Iwate Prefecture's Morioka whose names begin with a number and end with the character for door or gateway, pronounced in this case "hè," connected with the conjunctive particle "no."

Gateways number one, two, three, five, and seven (Ichinohe, Ninohe, Sannohe, Gonohe, and Shichinohe) are lined up in numerical order from south to north along Highway 4, with the sixth gateway (Rokunohe) slightly out of place as a suburb of Towada City. The eighth and ninth (Hachinohe and Kunohe) gateways bend back towards the first, touching the Pacific Ocean and coaxing the Tōhoku Main Line to take a similar eastward jog. The fourth gateway no longer exists, possibly because the number four is not a great favorite of the Japanese. Although different characters are used, "shi" can mean both four and death. To the superstitious, living in Shinohe would be like living on the thirteenth floor to the Western mind, and for the same reason many older Japanese buildings have no fourth floor or room number four.

The Nohes were horse-breeding areas in old Japan. No one knows when they were actually named (numbered), but they do appear in Kamakura-period (1185–1336) documents.

At one time all the Nohes belonged to the Nambu clan of

Morioka. But when the Meiji emperor brought an end to the feudal period and rearranged the former lords' holdings into prefectures, he left only three of the Nambu gateways still to be ruled from Morioka, which became Iwate's prefectural capital. The descendants of former Nambu subjects who live in what is now eastern Aomori Prefecture are still proud of their roots and, in many ways, feel closer to their Iwate neighbors than to fellow Aomori residents from the Tsugaru side of the prefecture. Subtle traces of the traditional rivalry between the neighboring clans remain today; just ask someone from Hachinohe for an opinion about the Hirosaki accent.

Today Iwate's three remaining gateways are small towns in the scenic rolling hills north of the capital city. National Highway 4 passes through two of them, first weaving through Ichinohe's narrow streets (left over from the days before the Hino diesel) and then taking a mercifully straighter and wider path through Ninohe. Tiny Kunohe, which lies between Kuji on the Pacific Coast and Ichinohe, gets bypassed altogether by all but local traffic.

Going through Ichinohe is a real irritant for most through-traffic, but for the first-time visitor to this area the town's old wooden buildings lining the narrow main road are a charming diversion. Ninohe's comparatively new route through town by-passes its old buildings, but they are there on the side streets for those with the time to discover them.

Aomori's Nohes hold varying degrees of interest for the foreign visitor. Sannohe has bits of its old castle-town charm remaining; Gonohe is now the gateway to the grave of a famous foreign VIP who came to the back country long ago; and Rokunohe and Shichinohe are typical, small Tōhoku rural communities. The Nambu lords' eighth gateway, the only one opening to the sea, is the only Nohe to make it really big: Hachinohe is Aomori's second largest city and its industrial center.

Coming up from the south along either Highway 4 or the

Tōhoku Main Line, the first Aomori Nohe you'll meet is Sannohe. This third Nambu gateway is now a sizable country town in the idyllic setting of forested hills, apple and cherry orchards, truck farms, and small rice paddies all tucked along a broad meandering river at the foot of another of Japan's innumerable Little Fujis, the imposing Mount Nakui.

Sannohe was the first home of the Nambu clan after they came into power in the late twelfth century. Their sixteenth-century castle, built after a fire ruined the original, was itself destroyed at the start of the Meiji era, as Japan attempted to exorcise itself of its feudal past. Wooded Shiroyama Park, where the early Nambu castles once stood, now offers only cherry blossoms in season, recreational facilities for the local ball teams, and a small circa-1967 castle-like museum.

Another piece of Nambu history is a short taxi ride from Sannohe Station. The ancestral shrine of Nambu Toshiyasu, a Momoyama-period (1568–1603) gold and lacquer structure, is an Important Cultural Property of Japan. It is now housed in a modest protective building that the caretaker will unlock for visitors.

Buses from Sannohe Station go to Yasumiya on Lake Towada, passing through some beautiful farm country along Highway 104. In the late summer, picturesque farmhouses and outbuildings are nearly hidden behind the summer's crop of garlic bulbs strung to dry in neat rows that completely cover the walls. If you can find an uncovered barn window, you'll see that the interior space of the outbuildings is also filled with rows of garlic bulbs, strung across the room like laundry. Along this stretch of highway you'll probably see more garlic than most people will see in a lifetime, but, surprisingly, the smell is not nearly as overwhelming as the sight itself.

Although the Sannohe–Yasumiya route to the famous lake is hardly the most popular one, an even less well-traveled route to the north stretches from Highway 4 or the Tōhoku Line's local station at Gonohe to Utarube on the lake. This route passes the Youth Travel Village at Mayoigatai Plateau, which offers good camping—and it also passes something else that needs a bit of introduction.

Rural places all over Japan have their legends of visits from famous historical figures, with or without the support of historical records. In any case, the towns themselves will all have solid evidence of these visits: the famous person sculpted a statue, founded a shrine, fought a battle, drank from a spring, or wrote a poem. The Minamoto clan's Yoshitsune, for example, figures in much of this legendary tradition throughout rural Japan.

But the folks of Shingō, a tiny community between Gonohe and Lake Towada, have a story a cut above the run-of-the-mill Yoshitsune-slept-here tales of other rural villages. Shingō, you see, is the site of the grave of Jesus Christ.

The grave is identified by a cross and signs in Japanese and English donated by the local bus company that explain this strange twist to the more popular account of Christ's life and death. A Star of David on a white signpost tells the visitor when to turn off the highway to find the grave. The tale may sound like a tall one, but Shingō has hard evidence that Christ, or a reasonable facsimile, did indeed spend time in this tiny community and just may be buried here as well.

According to the story, Christ came to Shingō on his second trip to Japan (he had come previously when he was 21 to study theology). This second visit was to escape death; his brother died on the cross in his place. After a troublesome journey, Christ finally settled in Shingō, where he died at the age of 106. His brother's grave is next to his, although there is no explanation of how he, too, got to Shingō.

That's the legend. To back it up, the villagers offer the following facts. The old name of Shingō Village was Herai, close in sound to Heburai, or Hebrew. More convincing is "Nanyado," Shingō's local song. In Japanese its words are meaningless sounds, but in Hebrew the sounds form the words. "I praise your holy name;

we will destroy the aliens and we praise your holy name." Finally, Shingō is the only place in Japan where part of the traditional Shintō ceremony to bless new babies involves an unusual gesture: the sign of the cross.

In the face of such evidence, it does seem likely that at one time a foreign Christian missionary may have come to Shingō to convert the local population. Some people suggest this person's "troublesome journey" may have been an escape from southern Japan when all foreign missionaries were banished from the country in 1639 rather than an escape from crucifixion nearly 2,000 years ago. If you are in the area to enjoy its rural scenery, do consider dropping by this ordinary little village with an extraordinary tale to tell to pay your respects to whoever may lie beneath the bus company's two wooden crosses.

A DETOUR OFF Highway 4 heading east from Gonohe leads to the Nambu lords' eighth gateway, the one with perhaps the most to offer present-day travelers. Hachinohe is a major stop on the Tōhoku Main Line and its busy harbor hosts international cargo ships and ferries to Hokkaido, including a comfortable overnight ferry to Sapporo's port of Tomakomai. The city's industrial complex—producing paper, cement, chemicals, steel, and ships—ruins the skyline but supports the city's population of more than 220,000. Damaged by bombings in the last days of World War II, Hachinohe today is a product of new Japan, with a modern downtown and first-class hotels.

Visitors looking for preindustrial attractions can try beautiful Tanesashi Beach, Hachinohe's old-fashioned fish markets, Kabushima (Seagull Island), the Hachinohe City Historical and Folk Museum, the wooded Kushibiki Hachiman Shrine complex, and the city's enduring handcrafted wooden horses.

From Hachinohe Station the Hachinohe Line runs south to Kuji on the northern edge of Iwate's Rikuchū Kaigan National Park. The small train line passes some coastline that is equally as pretty but less touristy than much of the national park itself. The 8-kilometer-long stretch of grass, sand, pine trees, and rock formations along Tanesashi Beach are accessible from Tanesashi Station, where a grassy campground along the beach is located, and from Mutsu Shirohama Station, appropriately named for its popular white-sand beach. By car, Tanesashi Beach is a worthwhile detour from coastal Highway 45, which efficiently bypasses the winding but lovely coastline.

Closer to town along the Hachinohe Line is Samè Station, the location of one of Hachinohe's busy fish markets. The Samè market is a survivor from the days when Hachinohe harbor hosted mainly family-owned fishing boats. The small vessels are still there, now dwarfed by huge international carriers. However, a night view of the dark ocean beyond the harbor, liberally sprinkled with the lights of hundreds of squid fishermen, joins the bustling early-morning fish markets in declaring that food from the sea is still an important part of the industrial city's economy.

In the streets of Samè you can observe the noisy commotion as the day's catch begins its journey to sushi shops and supermarkets. The narrow roads and boisterous buyers and sellers dressed for fish trading make this area one of the more colorful spots in an otherwise sterile, modern postwar city atmosphere.

Not far from the Samè fish market area is Kabushima island, now a peninsula, but still the summer home of tens of thousands of raucous umineko, the rare and protected black-backed seagulls. Called sea cats because of their meow-like screeching, the birds come to Hachinohe harbor's Kabushima to breed between March and August every year. During this time, the birds literally cover the two rocky projections into the harbor. For a close look at them, you can visit the "island" with the small fishermen's shrine. Bear in mind, however, the risks of such close scrutiny: some people actually carry umbrellas to protect themselves from showers of bird droppings.

A short walk out the main entrance of the Hachinohe Line's

Hon-Hachinohe Station is the city's interchangeable modern downtown. But another short walk behind the station leads to something unique to Hachinohe: the small factory in which Yawata Uma, Hachinohe's wooden horses, are handcrafted.[1] Actually more of a workshop than factory, the small building turns out all the brightly painted chunky wooden horses you see everywhere in the city, from the huge one in front of the civic center to the more practical-sized animals sold as souvenirs all over northeastern Tōhoku. To appreciate the handwork involved, visit the workshop where much of the woodworking and all of the painting is still done by hand, down to each tiny handpainted dot on each bridle.

Yawata Uma, sometimes called Hachinohe Uma, have been made in the city for about 700 years, since the time Hachinohe was a lesser castle town of the Nambu clan and yabusame, or horse-back-archery, contests began at the Yawata Shrine, now called the Kushibiki Hachiman-gū. As the contest drew more and more spectators, a business-minded wood and lacquer artisan from Kyoto began producing recreations of the contest's lavishly adorned horses, which he sold as souvenirs. The idea was copied by neighboring farmers as a winter pastime, and the angular horse, with a square face like a bulldog's and a chunky body as bright as merry-go-round horse's, became the city's symbol.

Yawata Uma make good souvenirs of a trip to this area because of the symbolism in their painted trappings. Some larger horses have the Nambu family crest, two mirror-image fan-tailed cranes; the diamond-shaped crest of the Takada clan, which preceded the Nambu; and a splash of flying umineko. Even the tiniest Yawata Uma is painted with the elaborate trapping of the

1. Yawata Uma Manufacturing Co., 7, 2-chome, Shiroshita, Hachinohe-shi, Aomori-ken 031; tel. (0178) 22–5729
   八幡馬製造合資会社　〒031 青森県八戸市城下二丁目 7
2. Jinya, 11–18, 4-chome, Shiroshita, Hachinohe-shi, Aomori-ken 031; tel. (0178) 43–8738
   陣屋　〒031 青森県八戸市城下四丁目 11–18

yabusame horse of long ago, each tiny painted dot representing a metal bell on a real horse's bridle.

A short taxi ride or a reasonable walk from the factory to the Highway 45 bypass leads to Jinya,[2] one of the city's more interesting restaurants. The restored Nambu-style farmhouse has two floors of dining rooms separated by the original woodwork and furnished with old chests, clocks, and pottery, formerly the possessions of Nambu farm families. The exterior is gleamingly restored, down to a final touch of plastic lanterns to attract traffic from the bypass, but the inside is still faithful to the original, with huge beams, time-smoothed woodwork, and cozy room-sized tatami dining areas. The menu is in Japanese, but you can order their specialty: a two-tiered lacquer box of homemade soba and tempura. Get your noodles either warm (Chōja Soba) or cold (Tenjin Soba). In each category the "A" dinner is standard, the "B" has more tempura, and the "special" offers sashimi as well. Or order whatever the others in your small dining room are having that looks good. A word of warning to the squeamish and an invitation to the adventurous: those rich, deep red strips of thinly cut meat on Jinya's picture menu (of the Yoshitsune Nabe), represent Jinya's other specialty: horsemeat. A few strips also come with sashimi platters, a tribute to the Nambu region's tradition of raising horses.

The Hachinohe City Historical and Folk Museum is about a 15-minute ride from Hon-Hachinohe Station on the road leading from the station that passes between the Marumitsu and Nagasakiya department stores. A bus from Mikka-machi near the stores for Korekawa will take you to Kokokan-mae, a 2-minute walk from the museum.

Over 6,000 artifacts from the prehistorical Jōmon period were unearthed on the Izumiyama Farm, where the museum now stands. These relics, along with items from later periods in the city's past, are on display in a small, modern building. There are also two replicas of Jōmon-period dwellings on the grounds along with a small gift shop featuring Hachinohe-yaki, an unusual green-colored local pottery that died out during the Edo period but has recently been revived.

Another historical item of note in Hachinohe is the latest and northernmost kofun, or ancient burial mound, found in Japan to date. This eighth-century mound came as a surprise to archeologists, who previously believed that Japan's Tumulus-period culture existed only in southern Japan and only in the third through the fifth centuries.

A storehouse of later Hachinohe history is the Kushibiki Hachiman Shrine, a 5-minute ride or 2-kilometer walk from Hachinohe Station across the Mabuchi River. Cryptomeria said to be 800 years old line the path leading to the new shrine building, a 330-year-old structure that replaced the original one built in the early thirteenth century. The city's Meiji-era public library building is also preserved on the grounds.

The shrine's main attraction is a set of armor that once belonged to the fourteenth-century emperor Chōkei. The only other set of imperial armor from the late Kamakura period is stored in Nara, far to the south. The armor displayed here got to the back country through the seventh Nambu lord, who received it from the emperor in recognition for his help in repelling an attack by a rebellious lord in southern Japan. The red-threaded armor is locked in the shrine's storehouse along with a white-threaded set from the later Muromachi period (1336–1568). For a small fee, the caretakers will open the building for you, light the display cabinet, and start a recording in Japanese that gives all the details. Each set of armor weighs forty kilograms; imagine if you can a Japanese warrior of 650 years ago, smaller in stature than today's milk-and-meat generation, doing battle thus encumbered. His only hope was that the other side would carry an equal burden.

Two pony-sized wooden Yawata Uma are also stored in the shrine compound, on the site that long ago spawned the still popular craft.

Before you leave this big industrial city with its scattered patches of history, mention must be made of its traditional celebrations, which also serve as links to the past.

In the early morning chill each February 17th, groups of costumed farmers arrive on the snow-packed grounds of Chōja Shrine near the main shopping district for the Emburi festival. They will offer prayers for the success of the new year's crops, the seeds for which they will be planting as soon as the frozen ground becomes warm and workable. A dance reenacting the motions of planting, harvesting, and all the steps in between gives the gods an idea of what the farmers hope to reap in the coming season, and it gives spectators great photo opportunities. Many of the dancers wear eboshi, tall colorfully painted hats similar to the ceremonial headgear of court nobles, but their eboshi, however, symbolize a horse's long neck, complete with streamers for a mane.

As in many snowbound Tōhoku towns, the parade down the main streets later that day gives the residents a joyous diversion from the drudgery of winter. But the early-morning shrine ceremony is particularly touching in that, unlike many of today's festivals, it is not simply a reenactment but a true continuation of an ancient and important tradition. Emburi, named for the tool used to prepare the ground for the new crops, has been celebrated for 800 years. If you watch the intensity and soberness with which the costumed farmers pray once they reach the shrine and notice farm families in everyday dress also in line to offer their prayers, you'll realize that this ceremony is the real thing. Farming in the back country is tough; some winters farmers must leave their families for jobs as day laborers in Tokyo to prevent the financial disaster caused by crop failure. Yet each February these hardy people will once again offer their prayers, and then, full of hope, plant the new crop in the late spring sun.

Hachinohe's summer festival, August 21st through 23rd, is like most in Tōhoku—local groups form dance teams and build floats for a downtown parade; booths sell the junk food that tastes so good in a festival atmosphere; and everyone comes out to celebrate, dressed in crisp summer yukata.

On the second day, though, the kiba-dakyū games add a different touch to the festivities. Carrying on a 200-year-old tradition, mounted and costumed contestants participate in the polo-like game at Chōjasan Park. Hachinohe's kiba-dakyū is one of only three such traditional matches left in Japan; the others are held at the Imperial Palace in Tokyo and in Tōhoku's Yamagata Prefecture.

The northernmost of the Nohes, Shichinohe, deserves a concluding note not only for its refreshing back-country small-town atmosphere and its old Meiji-era post office, but also for its very modern Michinoku Toll Road just north of it on Highway 4 near Temmabayashi. The toll road offers a shortcut to Aomori, saving about thirty minutes of travel time in bypassing the pretty stretch of Highway 4 along Mutsu Bay. It also cuts out one of the highway's worst bottlenecks through the string of little fishing villages that, like Ichinohe, further south on the highway, attract only those with extra time to enjoy them.

There is much to experience around the Nambu clan's gateways, but your explorations will eventually lead you into rival Tsugaru clan territory—the other side of Aomori Prefecture's part of the back country.

Prefecture.

Misawa

THE CITY OF MISAWA is known on the Tōhoku tourist beat as
one of the "gateways to Lake Towada" and as the home of
Aomori Prefecture's only jetport from which A-300 airbuses
connect Honshu's northernmost prefecture with Tokyo's Haneda
Airport. The city is also on JNR's Tōhoku Main Line, a
20-minute jog off Highway 4 from Towada City and the site
of the Komaki Onsen[1] complex, with its gigantic rock hot-spring
bath, an outstanding folk museum, and acres of restored and
replicated pieces of Japan's heritage.

But Misawa's days as a typical Tōhoku farming, fishing, and
horse-breeding community were numbered long before the appearance of Komaki and the modern airport.

A walk down Misawa's main shopping street will give you
an idea of what has happened to this once-ordinary rural village.
Listen to the accents of the shoppers around you: you'll be
surprised to hear the sounds of Korean, Thai, Tagalog, Chinese,
and Vietnamese. Recognizable Japanese will be mixed in there,
too, but it is as likely to be the soft Kansai or standard Tokyo
dialects as the local patois. And now and then you'll start at the
sound of a Texas drawl or a Bronx "Gimme two a dose."

1. Komaki Onsen, Eki-mae, Misawa-shi, Aomori-ken 033; tel. (01765) 3–5151
   古牧温線　〒033 青森県三沢市駅前

Misawa, although still a small city of 40,000, is now one of the most cosmopolitan cities in all Tōhoku. The reason is sandwiched between the modern downtown area and the south shore of Lake Ogawara—Misawa Air Base, a sprawling compound shared by thousands of Japanese and American troops and their families from all over Japan and the world. Hence, the hodgepodge of tongues and faces, the jetport, and the fact that you as a foreigner in Misawa will both lose your celebrity status and regain the luxury of communicating in your native tongue.

The prewar construction of a big air base was not the first attempt by outsiders to change the community. In the late 1800s samurai families of the Aizu clan who resisted the Meiji Restoration were exiled to this area from what is now Fukushima Prefecture. (See Fukushima's Aizu-Wakamatsu section.) Thousands came to the northernmost reaches of Honshu and to Hokkaido, some by boat and many on foot, leaving possessions behind and suffering hardships both on the journey and in their attempts to settle the poor back-country frontier. Not a few of the prefecture's business and political leaders today are descendants of these hardy Aizu pioneers.

More outsiders came to Misawa in the 1930s. They were much fewer in number, but they moved the village even further from typical, this time toward international fame. Misawa's Sabishiro Beach was the site of the takeoff of the Miss Veedol on October 4, 1931. When the Bellanca monoplane landed in Wenatchee, Washington, forty-one hours and thirteen minutes later, Clyde Pangborn and Hugh Herndon became the first flyers to cross the Pacific Ocean nonstop.

Pangborn and Herndon were the fourth team of American flyers who took off from Sabishiro Beach's 2,000-meter-long packed-clay runway in an attempt to claim the $25,000 prize offered by one of Japan's newspapers, the Asahi Shimbun, for a nonstop transpacific crossing. For over a year, the "typical" poor Tōhoku village intermittently hosted invasions of American flyers, their contingents, and the attending Japanese and international press, since nearby Sabishiro Beach was Japan's only unobstructed runway site long enough to accommodate the fuel-laden aircraft.

Today there is only a lonely wooden memorial to the Miss Veedol hidden in the windbreak behind Sabishiro Beach, but the prefecture does have some tentative plans to develop the historic site into a park to commemorate the fiftieth anniversary of the flight. The monument is near a wide sand beach (with a treacherous undertow) about 5 kilometers north of the intersection of Misawa's main road through downtown and coastal Highway 338. There is a small sign in Japanese on the left of the highway. A gravel road through the trees on the right takes you to the monument marking the spot from which the Miss Veedol dramatically lifted off the ground, barely missing the beginning of the soft sand.

The excitement of the foreigners, the aircraft, the international notoriety, and the community's first telephone (to accommodate the press)—it all happened over 50 years ago, but old-timers still have vivid memories of the outside world's abrupt intrusion into their thatched-roof, dirt-laned, sparsely populated village.

Chiyo Kohiruimaki, the first daughter-in-law of Misawa Village's mayor, and in whose house the flyers stayed, tells wonderful stories of those days. Then a young wife of twenty-five, she remembers having to send to Hachinohe, the nearest city, for such novel foods as meat, butter, bread, and coffee; asking a local craftsman to make bamboo copies of her few metal forks so there would be enough to go around; hastily ordering a Western-style toilet fixture from Tokyo to fit over her floor-level toilet; and piling seven or eight futon on top of one another to create the illusion of beds for her uninvited houseguests.

Masao Kohiruimaki, her cousin, remembers as a young boy smelling for the first time the delicious aroma of coffee brewing for the foreign visitors. He excitedly gulped down his first cup of coffee and can still feel the shock of the sweet-smelling liquid's bitterness on his tongue.

And Miyo Sekikawa remembers her delight as a child when the schools closed so that everyone could join the flag-waving crowd of well-wishers as each of the four planes took off. Her husband, Yūtarō, who was twenty-one at the time, and who was assigned to guard the planes during the days before the takeoff attempts, has spent the past fifty years collecting documents and photos so that the event that put humble Misawa Village on the map will not be forgotten by the rest of the world. While much of the documentation stored in Tokyo was destroyed in wartime bombings, his original newspaper clippings and photographs survived, carefully wrapped in a furoshiki (wrapping cloth).

You may not have time to visit remote Sabishiro Beach, but, as you travel through the still provincial countryside around eastern Aomori, imagine what the area was like fifty years ago when the Western world suddenly showed up saying, "Hello. Can you take us in for a week or so? We usually have bacon and eggs, over easy, for breakfast." The unflappable hospitality of the Japanese people is indeed remarkable.

It is no wonder that today's Misawans take in stride the presence of a polyglot foreign population in their midst. At least the new wave of foreigners brought their own Western plumbing and beds, and the changing times have brought to Misawa most of the other comforts of progress.

Between Sabishiro and the eastern shore of Lake Ogawara is the Misawa City Park recreation complex. This extensive development includes wooded nature trails, an obstacle course, athletic fields, a sand beach with showers and camping facilities, a small onsen and rest house, and, of greatest interest to the visitor, the Misawa Historical Museum. Displayed here are examples of the Jōmon-period pottery that continues to be unearthed in the area, items from later historical periods (including items related to the transpacific flight from Sabishiro Beach), and local flora and fauna. Buses from Misawa Station leave for the city park during the summer months.

IF YOU GET OFF the Tōhoku Main Line at Misawa Station to get on a bus for Lake Towada, plan to spend at least a few hours exploring the Komaki Onsen complex next door to the station. Komaki, another ambitious attempt to move Misawa further from the mere typical, is an amusing mixture of Japan old and new: attractions range from restored farmhouses to twice-daily variety shows.

Komaki's three focal points are its hotels—the original Komaki Onsen Hotel, the Komaki Grand Hotel, and the new Second Grand Hotel. Each building is more elaborate, more Western, and more expensive than the preceding one. The original onsen hotel is the only one with any old-fashioned charm; so if you're planning to spend the night, be sure to request a room there.

When Yukio Sugimoto, Komaki's innovative, Shizuoka-born owner, built the original Komaki Hotel in 1961, he expressed his appreciation of the simple beauty of things Japanese by adding a folkcraft museum, a small teahouse, a replica of the famous Hiraizumi open-air Noh stage, and several small carp-filled ponds and gardens tucked here and there.

Today the museum is one of the best in Tōhoku. It includes a small thatched-roof house, a bear-hunter's cabin complete with tools of the trade, and extensive displays of everyday articles used by Tōhoku farmers and fishers. Particularly interesting is the collection of kogin clothing, work clothes painstakingly covered with stitching in complex patterns to make them wear longer. Kogin is one of the true mingei, or folk, arts of this area—utilitarian in origin and now valued for its simple beauty and its part in Tōhoku's history.

Over the next twenty years, Sugimoto continued to add on

to his hotel complex. Besides the two grand hotels, he has built the largest rock bath in Tōhoku, an Olympic-sized indoor pool, a bowling alley (whose giant rooftop pin ruins otherwise great photos of Komaki's traditional roof lines), a copy of the wedding hall at western Japan's Izumo Shrine, two large restored farmhouses representing the Nambu style of northeastern Tōhoku and the Tsugaru style of northwestern Tōhoku, a rock garden, a replica of Kyoto's Sanzen-in temple, and more.

His latest improvement is Saigyodō Park, a new section of restored and duplicated old houses, teahouses, and temples from various parts of Japan placed around a small lake. He even built the lake, from a former swamp that he had drained, dredged, and refilled with layers of carefully chosen rock and sand.

Obviously, several hours are needed to cover Komaki, not counting time for the giant rock bath, which is included in the admission price. The various attractions are connected by tunnel-like passageways, themselves mini-museums lined with ink paintings, antique pottery, and classic furnishings. Just keep wandering till you've seen it all; the attractions are located roughly in the above order, the original hotel being the building nearest the train station.

Komaki's hot bath deserves further elaboration, because you may never see (and may never want to see) anything like it again. Really a series of indoor hot water pools and waterfalls, the entire structure is supported by twenty-one giant tree trunks of concrete. The men's and women's sections taken together represent a miniature of the Oirase River, which empties into famous Lake Towada.

Bathing at Komaki is a different sort of experience from the relaxing Japanese bath you may have come to expect. The onsen can hold thousands of people, and, if you're there when the tour buses unload, you may get the feeling that it actually does. Another feature that may either detract or add to the experience, depending on the individual, is that the two sections of the bath are only partially divided, and peeking, a big game for some of the bathers.

A waist-high open-weave fence partially filled in with plastic flowers gives the women some privacy, but the men, whose baths are at a lower level, are in full view of giggling groups of school girls. The men, however, can get their turn by peering through their large waterfall at the women who must pass behind it to reach the "Lake Towada" pools on the other side. Many women carry bath towels with them in order to get past the falls with dignity. (Other women, protesting that the big falls is reserved for men, have integrated it, and no one really complains.)

Komaki representatives claim that they are preserving the natural atmosphere of the baths by leaving inadequate separations between bathing areas. Once warned of what to expect, both modest and bold bathers can prepare to enjoy an unforgettable experience.

Sugimoto says that he is far from finished with Komaki. The self-made millionaire is now retired and lives modestly on the grounds of the Komaki complex. After his Aomori lumber business made him wealthy, he made it his goal to develop the area into Tōhoku's number one tourist attraction. His credits so far include Lake Towada's Towada Grand Hotel, the lake ferries, and the Towada tour buses; Noheji's Makado Onsen, a mini-Komaki; and the Hotel New Yagen on the Shimokita Peninsula. Komaki is still his pet project; you'll see his own calligraphy hanging in the tearooms of Saigyodō Park and may even see Sugimoto-san himself wandering through the grounds in his windbreaker and ball cap.

As the son of a poor widow who was later the protégé of Keizō Shibusawa, a former Minister of Finance and ex-head of the Bank of Japan, Sugimoto expressed his gratitude to his mentor by building a memorial museum to Shibusawa at Komaki. The former Finance Ministry summer house is also in Saigyodō Park, and the park itself is named for Shibusawa's pen name, a further tribute to the former political and business leader.

One wonders about Sugimoto and the other outsiders who just wouldn't leave rural Misawa alone. But with characteristic Tōhoku reserve, the local farmers and fishers take little notice. They just keep coming to town in their rubber boots, baggy work pants, and traditional quilted jackets, greeting each other in their enigmatic dialect and stubbornly ignoring the obvious—that the outside world has made Misawa something more than a typical Tōhoku town.

The Shimokita Peninsula

SHAPED LIKE AN AX hovering over the rest of the island, the Shimokita Peninsula, Honshu's northernmost projection, is the Tōhoku story in microcosm. Tōhoku, the back country, is well represented by Mount Osore, or Osore-zan (Mount Dread), in whose sulfuric crater remnants of a folk religion predating both Shintoism and Buddhism are found within a "more contemporary" 1,100-year-old Buddhist framework.

Modern Tōhoku is here also—in the busy modern city of Mutsu—whose downtown looks as if it belongs along a Tokyo suburban train line rather than far into the back country—and in the Japan Self Defense Force's big Ōminato Naval Base on the northern shore of Mutsu Bay.

Finally, Tōhoku's diversity of natural beauty is represented both on the coastlines and in the mountainous interior of the peninsula. Shiriyazaki (Back Room Point) is the Pacific shoreline's cape of green pastures shared by grazing cattle, shellfish gatherers, campers, and photographers. The Tsugaru Straits' Hotokegaura (Buddha's Strand) Coast of huge, white, sea-carved cliffs is reachable only by boat or the hardiest of land vehicles, and the snow monkeys of nearby Wakinosawa form the world's northernmost community of wild monkeys. Inland is the remote onsen community of Yagen, tucked deep in a forest along a rugged river valley beautiful enough to rival Towada's famous Oirase Valley and with only a fraction of its tourists.

In short, Shimokita has enough variety to warrant its monopolizing your entire vacation, with you still going home feeling you've seen the many faces of Northern Japan. If you only have a short time to spend on the peninsula, don't miss awesome Mount Osore, guaranteed to raise more than a few goose bumps and to be one of the most unforgettable scenes of your trip north. Then, before you head back down its narrow ax handle, see what you can of the rest of Shimokita's diverse offerings.

The peninsula is connected with the rest of Honshu by JNR's Ōminato Line from Noheji, a stop on the Tōhoku Main Line. The Ōminato Line then connects with the Ōhata Line at Mutsu City's Shimokita Station for the remaining 18 kilometers to the top of the ax head, terminating at the coastal village of Ōhata. JNR keeps threatening to discontinue these small, unprofitable lines, and residents keep protesting; so, for the time being, it's a standoff and the trains are still running.

Buses cover the same route on Highway 279 and also run along the less-traveled Pacific Coast route, Highway 338, a very pretty ride.

MUTSU CITY IS the starting point for a tour of the peninsula. Most intercity buses leave from Tanabu Station on the Ohata Line. There is a youth hostel near Shimokita Station, and most other types of accommodation are available in the city, including the modern Mutsu Kankō Hotel[1] along the bypass.

The narrow mountain road leading to Osore-zan is lined with Buddhist statues carved from stone that once marked the way for religious pilgrims walking up the sacred mountain. The road twists and climbs through a thick forest, one of the three finest in Japan, until it abruptly ends at Mount Osore's barren crater.

1. Mutsu Kankō Hotel, 4 Shitamichi, Tanabu, Mutsu-shi, Aomori-ken 035; tel. (01752) 2–2331
   むつ観光ホテル　〒035 青森県むつ市田名部字下道 4

Along the way is a spot where icy water channeled from a mountain stream is supposed to guarantee long life to those who stop for a drink. You may feel the need to do so (or to use the public toilet across the road) after a few sharp curves where wide uphill buses jerk to a stop as they come face to face with wide downhill logging trucks.

After the final curve through the trees comes a shock to the eye when all at once the gray desolation of Osore-zan appears, a grayness broken only by the dark blue and deathly still Lake Usori in the crater's center. At the same time, the smell of rotten eggs assaults the nose. It's easy to see why the peninsula's early inhabitants believed that this barren and forbidding scene had to be of another world—and why many present-day residents still do.

The strong sulfuric odor comes from the crater's many bubbling hot springs, which range in color from blood red to bright yellow. Jagged, low rock formations also dot the landscape, some warm to the touch, others with wisps of steam escaping from surface cracks, and others as cold as their gloomy surroundings.

If you were a departed spirit and wanted to return for a brief visit, wouldn't you feel rather at home in this setting? Many Japanese people think so, especially people from Tōhoku, which, as the last part of Honshu to be "civilized," is unusually rich in ancient folklore. Believers consider Mount Osore to be one of the three sacred spots in Japan where the spirits of the dead reside and can be contacted through mediums.

Once a year from July 20th to the 24th, specially trained blind women called itako will contact the spirit of a departed loved one for you. Unfortunately, the departed only communicate in the medium's strong Shimokita dialect, so you won't understand much. Many local people, however, claim they have indeed exchanged greetings with the dead during this Itako Festival. In fact, the local idiom for "kicked the bucket" is "gone to Tanabu" (Osore-zan is in this district) or "gone to the mountain."

Although you can converse with the spirit world only during

the festival, you can't help but feel the eerie sensation of its presence any time you walk the strange landscape—preferably not by yourself.

Early folk religion had already marked Mount Osore as sacred when Buddhism enveloped the desolate scene in its own lore as early as 845 A.D. with the establishment of the Entsū-ji Bodai-ji temple. Today, the temple complex is spread out among the rocks and bubbling ponds. As you walk through the grounds, you'll note the shiny stainless steel roof of Jizō Hall, the building nearest the lake. The choice of roofing material doesn't seem so strange when you consider the effects of Mount Osore's sulfuric atmosphere on the more traditional copper.

You'll also run into several small wooden bath houses, which are free to anyone who doesn't mind the smell, extremely hot water, and curious passers-by peeking in. The temple also runs a modern inn with very low rates, but temple officials say they would rather rent their rooms to religious pilgrims than to tourists.

The manifestations of the modern religion on the ancient holy grounds that most delight photographers are the Jizō statues scattered between the temple buildings and the lake. By the end of the summer pilgrimage season, the stone figures are covered to the point of being completely hidden with colorful offerings of clothing, and their bases overflow with coins, food, drinks, and even toys.

The infant-sized, hand-knit sweaters, small dolls, and other accoutrements of childhood donated to the Jizō statues lend an even more somber note to Mount Osore's already far from jolly atmosphere. Jizō is the guardian deity of children, and the offerings are to help him look after those children who have left our world and are making their way to the next.

You'll also see donations of straw sandals around the statues. These are for Jizō's other role as guardian of the spirits of the dead of all ages. Jizō makes nightly patrols of the land between this world and the next, Sai-no-kawara, and its rocky riverbed causes the thin straw sandals to wear out rapidly. On his rounds he comforts homeless spirits who are busy piling up stones for stupas so they will be allowed to enter paradise. He also scares away the ever-present demons who are continually knocking down these piles. Some visitors to Mount Osore lend a hand to the struggling spirits by creating small rock piles for them or by adding a stone or two to existing ones.

Osore-zan hasn't completely been turned over to the spirit world, however. The soba shop outside the temple features sansai, or mountain vegetables, that are supposed to prolong your stay in this world. There is also a modern rest house nearby.

IF YOU'RE GOING TO STAY on the peninsula for a while, pick up a detailed map of Shimokita at Mount Osore, and press on to the peninsula's more cheerful attractions.

Because mountains take up most of the sparsely populated interior of the peninsula's ax head, there are only a handful of interior roads, mostly narrow gravel lanes which in places barely hang onto the mountainsides. These are the most direct connections between places of interest on Shimokita peninsula, but most visitors, understandably, choose to backtrack to Mutsu City, the peninsula's focal point and population center, from which paved bus routes fan out in all directions.

Coming in a close second for the best of Shimokita is the hot-spring resort of Yagen. From Mount Osore a gravel road climbs the hill separating the two attractions in 40 minutes of teeth-jarring, dusty curves. It takes twice as long to go back to Mutsu, then north to Ōhata and 10 kilometers inland along the Ōhata River, but the scenery is pleasant and the roads are good. The bus trip from Shimokita's Tanabu Station to Yagen takes 50 minutes.

Yagen is for those travelers who like to venture out into the wilderness without giving up their creature comforts. You are definitely far into the rugged back country as the gentle Ōhata

River turns into rapids deep in an interior forest lushly green in summer and brilliantly tinted in fall. Yet the five-story, thoroughly modern Hotel New Yagen,[2] with its chalet-style facade, is discretely tucked into the wild landscape on the banks of the surging Ōhata Rapids. There are also several ryokan clustered near the hotel including the Furuhata Ryokan[3] with its Japanese cypress bath featuring the resort's clear, non-sulfuric water. For those who'd rather give up comfort in deference to their surroundings, there is also a campground nearby.

There's not a lot to do at this isolated onsen other than relax, bathe in waters recommended for tired muscles and tense stomachs, and enjoy a walk along the beautiful rapids on a 4-kilometer-long trail. For travel-weary spirits, this may be entertainment enough. Fishers also like the opportunity Yagen gives them to catch small trout in the absence of the busloads of tourists who flock to the more famous Oirase Rapids near Lake Towada.

The walking trail ends at a second onsen community, Oku Yagen, which has a few more ryokan and a riverside open-air hot-spring bath. You can see the bath (and so can everyone else!) along a tributary of the river that is crossed by the road. The mixed bath is free, and there are no dressing rooms. But if you're feeling as free as the natural scene around you, why not give it a try?

Yagen gets its name from the yagen dai, or druggist's mortar, symbolizing both the shape of the original hot water source and the pre-tourist-era occupation of early residents, gathering and preparing medicinal herbs. The old bear rifle displayed at the Furuhata Ryokan is a reminder that bear hunting in the surrounding forests was also once a popular livelihood for the community's

2. Hotel New Yagen, Yagen Onsen, Ōhata-machi, Shimokita-gun, Aomori-ken 039–44; tel. (017534) 3311.
   ホテルニュー薬研　〒039-44 青森県下北郡大畑町薬研温泉
3. Furuhata Ryokan, Yagen Onsen, Ōhata-machi, Shimokita-gun, Aomori-ken 039–44; tel. (017534) 2763.
   古畑旅館　〒039-44 青森県下北郡大畑町薬研温泉

handful of residents, some of whom claim to be descendants of a samurai who escaped Tokugawa's siege of Osaka Castle in 1615 and settled in what was then known as Furuhata—the name the samurai took as his own.

Most of the peninsula's Pacific coastline is inaccessible, with the exception of Shiriyazaki, or Cape Shiriya, on the northeastern tip. And Shiriyazaki is also a photographer's dream come true. Rolling fields of green dotted with grazing cattle lay beside a jagged shoreline with a turn-of-the-century lighthouse for a backdrop.

A one-hour bus ride from Tanabu Station will take you all the way to the cape during the tourist season, but the rest of the year the bus route terminates at the nearby town of Shiriya, leaving you with a very pretty and not unreasonably long walk through the fields and along the beach to the lighthouse. Shiriya offers a few minshuku and a youth hostel for overnight guests and the beach has beautiful campsites to be shared with cows and early morning shellfish gatherers. Signs posted throughout the area ask that you do not disturb the grazing cattle's peaceful routine—which is the least you can do in return for their good-natured posing in the foreground of your camera-captured seascapes.

The area's human residents have a unique custom you may be able to observe. If you pass a beach near the town that's lined with cars and crowded with chattering people, you probably have stumbled onto Shiriya's community seafood gathering efforts, the results of which will be equally divided among the participants. You may also stumble onto remains of some very early residents of the cape. Archeologists have found many prehistoric relics in the area, including a shell mound and a small stone circle left by Jōmon-period people over 5,000 years ago. (See Iwate Prefecture's Hachimantai section for more on stone circles.)

The only blight on Shiriyazaki's idyllic peace and contentment is a gigantic limestone mine and processing plant—an eyesore to the tourist, but a great boon to the remote community's economy.

Luckily, it is far removed from scenes of cows, grass, pines, cliffs, crashing waves, and a regal lighthouse, all of which the photographer can, if so desired, include in a single frame.

IF BY THIS TIME, you're hooked on discovering more of this beautiful and diverse peninsula, head west along the northern coastline beyond Ōhata for the highly sulfuric coastal onsen of Shimofuro. Although the characters for Shimofuro mean lower bath, appropriate enough for an onsen community, the name is said to originate from the even more appropriate Ainu words shumo fura, or sulfuric rocks. Your nose will have no difficulty in agreeing with the latter derivation. What is unique about this onsen is that it looks like another typical Tōhoku weathered fishing village, rather than an onsen community, except for the clouds of steam rising from its hot water source. If you can get past the strong odor, a dip in the community bath (kyōdō yokujo) will cure any skin ailment—from athlete's foot to a bruise—you may be in possession of. For overnighters, several ryokan, minshuku, and a locally-run kokuminshukusha are available.

Further west, and as far north as you can go and still be on Honshu, is Ōmazaki, only 17 kilometers from Hokkaido. Ferries leaving from Ōma harbor take less than two hours to reach the port of Hakodate, and are twice as fast as the Aomori City ferries. The area around the town has been used grazing for horses and cattle since Edo times.

South of Ōma along the western coast is the fishing village and lumber port of Sai, uninteresting to the traveler except that it is the northern gateway to the area's famous, sea-carved, white cliffs of Hotokegaura. Roads along this rough coastline range from poor to nonexistent, so your selection of transportation to the tall limestone cliffs consists of either a 2½-hour round-trip boat ride or a boat ride one way. If you've come by bus, a one-way ticket will enable you to catch another tour boat at Hotokegaura for its southern gateway, Wakinosawa.

Speaking of one-way tickets, there is some irony connected with the cliffs' tongue-twister name. Hotoke means Buddha, and the individual rock formations both resemble and are named for various Buddhist images. Poet Keigetsu Ōmachi once observed that the 2-kilometer-long stretch of weird rocks must have been sculpted by something beyond our world. But hotoke also means corpse— and the bodies of most victims who drown in the Tsugaru Straits usually wash up on the rocky shores of their namesake, Hotoke-gaura, supposedly because of the way the currents flow.

Wakinosawa is the home of the wild snow monkeys who some-times delight photographers by calmly sunning themselves on the rooftops of village houses or fearlessly scampering across the road. Some will even take food offered from a human hand, and others will boldly help themselves to food from a loosely held purse or picnic basket before it is offered!

Share what you want with these northernmost of the world's monkeys who must tread a fine line between being disdainful of their human neighbors and being dependent upon them for survival when nature doesn't come through in this harsh climate. Just re-member to hang onto anything you don't care to share and also that they are wild animals and can be vicious if they feel threatened.

The snow monkeys have not only had to learn to live abnormally close to man on the small peninsula, but have also had to adapt to the Tōhoku winters. Unlike their southern relatives, snow monkey babies cling to their mothers' backs rather than to their under-sides—to keep from being dragged through fresh snow before it packs down.

The monkeys are becoming harder for tourists to spot recently since dwindling natural food sources have caused them to help themselves to the local farmers' crops, leading to retaliation by the farmers who have a hard enough time as it is making a living on the mountainous peninsula. There is a walking trail at the road's end to a hillside that used to be the monkeys' stomping ground. However, if they aren't around on the day you come to visit, they are probably further back into the woods in search of something to eat. Maybe if you got the word out ahead of time about the goodies you intend to share . . . .

From Wakinosawa, a partially paved bus route will take you along the gentle northern shore of Mutsu Bay back to Mutsu City.

Who would have imagined that there was so much to see on the small northern ax hovering above Japan's main island? Shimokita may well end up as your favorite stopover during your Tōhoku itinerary.

Along Mutsu Bay

IF YOU BEGIN YOUR TOUR of Tōhoku from the top, by taking the Tōhoku Main Line from Tokyo as far as it goes, you could be spending your first night in the back country in an adequate but boring Aomori City business hotel. After nearly nine hours on the train in search of something different, you may view this situation as somewhat of a letdown.

But if you plan to get off the train a few stops before the end of the line at Noheji or Asamushi, you can instead spend your first evening in Tōhoku relaxing travel-weary bones in a natural hot-spring bath or walking the quiet beaches of Natsudomari, the nipple-like projection of land that juts into Mutsu Bay.

Noheji is a busy fishing community on the southeastern curve of the bay, a terminus for several Hokkaido-bound ferries. And at the end of a residential street in its suburbs stands its single tourist attraction, the imposing Makado Onsen Hotel.[1]

The giant modern but shabby structure and its slightly sulfuric natural hot water offer an interesting alternative to an Aomori business hotel in spite of the fact that it may be crowded with busloads of tourists.

1. Makado Onsen, 9 Yuzawa, Noheji-machi, Kamikita-gun, Aomori-ken 039–31; tel. (01756) 4–3131.
馬門温泉　〒039-31 青森県上北郡野辺地町字湯沢 9

Beyond several old thatched-roof structures moved onto the site for the sake of ambience is an impressive old wooden gate that leads to a locked glass door with an arrow directing the visitor to the more modest main entrance. Here you can buy just a hot bath, including a private "family bath," or bed and board.

Inside the locked glass door but reachable from the souvenir shop is a photo and memorabilia collection documenting the Hakkōda Death March of 1902 in which about 200 Japanese soldiers froze to death trying to cross the nearby Hakkōda Mountains during a winter exercise. (See the Hakkōda section for details.) Makado's exhibit includes graphic photos of the tragedy's handful of limbless survivors and the artificial feet of one of them in a glass display case.

If you'd rather be on the shores of placid Mutsu Bay than in Makado's soothing hot water, you can stay at Natsudomari's pretty new hotel and campground, the Hotel Kokumin Kenkō Shukusha[2] unobtrusively nestled among the pines near a pebbly beach on the peninsula's eastern shore.

You'll have to get off the limited express train at Noheji, transfer to a local train or a bus heading toward Aomori City, and get off at tiny Kominato Station. You then catch another bus for Natsudomari and the 13-kilometer-long ride to the hotel.

Once past the beautiful peninsula's very unglamorous entrance at a cement works, you'll see a shallow inlet with a narrow foot bridge leading to a tiny islet. If it's not winter you probably won't be overly impressed with Asadokoro Beach, but around mid-November every year the inlet fills with majestic whooper swans who come from Siberia to enjoy Aomori's "mild" winter. The large, graceful birds, protected by the Japanese government during their stay, come here to be fed, oogled at, photographed, and otherwise spoiled with VIP status.

2. Hotel Kokumin Kenkō Shukusha, 6–45 Shirasu, Hiranai-machi, Higashi Tsugaru-gun, Aomori-ken 039–33; tel. (01775) 9–2155
国民健康宿舎　〒039-33 青森県東津軽郡平内町大字白砂 6-45

The free eats also attracts several varieties of wild ducks and seagulls, dwarfed but not at all intimidated by the huge swans. If you come to Tōhoku in winter, don't miss seeing these beautiful birds, which also congregate in other northern Honshu bodies of water. The colored bands that can be seen around the necks of some were attached by scientists from various countries to study their movements, the green ones representing Japan, the blue, America, and the red, of course, Russia.

The people of Aomori, getting a slight jump on contemporary environmentalists, have been protecting their swans for the last 400 years, ever since the birds saved the day for the ruling Tsugaru clan. It seems that word reached a local military leader that Nambu clan warriors were on the way, a fact which sent him scurrying to the local shrine at Kominato to pray for divine intervention.

And it came—in the form of thousands of whooper swans, a beautiful but raucous sight.

Hearing the birds' screeching and flapping, the confused invaders thought the Tsugaru troops must be charging, so they hastily retreated without a fight.

The Tsugaru lord then ordered that the heaven-sent birds never be harmed and forbade the people from even collecting their feathers. After centuries of such deference, the haughty swans of today are fearless of human admirers and will come within a few feet to allow you the honor of tossing them a handout.

Natsudomari's narrow coastal road goes through several fishing villages on the way to the hotel. You will feel like you're almost inside the front door of many of the fishers' homes, which appear to come within a few feet of either side of the twisting road. You'll see piles of tempting glass fishing floats along the sides of buildings (as well as the not-so-tempting orange and black plastic floats). These are, of course, the villagers' tools of the trade. The souvenir ones some people come home with are strays that wash up on the sandy eastern shore of the bay along the Shimokita

Peninsula's long arm. For obvious reason, not too many glass floats arrive intact on Natsudomari's rocky beaches.

Although most travelers will want to head back toward the main highway after the hotel's lovely beach, if it's May and the camellias are in bloom, or if you just can't get enough of Natsudomari's pretty coastline, you can follow the winding coastal road around the peninsula.

Yet to come are Tsubakiyama (Camellia Hill), a hillside of tree-sized camellias, and Ōshima, a tiny island named Big Island, at the tip of the peninsula. Hikers and campers can use a sturdy foot bridge to reach the island and then hike through brush to reach the lighthouse on the very last bit of land jutting out into the bay. Shortly beyond Ōshima, the road turns inland to intersect with Highway 4.

Before you leave this stretch of Mutsu Bay, you must sample its specialty, the famous Mutsu Bay hotate (cultured scallops). Mutsu Bay scallops are so fresh and delicately delicious deep-fried, sauteed in butter, or raw in sushi or sashimi, that they will win over even non-fish-eaters.

But Mutsu Bay didn't always have its delicious scallops. In its pre-scallop days, Mutsu Bay fishers were extremely poor, living in weathered wooden houses and going out in even more weathered wooden boats, grateful for whatever the sea chose to give up each day. Then they started scallop cultivation and instant prosperity came their way.

You'll see much evidence of the scallop impact on the fishing villages between Noheji and Aomori. You'll see veritable hills of scallop shells with crews of old women patiently placing the best ones on strings to be used to cultivate more scallops, carefully picking up a shell at a time from the giant mounds. And you'll pass one drive-in shop after another along busy Highway 4, most with no more advertising than the word "hotate."

Another indication of the scallop impact is the "scallop house." boom." The sarcasm-laden term is used by local big-city sophisticates to describe the sprawling and often gaudy new homes of the scallop-growing nouveaux riches. It carries the implication, tinged with envy, that the scallops have brought Mutsu Bay fishing families' wealth but not the refinement class-conscious Japan expects owners of such expensive houses to possess.

If you can, spend some time observing the hardworking fishers of Mutsu Bay. Glance at their rough, nearly raw hands and their sturdy, lined faces—and imagine the frigid winters they face each year. It's not hard to conclude that their years of struggling with the sea have justly earned them every ornately carved roof doodad and multi-colored exterior wall on their precious "scallop houses."

There is one more onsen along the bay before the Tōhoku Line and Highway 4 both terminate in Aomori City. Asamushi is really a town of onsen. It is also one of the handful of places in the prefecture your friends in southern Japan may have heard of.

Its therapeutic waters were discovered by a Buddhist priest 700 years ago as he watched a wounded deer heal itself by bathing in the hot springs.

Since then, humans have taken the place over. Today the site is cluttered with various-sized hotels and inns standing side by side in two solid lines down the main street.

Examples of charming old-fashioned onsen are hard to come by here, so don't come with high hopes of lots of traditional ambience. The Japanese tourists flock here by the busload to relax, party, and spend, so don't expect to find any bargains either.

On the other hand, the hotels are very near the station, a convenience both Makado and Natsudomari lack. Besides, a comfortable place to sleep and a refreshing bath can help one overlook almost anything. And you'll need both to prepare for the busy days ahead exploring the western side of the prefecture.

Aomori City

AT FIRST GLANCE you may decide to write off modern, bustling
Aomori City as not quite what you were looking for on a trip
to Japan's back country. But don't take off too soon.

Modern Aomori is on the site of a city which World War II
left seventy percent destroyed. As you travel down its wide streets
past the glass and chrome multistoried buildings, you can't help
but be impressed at the fine prefectural capital that has emerged
from the ruins. But, in spite of the fancy facades used to rebuild
the city, a tragic omission seems to have occured—Aomori City
has forever lost her distinctive personality.

Aomori is indeed a nice city, but it's a city nearly indistinguishable from the many others constructed in postwar modern all
over Japan, with its tall department stores, large office buildings,
overdecorated coffee shops, and modern houses. There is even
a U.S.-suburban-style enclosed shopping mall complete with
a bubbling indoor fountain and free parking. Even the Aomori
Prefectural Museum, the storehouse of its history, is encased
in sterile white stucco and glass.

Yet once a year, during the first week of August, sparks of
old Aomori emerge with a real bang. The Nebuta Matsuri, one
of Tōhoku's Big Three festivals during this week (the others being
Sendai's Tanabata and Akita's Kantō festivals), brings nighttime

193

parades of gigantic illuminated monster floats interspersed among thousands of frenzied dancers chanting old nonsense rhymes, drinking sakè, and entertaining the spectators whom they seem to outnumber.

However, after this week of madness, the city once again contentedly settles into its pursuit of all that is modern, and traces of old Aomori become harder to find. But they are there. Much of old Aomori is preserved in her three museums and some is alive and well at the old fish market near the station.

The modern city which greets the traveler is the major transportation terminus for northern Tōhoku. Both eastern Honshu's Tōhoku Main Line and western Honshu's Ōu Main Line terminate here, as do National Highways 4 and 7 and the Tōhoku Expressway. And much of the ferry traffic between Honshu and Hokkaido passes through busy Aomori harbor. The city is also one of the "gateways" to famous Lake Towada and a terminal for tourist and local buses destined for most other local places of interest.

As you leave Aomori Station, you'll come face to face with Shinmachi, an interchangeable Japanese-modern downtown. Don't pass through too quickly or you'll miss the only active remains of prewar Aomori hidden behind the city's modern facade.

Look between the buildings on your right as you leave the station and you'll see the dark alleyways of the old fish market lit with bare bulbs strung between open-air stalls. Busiest during the early morning hours, it is charming any time of the day. Here you'll see very few of Shinmachi's business suits and high heels, but lots of hard-working people going about their business in old-fashioned work clothes and rubber boots. This is the place to take your "people shots" with a fast-film-loaded camera.

If you're able to get by pretty well with the language in Tokyo, listen for a moment to the strong local dialect spoken here and see why even native speakers find it nearly impossible to understand the locals. Soak up this living chunk of old Aomori, because once you hit daylight back in Shinmachi it will seem like it never existed.

Other remains of the prewar city are preserved in its three museums—the Kyōdokan Prefectural Museum, the Keikokan's private collection, and the Munakata Shikō Memorial Museum of Art honoring the famous woodblock artist who was born here.

If you have only a few hours in Aomori (and it's not Monday), after the fish market you must visit the Kyōdokan. Don't let the stark modern building mislead you; Aomori's history was intentionally housed in an edifice "with the whiteness of Greek monuments of culture" to commemorate the centennial of the Meiji Restoration of 1868.

The museum preserves the culture and history of the prefecture, from its prehistoric remains, which continue to be unearthed in abundance, to a fine collection of comparatively recent tools of daily life from the period when Aomori really was Japan's back country. A 20-minute walk from the station or a short cab ride will take you there. It is four blocks north and one block west of the intersection of Highway 4 and the road to Lake Towada, an important landmark for visiting drivers.

The Keikokan is a private museum occupying a modern (what else?) three-story cement and glass cube just beyond the impossible-to-miss Sunroad Shopping Mall on the road to Lake Towada. Watch for a multistoried gray office building on the same side of the road with a shorter "cube" in front.

Like the Kyōdokan, the Keikokan is dedicated to "collecting and preserving the artifacts of daily life of the area's common people." In 1971 six local credit unions merged and, in honor of the event, built the museum in front of their new headquarters. It is closed on Thursdays in contrast to most Japanese museums, which are closed on Mondays.

You may wonder at the first-floor collection of old phonographs, but more traditional examples of the area's "artifacts of daily life" will follow, including one of the best collections of old Tōhoku tansu and outstanding examples of Tōhoku pottery. Also interesting is the display of Ainu clothing and articles.

Most people think of the Ainu as native to Hokkaido, but in fact they once lived on Honshu until the Japanese gradually pushed them northward to Hokkaido where assimilation became the final conqueror. Logically enough, Aomori Prefecture was the last Ainu foothold before the big push across the Tsugaru Straits.

The third floor of the Keikokan is devoted to local artists, two of whom—Shikō Munakata (see below) and Junichirō Sekino—will be familiar names to collectors of modern Japanese woodblock prints. A separate room contains the writings of the famous author Osamu Dazai, who was born on the nearby Tsugaru Peninsula (see that section).

Everything in the Keikokan is tastefully and carefully displayed. Japanese folk songs playing softly in the background and a small mingei shop are additional details of an unusually well done presentation of old Tōhoku.

As long as you're in the neighborhood, you may want to stop by Sunroad Mall to see just how far the city has come since its fish market days. You can't miss the big red building with the Jusco sign on the roof, a three-story island surrounded by a parking lot. There is a small mingei shop on the first floor and inexpensive restaurants on the top floor.

Also nearby is the Murata Tsugaru Nuri Workshop.[1] Tsugaru nuri is Aomori Prefecture's contribution to Japanese lacquerware. It is the colorful culmination of a laborious forty-three-step process from which everything from toothpick holders to tables emerge covered with thousands of tiny circles within circles, looking like

1. Murata Tsugaru Nuri Factory and Showroom, 89–30 Okuno, Uramachi, Aomori-shi, Aomori-ken 030; tel. (0177) 75–4175
むらた工芸工場・展示場 〒030 青森県青森市浦町奥野 89–30

lots of miniature peacock feather dots. Try looking at it very long and you'll understand why it is also called baka nuri, or crazy lacquer.

You are welcome to tour the workshop to observe the painstaking process of creating Tsugaru nuri. If you want a piece for a souvenir, the factory showroom has lots to choose from and Murata will mail your purchases for you. It is a short taxi ride from the Keikokan or Sunroad.

If you go much further down the road, you'll be on your way to Lake Towada through the beautiful Hakkōda Mountains. But back up a bit if you've been in Japan long enough to get hooked on modern Japanese hanga, or woodblock prints.

Shikō Munakata is known throughout the nation for his strange, symbolic, wild-looking prints. In 1970, he was named a National Cultural Treasure, bringing great honor to the people of his birthplace. He lived long enough after this to aid in the planning of a local museum to house his works. No doubt influenced by his years down south, he chose the azekura style—very atypical of Tōhoku—for the building, complete with sculptured garden, stone bridge, and carp-filled pond.

The environment of the Shikō Munakata Museum is indeed novel for this area, but it is nonetheless a welcome and refreshing addition to the city, just as Munakata's unique works are welcome and refreshing additions to the world of woodblock prints.

If you like Munakata or are homesick for a stroll through what looks like the Japan you used to think was Japan, take the Tsutsui-bound bus from the station to Bunka Sentā (Cultural Center)-mae and walk westward for two minutes past the new public library. The museum is also a short taxi ride from the other museums. By car, turn south from Highway 4 immediately west of the river and turn right at the second traffic light.

A FEW WORDS ABOUT the Nebuta Matsuri are called for before going off back down the road through the mountains to the lake.

Those who enjoy crowds, sakè, noise, lots of local color, or any combination of the above will love Nebuta. Two million revelers crowd into the city between August 3rd and 7th each year to partake in parades of after-dark madness.

At sundown on the 5th and 6th, the music of traditional flutes and drums paces thousands of celebrants as they join hands to form small circles along the parade route, skipping and chanting to the baka odori, or fools' dance. Those on the sidelines will be merrily thrust into the action (especially foreigners), so don't stand in the front row if all you want to do is observe and photograph.

The raucous festival's saving grace is the entourage of beautiful illuminated papier-maché floats thinly interpersed among the merrymakers. They are huge monster-faced structures, pushed and pulled through the streets by cheerful groups of less-than-sober celebrants. The Nebuta floats make fantastic photos, but, after a short time, the noise tends to grate on the nerves, possibly the reason so much numbing sakè is consumed.

As the parade route finally clears of people after the last float and group of dancers have passed, another of the innumerable small things that make Japan such a nice place to be in begins. The street is now completely littered with trash. (A New Yorker was once overheard at this point commenting with a deep sigh, "It makes me homesick!")

But as soon as the humanity on the sidewalks thins, each shopkeeper, broom and blue plastic bucket in hand, begins policing the sidewalk and half the street in front of his or her shop. Thus, less than an hour after the festivities have ended, the streets look as if the evening's madness had never happened— and the visitor is left wondering if maybe the Nebuta Matsuri wasn't just a noisy and colorful dream. It's interesting to ponder just how long the streets of any other country would remain littered before "the city" came to scoop up the mess.

Traditionally, Nebuta's origins are traced to the seventh century, when the conquering Yamato warriors lured the rebellious Ezo out into the open by throwing a big party in the streets much like the present-day celebration.

Another version of the same tale tells of Nebuta dummies of men and horses being floated out to sea on barges one night so the native Ezo would think the Yamato troops had withdrawn. The native troops then returned to the city, only to be ambushed by their conquerors. The final night of the festival features a maritime procession of floats, reenacting this event.

A less gruesome and more credible explanation tells of a much later time when the Tsugaru lord of the late sixteenth century contributed a big colorful lantern to the Kyoto Obon (the Buddhist All Souls' Day) festivities. The lantern made quite a hit, bringing great notoriety to the back-country lord. If the southern sophisticates liked it, it had to be worth repeating—which is exactly what people from all over Japan continue to come to Aomori City each August to do.

Today's celebrants, however, seem to push origins aside and simply use the time to enjoy one final week of exuberant merrymaking before the tough work of harvesting the rice or returning to the classroom begins.

Normally quiet Aomori probably couldn't stand Nebuta madness for more than a week at a time, but tourists who come at other times of the year can still view the famous Nebuta floats at an amusement park called Nebuta-no-sato. Getting there will take you once again past Sunroad and the Keikokan, but this time much further out into the countryside. Also on this route out of the city are the ski resort of Moya, with its year-round Skyland Hotel overlooking the city, and the spacious greenery of Kaya no Chaya.

Although chaya means teahouse, Kaya no Chaya is actually much closer to a stateside city park. Its rolling grassy terrain dotted now and then with big shade trees makes you momentarily forget you're still in an island country which can afford so few of these spacious luxuries. It's a nice place for a picnic; camping is also permitted, but it would be rather similar to camping out in the local city park in the U.S.

The chaya in the park's name comes from the cups of free mugicha, or chilled barley tea, and samples of Aomori Prefecture's tasty walnut mochi (pounded rice cake), which are offered by the souvenir shops lined up along the road. The mochi is dusted in soy flour, and microscopic fragments of walnuts appear every now and then. It is attractively packaged in small, inexpensive souvenir-sized bundles.

The mugicha is another story. It seems that if you drink one free cup, you better drink two more. They say that if you drink one cup, you'll have added three years to your life; if you drink two, you can add on another three years; and, if you drink three, you'll live until you die. Using the communal cups provided (to be rinsed out in cold water before use) may just do the trick!

The scenery gets better and better along this route as you start to climb into the Hakkōdas, leaving Aomori's capital and largest city behind, but taking along impressions gleaned from the city's reminders of the past and showcases of the present.

The Hakkōda Mountains

THEY MAY LOOK like a beautiful cluster of docile mountains to you today, but the ten peaks collectively known as the Hakkōda Mountains appeared quite differently to the 210 soldiers in Corporal Gotō's regiment back in January of 1902.

The troops were training for possible battle in frigid Siberia during the tense times leading to the Russo-Japanese War of 1904. And what better place is there to prepare for Siberia than Tōhoku in winter?

The soldiers left their Aomori City base on January 23rd to trek over the snow-covered mountains to Tashirotai, a grassy plateau just to the east of the Hakkōdas. But an unusually severe blizzard caught them by surprise on their first day out. By the second night, 70 men had died or disappeared into the blowing snow and others were becoming delirious from the cold and strain of impending death as they blindly kept moving just to keep from freezing.

By the third day, only 30 men were still alive. It was at this point that Corporal Gotō became the hero of the disaster, setting out alone to find help. The next day rescuers searching for the overdue troops noticed a statuelike form, its face frozen into a mask, standing among the bare trees on a hillside near the village of Tashirotai. A bronze statue of Corporal Gotō now stands on this hillside. The rescue party then found 17 more soldiers still alive, but looking more like ice carvings than human beings.

Only Corporal Gotō and ten others made it through the ordeal, but most lost one or more limbs. Some people blamed the government for the tragedy because of its callousness in experimenting in cold weather warfare with human lives. But the facts that the blizzard was unexpected and unusually severe and that another regiment from Hirosaki made it safely across the mountains to Aomori at the same time should be considered as a partial defense.

You can see a graphic pictorial display of the tragedy and a small memorabilia collection at the Makado Onsen near Noheji (see the Along Mutsu Bay section). The drive-in near Corporal Gotō's monument also has a small photo display.

This adventure-packed disaster complete with a hero is the stuff exciting movies and novels are made of, so every Japanese is familiar with the Hakkōda "death march." This is what your Japanese friends will think of when you speak of traveling through the Hakkōda Mountains. You, too, may want to remember Corporal Gotō and his fallen comrades as you enjoy the now peaceful mountain scenery.

Although the mountain roads are now closed during the winter months, you can get a good idea of the severity of a typical Hakkōda winter in April after huge snow blowers cut through the snow to the asphalt, in some places six meters down. You will wind through the white maze created by steep walls of snow on either side of the road, a roofless and impressive tunnel of white.

Actually, the road is cleared from Aomori City as far as the Hakkōda Ropeway by mid-February so buses can transport skilled skiers from Aomori Station to the foot of Mount Tamoyachi. A 10-minute cable-car ride then takes skiers above snow-covered tree-tops, whose monster-like shapes are similar to those of Miyagi Prefecture's famous Mount Zaō.

The experts-only 4- to 6-kilometer-long downhill run is done in escorted groups; if the ski patrol doesn't think your skills are up to the challenging slope, you will be sent back down the mountain the way you came, carrying your skis rather than wearing them. Other Hakkōda peaks offer snow-covered slopes as late as August.

For most people, the Hakkōdas are much more appealing in other seasons as an area of great natural beauty and old-fashioned hot-spring inns and as the well-traveled connection between Aomori City and Lake Towada.

Once the roads are opened in the early spring, buses connect the prefecture's capital city and its biggest tourist attraction several times a day, stopping at the various onsen and places of interest along the way. The route winds through the western skirts of the mountains, intersects with Highway 102 at Yakeyama Onsen and continues through the Oirase River valley to the lake.

There is also an eastern route around the Hakkōdas, the one Corporal Gotō and crew were fruitlessly searching for. The turnoff for this road is identified with a road sign for Tashirotai between Aomori and the ropeway. The Gotō Monument is visible on a hillside where the road joins another coming from Aomori. Gotō's 199 fallen comrades are buried in a cemetery near the city along the Aomori road. The wide, grassy Tashirotai plateau has several onsen and campgrounds. This eastern route eventually rejoins the main road through the mountains north of Yakeyama.

IF THIS IS YOUR FIRST TIME through the Hakkōdas, you'll want to take the main bus route from Aomori to the lake. It will stop at the Hakkōda Ropeway, which keeps running for hikers and sightseers even when the snow monsters once again become a snow-bent but colorful forest. The cable cars take you to the summit of Mount Tamoyachi for a panoramic view that includes taller Hakkōda peaks, Mutsu Bay, Aomori, and, on clear days, even the Shimokita Peninsula to the east and Mount Iwaki to the west.

Two easy trails through alpine forest, known as the Gourd Line because of their combined hourglass configuration, take up to an hour to cover from the summit terminal. Serious hikers can go on to the trails over two higher peaks to reach Sukayu Onsen[1] in another two to three hours.

The more conventional way to get to Sukayu is to stay on the bus until it gets to an old-fashioned wooden inn absolutely reeking of sulfuric fumes from its strong waters.

Sukayu is an interesting spot to get off the bus for an hour or two. The old inn attracts a fascinating assortment of visitors: youthful new Japan in its designer skiing or hiking wear, portable stereo cassette players, and shiny white cars; old Japan here for a few weeks of therapeutic bathing, carrying on a hundreds-of-years-old tradition: and Japan-in-transition disembarking from the many tour buses which stop here, in kimono or western dress, enjoying the conviviality of the group experience more than anything else.

You'll see a variety of humanity browsing through the busy souvenir shop or eating "pure" soba, Sukayu's healthful all-buckwheat noodles. But the baths are the domain of old Japan. Long before the paved highway and Sukayu's modern sister hotel, and even before the dignified old inn itself was built, people were walking the 28 kilometers up the mountainside, bringing up their own food and building temporary shelters in order to spend at least ten days soaking their ailments away in the sulfuric waters.

Apparently General MacArthur never made it as far north as Sukayu because bathing is still mixed, although dressing rooms are separate. You can buy just a bath ticket, but if you're going just to leer, you may be disappointed to find yourself the sole representative of the under-sixty crowd.

It will be no problem keeping busy until the next bus if you decide to stop here. If you're coming from Aomori, get off at the

1. Sukayu Onsen, Hakkōda-san, Aomori-shi, Aomori-ken 030; tel. (0177) 38–6573
酸ケ湯温泉　〒030 青森県青森市八甲田山

onsen and continue walking down the highway. On the right beyond another parking lot and a campground is the Mount Hakkōda Botanical Laboratory of Tōhoku University, which has narrow footpaths leading through such exotic (for the Hakkōdas) plants as blueberries. Across the road is a barren pond with steam rising from it; that's Jigoku Numa (Hell Pond). In between the pond and the onsen are thirty-three Kannon dieties carved into rocks along a hillside path.

Just beyond the plant station is a gravel road leading to Manjū Fukashi, which translates as steaming buns. Although manjū does not share all the connotations of buns, Manjū Fukashi provides an opportunity to do just what the name implies. The visitor sits on thermal-heated wooden benches alongside a stream and steams his or her buns—it's supposed to be great for hemorrhoids! Even the non-afflicted will welcome Manjū Fukashi's permeating warmth on chilly or wet days.

Back at Sukayu, catch the next bus for Lake Towada. The next brief stop of interest will be Suiren Numa, a natural pond featuring the flora of mountain marshes and a fine view of five of the Hakkōda peaks in the background. Man's contribution to this idyllic setting is a wooden pier across the pond and a public toilet. From the road all you'll be able to see are a very small wooden sign, stone steps leading to the pond, and, possibly, some parked cars or buses.

If you've done your homework well, you will have made arrangements in advance to spend a night at Tsuta Onsen,[2] a truly classic piece of old Japan coming up soon after the bus takes a right fork in the road. Even if there are no rooms available, do take time for a look around this lovely old mountain inn.

Tsuta is a vintage 1908 wooden structure built at the site of a clear hot spring and a cluster of seven small ponds hidden by a

2. Tsuta Onsen, Towada-ko-machi, Kamikita-gun, Aomori-ken 034–03; tel. (017674) 2311
蔦温泉　〒034-03 青森県上北郡十和田湖町

lush forest. A gently climbing 3-kilometer-long walking trail from the onsen winds among the ponds. Along the way are several picnic sites and lots of mossy rich forest scenery.

Tsuta is the name of a vine which can grow into twisted tree-size proportions. The inn makes good use of this decorative wood as well as other woods in the original building and in the addition built into the hillside above. The two buildings are connected by a long steep stairway with heavy fire doors about halfway up. Tsuta's two large baths are made of beechwood (buna), with its natural hot water bubbling up between the floorboards.

If you appreciate the natural wood decor of pre-modular-plastic old Japan, you'll love Tsuta. Individual guest rooms are liberally decorated with beautifully shaped or grained woodwork, staircase banisters are of twisted tsuta, and even the urinals are divided by woodwork worthy of anyone's living room. Round hibachi made from highly polished sections of tree trunks hold real charcoal and are used to heat guest rooms. However, if you don't appear to be from old Japan, you'll be given a kerosene space heater unless you can prove you know how to use charcoal without asphyxiating yourself.

The fresh mountain air, a walk through the peaceful forest, a soak in the beautiful wooden bath and the refreshing natural atmosphere of the old inn are topped off with an outstanding meal in your room with mountain vegetables and fresh trout sashimi among a plethora of dishes.

Tsuta is an experience worth the ryokan prices you'll be paying. You will think you have indeed discovered old Japan alive and well in this secluded corner of the Hakkōda Mountains.

Savor this feeling of discovery—even though you are not the first to revel in Tsuta's offerings. When Tōhoku was really Japan's poorest back country and few Japanese could find in it any redeeming features, Keigetsu Ōmachi, a Meiji-era poet from Shikoku, traveled through the area writing about the beauty be found. (See the Lake Towada section for an example.)

When he discovered a newly built mountain inn near seven beautiful little ponds in the woods, the well-traveled poet decided he had at last found his paradise on earth. He spent as much of his remaining years as possible at Tsuta and his ashes are permanently buried on a small hillside across the highway from the inn—a more beautiful and peaceful resting place cannot be imagined. A bust of Ōmachi is between the stately old bathhouse and the trail leading through the ponds.

Before boarding the bus heading down the mountain, be sure to stop by the poet's grave and silently thank him for sharing his wonderful discovery with the rest of us.

At the foot of the Hakkōdas is the Towada-ko Onsen Hotel. This is where adventurous souls who plan on pedaling the remaining 16 kilometers along the Oirase River to Lake Towada can rent bikes and make arrangements to have their luggage waiting for them at the lake. Walkers should stay on the bus a little longer. (See Lake Towada section for details.)

The traffic light at Yakeyama Onsen a little further on signals the end of your tour through the Hakkōdas. If you had to pass up Tsuta and need a place to spend the nights, this ski resort and year-round onsen has all types of accommodations. The Hotel Kaikōen[3] is one of the larger hotels which stay open all year. It has both Japanese and western rooms, private and public baths, and a summer roof-top Genghis Khan barbecue.

Before following the beautiful Oirase River valley to the lake, there is one more stop that people who appreciate minka, traditional Japanese farmhouses, won't want to miss. By crossing the river one bridge east of the traffic light on Highway 102 (across the highway from Yakeyama's arched main entrance) and going about 2 kilometers to the left, you will find the thatched-roof Old Kasaishi House open for your inspection.

3. Hotel Kaikōen, 36 Yakeyama, Towada-ko-machi, Kamikita-gun, Aomori-ken 034–03; tel. (017674) 2141.
ホテル海幸苑　〒034-03 青森県上北郡十和田湖町焼山 36

When the Kasaishi heirs put the old farmhouse up for sale, local governments purchased and restored it and built the modern folk museum next door. The museum has a small collection of farm implements and other items local farm families once used daily. The architectural style of the museum, strangely unlike any in Tōhoku, turns out to be the best way to pick out the Kasaishi House. Otherwise, the old house simply blends in with the neighboring farms as it has for many, many years.

Unlike many minka on the tourist trail, the Kasaishi House is not elaborate, nor is it furnished. But it will give you an idea of how the ordinary Aomori farm family once lived—and how some still do.

You may be surprised to find that nearly half the house is really a stable, a winter-time convenience used by many snow-country farmers. Next to the stable is the kitchen, where smoke from an unvented clay stove rises right through the thatch. The dark "closets" behind the kitchen are the bedrooms. The house is even without the basic luxury of tatami, not to mention running water. Imagine the house on a stormy February night as cold wind coming through spaces between the wooden siding seeps into the smoky interior.

If you travel Highway 102 between Towada City and Yakeyama, you'll see more farmhouses like the Kasaishi's. The only difference is that the farm families and their animals are still using them. But after touring the Kasaishi House you may see them in a different light. They are still aesthically appealing, a part of traditional Japan that is sadly dying out, but they are also cold, smoky, gloomy, and uncomfortable. You cannot leave the Kasaishi House without a new respect for the hardy Tōhoku farm family.

Lake Towada

If you have a choice, live in Japan;
If you have a choice, play in Towada
And walk the 12-kilometer-long path
Along the Oirase River.
Keigetsu Ōmachi

LAKE TOWADA may be the only thing foreigners coming from southern Japan have heard of in Tōhoku. They mention plans to see the northern part of Honshu and their Japanese friends respond, "Ah, you are going to Lake Towada."

Thus, many foreigners come to Tōhoku assuming that a visit to the lake will be the focal point, if not the climax, of their trip.

They may be disappointed.

Not that Towada-ko (Lake Towada), the main attraction of the Towada- Hachimantai National Park, isn't a nice lake, but that is all it is—a beautiful crater lake.

But you must see Lake Towada, first of all, because you can't disappoint your Japanese friends with such a gross omission, and, secondly, because getting there is much, much more than half the fun—especially if you get there via the glorious Oirase River valley. You can reach the lake by bus or car from the south, west, or east. Either coming or going, however, you should travel the latter route along the Oirase. The tortuous river valley is a spectacular sight from bus or car, even better from a rented bike,

209

and, as the poet implies, it is just absolutely fantastic if you walk.

Tour buses traveling through the Oirase Valley to Nenokuchi and Yasumiya, the two largest tourist enclaves on the lake, leave from Misawa, Aomori City (via the scenic Hakkōda Mountains) and Towada City. If your feet plead mercy, you can ride the entire route since the buses make short stops or slow down for all appropriate falls, rapids, rocks, and at the public facilities at Ishigedo.

Even if your bladder is doing OK at Ishigedo, get off the bus if you want to walk the remaining 8.5 kilometers to Nenokuchi. The walking trail twists and turns with the river, past churning rapids, moss-covered boulders and steep cliffs dotted with foliage, and delicate waterfalls. It's a walk that most people, feet and schedules willing, won't want to miss.

There are rent-a-bikes available from the Towada-ko Onsen Hotel[1] on the Aomori City bus route at the foot of the Hakkōdas. You can arrange to leave the bike at Nenokuchi and pick up your luggage there. A disadvantage to cycling is that you'll be traveling with the big guys on the busy highway, a narrow bus and truck route, rather than on the rustic path along the river's edge.

The main attraction at Ishigedo is a huge boulder cockily perched on the river bank. The romantic legend associated with it is the story of Omatsu, who lived under the big rock. Omatsu was a beautiful young woman who asked travelers to carry her across the river and, midway across, killed and robbed them.

At any rate, after solemnly posing for a picture or two beside the rock, most tourists will return to their buses or cars, and the beautiful wooded walk along the river may be exclusively yours for the next few hours. But be prepared to share your walk with a few other admirers, especially when the valley is at its most beautiful (and populated), decked in autumn golds and reds.

1. Towada-ko Onsen Hotel, Yakeyama, Towada-ko-machi, Kamikita-gun, Aomori-ken 034–03; tel. (01767)4–2231.
　十和田湖温泉ホテル　〒034-03 青森県上北郡十和田湖町燒山

Once you near the big falls and catch up with the camera-clicking tour groups, you'll be very close to the Oirase's source.

Lake Towada itself at this point may seem anticlimatic after the breathtaking river valley (and breathtaking hike), but it is nonetheless a lovely sight with its wooded hillsides sloping to meet the water. Its volcanic origin will be readily apparent from a glance at the rounded shoreline opposite, but a subsequent eruption formed a second much smaller crater in the caldera, adding a crooked finger and a fat thumb into the pie on your side.

If you're interested in this series of events, the Towada Science Museum near the Yasumiya bus terminals has a detailed graphic display of the formation of Lake Towada and Japan's other caldera lakes with explanations in English. The small museum's four display rooms also contain pickled, stuffed, and photographed representations of nature's plant and animal contributions to the area as well as a collection of fascinating old farm and household implements.

At Nenokuchi you can follow the tour groups aboard the ferries to Yasumiya, which is located on the lake's "finger." This will give your feet an hour's rest as you very slowly tour the lake's tree-covered southern shores. However, your ears may not share your enthusiasm unless you can mentally tune out the continuous recorded commentary in Japanese relating in excruciating detail the lake's vital statistics.

Buses from Nenokuchi travel around the lake clockwise to Yasumiya and also counterclockwise, climbing Mount Ohanabe for a panoramic view of the lake high above its northern shore at Takinosawa Lookout. You can eliminate the steep mountain climb by taking a bus for the lookout from Yasumiya. Some buses for Takinosawa go on to Hirosaki via the onsen community of Kuroishi.

If you decide to hit Yasumiya, either by ferry or land, you will be greeted by one of the largest concentrations of tourist facilities in Tōhoku. The entire town is comprised of hotels, inns, and shop after shop crammed full of identical mingei and omiyage products from all over Tōhoku.

You will probably want to sample one or both of the local specialties here. Himemasu, or river trout, can be eaten fresh in one of the many restaurants or taken home smoked and vacuum packed. Kiri tanpo are the grilled miso-coated mochi "popsicles" that smell so good as you walk by. The slightly-pounded stick-to-your-ribs rice concoctions are found throughout the northern part of Akita Prefecture, which shares the lake with Aomori, but the tangy burnt miso coating is Towada's contribution to the local delicacy.

Walking eastward along the shore, you will eventually reach the end of the souvenir shops. Shortly thereafter, you'll see a bronze monument of two identical nude women facing each other with a lot of tourists posing for pictures beneath it. This is the famous "Maidens by the Lake," the last notable work of the well-known poet and sculptor, Kōtarō Takamura.

He completed the statue in 1953, before the lake's present development. At that time he wrote of his ladies who were then surrounded only by forest,

> Whatever the brutal power
> Of primitive nature,
> They'll stand forever.

Takamura was commissioned to do the work when he was seventy years old to honor three men responsible for developing the area for tourism, one of whom was the poet Ōmachi. But the subject of the statue was a memorial to his beloved wife, Chieko. Chieko was a would-be artist who died in 1938 as a schizophrenic patient in a mental institution; it is said that the statue's double image symbolizes her split personality.

Although Takamura was Tokyo-born, his wife was a Tōhoku country girl from Fukushima Prefecture who lived in the big city only to be with her husband. Takamura wrote after her death that "she could not maintain her health without occasionally breathing country air. She complained very often that there was no sky over Tokyo."

He wrote a poem entitled "Chieko's Sky" about his homesick wife as part of a collection of love poems written during and after their twenty-four years of marriage. He also wrote of his guilt feelings at having prevented her from returning to her rural Tōhoku roots. So perhaps the "Maidens" is an old man's attempt to return his beloved to the fresh country air he denied her in life.

After Chieko died, Takamura exiled himself to the mountains of Iwate Prefecture. Some say this act was self-punishment for his prowar poetry, but it is much more romantic to believe he made the move to feel closer to Chieko's rural Tōhoku spirit than was possible in skyless Tokyo.

The path behind the "Maidens" leads to a small shrine and then back to the shops. After visiting the science museum and a shop or two, there's not much else to cause the traveler to linger in the crowded tourist community.

Since Lake Towada is northern Tōhoku's biggest drawing point, the large concentration of hotels, ryokan, minshuku, youth hostels, and campgrounds on three sides of the big lake shouldn't come as a surprise, but be aware that nearly everything gets booked up during the busy tourist season from August through early October. There are four campgrounds around the lake, the prettiest being on the lake's thumb at Utarube. You can find youth hostels at Wainai and at Yasumiya, and kokuminshukusha at Utarabe (Kokuminshukusha Towada),[2] at Wainai (the Towada Caldera),[3] and at Yasumiya (Kokuminshukusha Towada-ko).[4]

2. Kokuminshukusha Towada, 361 Towada, Okuse, Towada-ko-machi, Kamikita-gun, Aomori-ken 018–55; tel. (017675) 2536.
   国民宿舎とわだ　〒018-55 青森県上北郡十和田湖町奥瀬十和田 361
3. Towada Caldera, Ōkawatai, Towada-ko, Kosaka-machi, Kazuno-gun, Akita-ken 018–55; tel. (017675) 2821.
   十和田カルデラ　〒018-55 秋田県鹿角郡小坂町十和田湖大川岱

But if Towada-ko has moved too far from the "primitive nature" of Takamura's time for your tastes, you may want to press on. There are several old-fashioned onsen to the west towards Kuroishi and to the northeast in the Hakkōdas. A peaceful night in a quiet mountain inn seems like the perfect setting for sorting out the day's memories of the Oirase valley and Lake Towada, impressions of how truly lovely nature can be.

4. Kokuminshukusha Towada-ko, Yasumiya, Towada-ko-han, Kamikita-gun, Aomori-ken 018–55; tel. (017675) 2041.
国民宿舎十和田湖　〒018-55　青森県上北郡十和田湖畔休屋

Kuroishi and Hirosaki

LONG, LONG AGO the Aseishi River carved a valley through the volcanic slopes leading from the water-filled crater we know today as Lake Towada toward what later became Hirosaki, the castle town of the Tsugaru clan and later the cultural and educational center of Aomori Prefecture. A series of onsen and later a highway sprang up along this river. The Aseishi River valley through the mountains is now the prettiest and most relaxing route for tourists on their way to Hirosaki.

THE ONSEN RESORTS, large and small, from tour-bus modern to oil-lamp traditional, between Lake Towada and Hirosaki along Highway 102 collectively make up the Kuroishi Onsen Prefectural Natural Park, named for the largest community among them. Kuroishi City itself, now practically an eastern suburb of Hirosaki, is the location of the unusual Meiji-era Seibi-en garden. The other onsen resorts in the park also claim a few attractions of their own, including a shrine surrounded by a hillside of maples, a lovely but lonely temple nearly inaccessible on the top of a mountain, a community of kokeshi doll artists, and more of the natural forests and curative waters that abound throughout the back country.

Buses from Yasumiya and Nenokuchi on Lake Towada take

Highway 102 to Hirosaki. From Aomori or Hirosaki, the Ōu Main Line stop at Kawabe connects with the Kuroishi Line to Kuroishi City. The Kōnan Tetsudō Line, a small private line, runs between Hirosaki and Kuroishi. From Kuroishi Station, only buses go further east through the various onsen towns and eventually to the lake.

Coming from Lake Towada, the first of the park's quiet, secluded onsen is Nurukawa,[1] a kokuminshukusha standing alone in the woods just off the highway. The ambience of the peeling modern hotel itself is rather bland, but the setting, if you're in the mood for wooded isolation, couldn't be better, and the prices are kokuminshukusha reasonable.

Kuroishi's most interesting onsen, the one guaranteed to make you feel you're far into the back country of 100 years ago, the one with the outdoor rock bath of old Japan, is also the most challenging to reach. Aoni Onsen[2] is about five kilometers of winding, climbing gravel road into the mountains beyond the Okiura Bus Stop. But, if you make arrangements by mail beforehand, Aoni's car will pick you up at the Kōnan Tetsudō Kuroishi Station.

Aoni's symbol is the oil lamp, its proud statement to the twentieth century that it doesn't need ugly poles and wires for the power to make its guests comfortable. A night savoring the ryokan's peaceful isolation along the Aoni Rapids will no doubt more than compensate for the effort in getting there. You can also hike, fish, and camp along the beautiful mountain stream.

The three onsen communities of Itadome, Ochiai, and Nuruyu, spreading into each other where the river valley broadens, offer more overnight choices and a little sightseeing as well.

The first community you come to is Itadome, where the Nishi

1. Nurukawa Onsen, 71–2 Tsunekawamori, Kiriake, Hiraka-machi, Minami Tsugaru-gun, Aomori-ken 036–04; tel. (01725) 4–8555.
   温川温泉　〒036-04 青森県南津軽郡平賀町大字切明字津根川森 71 の 2
2. Aoni Onsen, 1–7, Taki-no-ue, Aoni-sawa, Okiura, Kuroishi-shi, Aomori-ken 036–04; tel. (01725) 2–3243.
   青荷温泉　〒036-04 青森県黒石市大字沖浦字青荷沢滝ノ上 1 の 7

Towada Youth Hostel is located. As the town melts into neighboring Ochiai, you can see, if you look south into the next town, a towering, pink, angular structure. That is the Nishi Towada-so kokuminshukusha,[3] run-down but reasonable, with a big mixed bath on the top floor.

On the other side of the highway at this point is the Ochiai Bus Stop. There, a narrow road starts its climb into the hills above the valley, eventually reaching Sukayu Onsen in the Hakkōda Mountains. Local buses head up this road, stopping to let visitors off at Nakano Momijiyama and Jōsen-ji Iriguchi stops.

Not far up the hill on the right is a red torii, the entrance to Nakano Momijiyama, or Maple Mountain. During the feudal period a local Tsugaru lord had a castle here and ordered over 100 different kinds of maples from all over Japan to be planted around it. Today Nakano Maple Mountain, at its colorful glory in mid-October, also boasts a brightly painted shrine and a small rushing stream, both nice companions to the beautiful trees.

Jōsen-ji Iriguchi Bus Stop is at the end of the second gravel road on the left after Momijiyama. At this point all that separates you and the Jōsen-ji temple is a 40-minute hike or winding dusty drive up Mount Kuromori.

Jōsen-ji's well-kept buildings and grounds are a great surprise considering its location. Its small iris garden blooms in mid-July, but the orderly grounds are pretty anytime. The temple complex was once a Buddhist school and also a retreat.

Nuruyu Onsen is the last of the trio of communities clustered in the valley. It has accommodations of all types and, in addition, is the headquarters of the Tsugaru Kokeshi Guild, an organization for the makers of Aomori Prefecture's most famous contribution to Tōhoku's folkcraft.

Tsugaru kokeshi dolls are distinctive among Tōhoku kokeshi

for their painted designs representing local symbols. Some Tsugaru kokeshi have a peony painted on their narrow bodies, the same peony which appears on many floats during the Nebuta Festival. Others have the skirts of various Nebuta monsters leering far beneath their more pleasantly painted heads. All Tsugaru kokeshi have the scalloped border designs of the Ainu who lived in the area before being pushed off the island to Hokkaido.

Probably the easiest kokeshi kijishi, or wood artisan, to find is Abo-san, who set up his small workshop right off Highway 102 between Nuruyu and Kuroishi. His giant kokeshi sign is hard to miss. Craft shops in Hirosaki have good selections from other guild members as well.

Kuroishi itself is a city, unlike the other small onsen communities surrounding it. The old komise, or covered arcade-like sidewalks, still seen here and there in the city date from Edo times and have been designated as Important Cultural Properties by the Japanese government.

Between the city proper and Hirosaki is a turnoff for Onoe Town, home of the Seibi-en garden. The garden is a 15-minute walk from Tsugaru Onoe Station on the Kōnan Tetsudō Line.

Seibi-en garden is an attractive yet strange place. A thatched-roof farmhouse stands with its kura, or storehouse, just outside the garden entrance. But inside the kura of this deceptively simple back-country homestead is the elaborate family sanctuary of the Seitōs, the wealthy builders of the garden. Inside are walls of gold maki-e, black lacquer decorated with gold leaf, done by an Imperial Palace artist. The Kamakura-period (1185–1336) image enshrined within the sanctuary is the oldest in the area. You may have to ask the caretakers to open the kura for you; a peek inside comes with your admission to the garden.

The beautiful garden is one of the three best gardens of the Meiji era. It took a Kyoto master nine years to complete it in the early 1900s. The central pond is surrounded by man-made hills covered with meticulously groomed shrubbery. The view of the mountain in the distance is also part of the garden.

But it is the garden house that will attract most of your attention. The first floor is typically Japanese; sliding paper-covered doors separate the spartan tatami rooms from the wood-floored engawa, or enclosed verandah, overlooking the garden.

The second floor looks like an architect's practical joke or colossal mistake—an English manor house's top floor and turreted roof sit atop the Japanese garden house. The Seibi-en garden is an outstanding example of Meiji-era Japan's zeal for Westernization clashing head on with a refusal to abandon the best of traditional Japan. To the Seitō family, their unusual garden house must have been the ideal compromise.

If you find the Seitō's first floor somehow much more appealing than the second, you'll love the place where Highway 102 dead ends at busy Highway 7—the Tsugaru castle town of Hirosaki.

THE CITY OF HIROSAKI was left without the political power it had enjoyed since Lord Tsugaru Tamenobu founded it in 1603, when the Meiji Restoration joined the rival Nambu and Tsugaru territories into a unified Aomori Prefecture, and the port city of Aomori become the new capital. But to this day neither Aomori City nor any place else has been able to usurp Hirosaki's title as the cultural and educational capital of Aomori Prefecture.

American World War II bombers left Hirosaki untouched while reducing most of old Aomori to rubble, so, unlike the capital city, Hirosaki is liberally splashed with bits of its feudal past—the temples, the castle gates (lightning got the castle itself), a few old houses and shops, and even the narrow winding roads (to the despair of present-day conveyances and their drivers).

A mood of quiet refinement permeates the city in contrast to the harsh climate, and the roughness induced by the struggles of daily life in much of the back country.

Even the Hirosaki accent is soft and elegant, unlike the shrill and guttural sounds often heard elsewhere in Tōhoku. This accent is a mattur of local pride, a symbol of a distinctive heritage that Hirosaki residents refuse to compromise. Thus, even native Japanese tourists have problems asking directions—or rather, in understanding the replies. But the people of Hirosaki are just as proud of their city itself and do want to help the visitor discover it— even the English-speaking visitor. The Hirosaki Tourist Information Office[4] has published a very good guidebook in our language. As Hirosaki is a university town, your chances of running into an English-speaker when in need are greater than in other parts of Aomori.

Although no single attraction is an absolute don't miss, the city's various offerings combine to make you feel in communion with the Tōhoku of feudal times during your stay.

In the true feudal spirit, the first Lord Tsugaru cleverly designed his castle town so that invaders would have to travel through a maze of winding and backtracking lanes and cross three moats to reach him. Today's invaders, although on friendlier missions, still may fall victim to the feudal lord's original intent to confuse and frustrate the newcomer. Hirosaki is a town in which you should be prepared to stop every now and them to confirm you're still heading in the right direction or to use taxis. On the positive side, the town is relatively compact and the narrow, winding streets create a quaint atmosphere that can be enjoyed best by walkers and bikers. You can join the latter category by renting a bicycle from the Tourist Information Center just to the left of the train station. Free city maps can also be picked up there.

Present-day Hirosaki is a modern city in spite of its surviving relics of the past. The main street, Dotemachi, which heads from the station to the old castle area—with a few of Lord Tsugaru's

4. Hirosaki Tourist Information Office, 1 Kami Shirogane-chō, Hirosaki-shi, Aomori-ken 036; tel. (0172) 35–1111 ext. 250.
弘前市観光課　〒036 青森県弘前市上白銀町 1

twists and turns—is lined with modern storefronts. But a pleasant stop about halfway through the downtown area will get you in the mood for the old Hirosaki to follow. Suzuro, a traditional Japanese pastry shop, is off to the left down a side street, near the Kōnan Line's Chūō Hirosaki Station, just before you cross the river.

Downtown eventually empties into Hirosaki Park, site of the castle and the center of old Hirosaki. Two mingei shops are appropriately located at this junction of old and new.

Several gatehouses still stand in the park, one of which contains a small exhibition of Hirosaki history. Sections of the three moats and a small castle keep join thousands of old pines and cherries to make the park the most refreshing spot in the city.

The cherries were planted at the beginning of the Meiji era when the fortress was turned over to the common people. One hundred years later, cherry viewing at Hirosaki Park is still one of the most popular annual events for the people of Aomori Prefecture. The Cherry Blossom Festival is from April 24th to May 7th. During the day, the cherry blossoms framing Fuji-shaped Mount Iwaki in the distance, and at night, the illuminated blossoms and the castle buildings all keep photographers equally busy.

In the fall the park's maples and a chrysanthemum display overshadow the long-past cherries in a celebration of autumn colors lasting from October 1st through November 10th. Then during the second week in February, just when everyone is getting sick of winter's icy roads, dead car batteries, and shoveling chores, the Snow Lantern Festival reaffirms that winter in Tōhoku can also be beautiful and fun as well as frustrating. Snowcarved lanterns, illuminated at night with candles, and Sapporolike snow sculptures keep spirits high until the cherry blossoms can take over once again.

The second Tsugaru lord married the daughter of the shogun Tokugawa Ieyasu and was therefore a big supporter of the shogunate's ideals, including a great devotion to Buddhism. During his time, all Zen temples in the Tsugaru territory were brought to Hirosaki and reestablished on the grounds of the Taihei-zan Chōshō-ji temple. Some say that the high wooded temple site, protected by rivers and offering an excellent view of the surrounding Tsugaru Plain, was the first choice for the castle, but that the Shogun wanted the powerful clan a bit more vulnerable and refused permission for the project. So a temple was built here instead, but it was a temple that could meet military as well as spiritual needs. You can get a feeling for Chōshō-ji's strategic importance by walking past the unattractive modern stone temple to the right of old Chōshō-ji for an overview of the plains below—and majestic Mount Iwaki looming ahead.

Outside Chōshō-ji's 350-year-old Sangedatsu Gate is a street lined with newer versions of the different temples gathered here in the early seventeenth century. Each temple has its own personality, and discovering a small statue in one courtyard or an unusual tree in another makes for an interesting stroll.

Inside Chōshō-ji's impressive gate is a fourteenth-century temple bell, and inside the main hall are many other historical treasures of the Tsugaru clan. The temple still has the creaky floors which were intended to announce all intruders to both the religious- and the military-minded residents of feudal days. Today, the most interesting resident of Chōshō-ji will take no notice of your creaks. The twelfth Lord Tsugaru is now 150 years old and, except for the first seventeen and last thirty years of that time, has been buried deep under the temple grounds. In 1954 his naturally mummified body was found and, since he was so well preserved, the decision was made not to cremate him but to allow him to remain in his ancestral temple as is. You can pay him a visit for a small fee. The Chōshō-ji complex is a 15-minute walk southwest of the park.

Hirosaki has other Edo-period religious structures still standing around the former castle. The eighteenth-century Seigan-ji temple gate is just west of the park and the five-storied Saishō-in pagoda, built in 1667, is a 15-minute walk to the southeast of the park. Another street of temples, Shin-Teramachi, is located west of the pagoda. The Tōshō-gū shrine, like its well-known sister shrine in Nikkō, was built as a memorial to shogun Ieyasu. But, unlike most other brilliantly painted Tōshō-gū, this one was never painted at all. It is a short walk east of the park.

As you wander the streets of Hirosaki, you may run into remnants of later times as well. The stately Aomori Bank of 1904 has been preserved near the southeast entrance to the park. Similarly, the Meiji emperor's reopening of the country to foreign missionaries is evidenced by several turn-of-the-century church buildings around the city.

As stated earlier, Hirosaki is a mood rather than a set of attractions, a mood carried out in various ways. From August 1st through the 7th each year, the Hirosaki Neputa Festival features nighttime parades of illuminated fan-shaped floats, a celebration of similar origin to Aomori City's more famous and less provincial Nebuta Festival.

Tsugaru mingei industry, too, is kept alive in the area's cultural capital. Tsugaru lacquerware, discussed in the Aomori section, is also produced here, as are Tsugaru kogin-embroidered cloth; akebi vine baskets; hatobue, or pigeon whistles; boldly painted kites; and local pottery.

Kogin is true mingei, developed out of necessity and gradually refined to the level of an art, replaced by modern processes, and finally revived in the nationwide mingei movement of the 1930s.

In feudal times, Tsugaru farmers were not permitted to wear cotton clothing and had to somehow make their loosely woven hemp kimono warm enough for a Tōhoku winter. Since cotton yarn was available, the women developed a technique for embroidering sections of hemp clothing with the white yarn, adding both strength and warmth. The various intricate patterns of kogin embroidery evolved as Tsugaru women attempted to make their families' clothing attractive as well as practical.

When cotton cloth became plentiful in the late Meiji period, the women gladly abandoned the tedious skill. Today the craft is employed in making coin purses, placemats, and the like—only as reminders of the hard times of the past and the creativity and spirit of the women of Tsugaru.

You'll find samples of the other Tsugaru crafts along with kogin in the city's mingei and souvenir shops. The pigeon whistles are hand-painted molded clay pigeons that coo when you blow into their tails. Colorful Tsugaru kites reflect the area's Nebuta/Neputa traditions. The dark tones of Tsugaru pottery and akebi baskets are also on local shop shelves, the latter sometimes in the form of an unusual sakè bottle holder.

If you want to spend the night in old Hirosaki, you can stay at the Kobori Ryokan,[5] an old wooden inn near the castle site with ryokan prices. The alternative business hotels of new Hirosaki are clustered around the station. Or, if you're heading towards the Sea of Japan, you may want to hold out for the Iwaki-sō kokuminshukusha,[6] a 35-minute bus ride out of the city near the Iwaki Shrine at the foot of the ever-present extinct volcano which looms over the city and the entire Tsugaru Plain.

MOUNT IWAKI, and its 1,600-meter-high summit can be reached without much difficulty if you're so inclined. Buses leave from the Kōnan Bus Station near Hirosaki Station and climb the sixty-nine hairpin curves of the Iwaki Skyline Toll Road. At the end of the toll road it takes a chairlift ride and about a 40-

5. Kobori Ryokan, 89, Honchō, Hirosaki-shi, Aomori-ken 036; tel. (0172) 32–5111.
   小堀旅館　〒036 青森県弘前市本町 89
6. Iwaki-sō, Hyakuzawa Onsen Kyō, Iwaki-machi, Naka-Tsugaru-gun, Aomori-ken 036–13; tel. (017728) 2–2215.
   岩木荘　〒036-13 青森県中津軽郡岩木町百沢温泉郷

minute hike to reach the summit. The toll road and lift are popular with skiers once the mountain reopens in April after four months of heavy snowfall.

At the foot of Mount Iwaki are several onsen, including Hyaku-zawa, location of the Iwaki-sō and also of Tsugaru's back-country Nikkō. As at the real Nikkō, tall cryptomeria trees line the path leading to the Iwaki Shrine, which is a well-preserved old complex with the Hirosaki aura of quiet dignity.

Things aren't so quiet, however, around the third week of September each year when local farmers participate in the Oyama-sankei, a pilgrimage to the small shrine at Iwaki's summit. They form a procession from Iwaki Shrine carrying poles with colorful streamers for the four-hour hike up the mountain where they will relay their appreciation to the mountain gods for the rice they are about to harvest. The Hirosaki Oyamasankei is, like the Itako Matsuri at Osore-zan, an example of how pre-Buddhist pantheistic beliefs already in place were easily incorporated into the religions that migrated up from the south. And like Hachinohe's Emburi Festival, this annual event is a continuation rather than a reenactment of ancient tradition.

If you've come too late in the year for the Oyamasankei, you may be just in time for another big event which takes place in the fall months all over the Tsugaru plain—the harvesting of the famous Aomori apples. Over half the nation's apples are grown in Aomori Prefecture, most of them on the Tsugaru Plain. You can pick your own at the numerous apple orchards near the city including the orchards around Ringo Kōen, or Apple Park, on the southwestern outskirts of Hirosaki. Or stop by one of the innumerable apple shops that appear this time of year all over the prefecture and ship to anywhere in Japan a sampler box of several varieties of huge, flawless Aomori apples. Other times of the year, dried, sugared apple rings and soft apple-honey candy are delicious souvenirs of your trip to Hirosaki, the center of Japan's apple heartland.

The Tsugaru Peninsula

IN RURAL AREAS EVERYWHERE a local who makes a splash in the big world becomes a beloved source of pride for the folks back home—and Japan's back country is no exception.

Aomori Prefecture claims two such national celebrities, Aomori City's famous woodblock artist Shikō Munakata and the Tsugaru Peninsula's youth-cult novelist Osamu Dazai.

Dazai was the son of the extremely wealthy Tsushima family who in 1908 built a lovely East-meets-West manor, now a ryokan, in their hometown of Kanagi. A night in this fascinating old house, renamed the Shayōkan in honor of Dazai's most famous novel, *Shayō*, will be one of the most interesting stopovers of your trip. And, if you have an extra day to explore the stubby western arm of Honshu, you can also include visits to the sites of the world's longest tunnel, the Seikan undersea tunnel to Hokkaido at Cape Tappi, and a nineteenth-century American shipwreck at Shariki —and, of course, more of the coastal and rural scenes you've come up north to find.

ALTHOUGH KANAGI GIVES YOU the opportunity to experience the Tsushima family's former home in its own right, you can make your visit even more meaningful by reading the English translation of *Shayō* (The Setting Sun) before you arrive. The novel dramatizes the painfully difficult adjustments of the former Japanese aristocracy as they struggled to find their place in postwar egalitarian Japan. Dazai's troubled characters are said to reflect feelings of normlessness and uselessness experienced by his own family and their peers in the new society. In translation you'll be missing out on Dazai's masterful use of language much admired by the Japanese, but his sensitive characterizations and insights into the last days of an era in modern Japanese history may make you a devoted Dazai admirer.

Dazai has a James Dean-like appeal to Japanese youth, in part due to his own colorful life as a bitter nonconformist who died by his own hand before he had a chance to mellow into a graying conservative. He considered his family's wealth and status a great embarrassment and showed his contempt by spending his parents' money for five years at Tokyo University without attending a single lecture. He culminated a dramatic string of five suicide attempts by throwing himself into the Tama Reservoir near Tokyo on June 13, 1948. His body was found six days later, on his thirty-ninth birthday.

If Osamu Dazai, respected novelist and offbeat personality, is famous throughout Japan, you can imagine how those of back-country Japan feel about one of their few claims to national recognition. All over the Tsugaru (western) side of Aomori Prefecture you'll run into stone monuments saying, "Dazai came here" or "Dazai wrote the following about this spot. . . ." The Keikokan museum in Aomori City devotes an entire section to the novelist.

But nowhere will you find the memory of the sensitive young writer so alive as in the tiny town of Kanagi, his birthplace. During school vacations, the Shayōkan fills with his eager, young devotees, and the topic of conversation in the big Japanese-style first-floor dining room is, of course, the life and works of their de facto host. You can try gazing out onto the compact Japanese garden or admiring the fine woodwork of the old house, but you'll probably be swept up into the lively discussions anyway—so do your homework! You will find the conversation, however, a pleasant change from the "do you like sports" variety long-time residents become skilled at avoiding.

Dazai's works are filled with contempt for the pretentiousness of the fading aristocracy of his parents' generation, and the house's present owners have unwittingly reflected this opinion. In an action comparable to the Chinese government's placement of a souvenir stand in the final chamber of a Ming emperor's elaborate tomb outside Beijing, the staff of the inn has added tatami matting to the prissy Meiji/Victorian décor of the master suite.

Actually, circumstances made this defacement necessary, but the result is still amusing to the Western eye. The dilemma involved the facts that a ryokan beds down its guests on futon, that futon can't be laid on rugs (don't ask why not; it won't do any good), that Western-style doors open inward unlike sliding Japanese fusuma, and, finally, that these Western doors don't open very far when inches-thick tatami, usually recessed into custom-built floor wells, are laid atop door-level Western-style flooring.

This seemingly unresolvable clash of East and West was cleverly handled by cutting squares out of the tatami large enough so that the doors could open. Thus, a flooring of patchwork tatami lies amidst the suite's very European dark, heavy draperies, ornate chandeliers, and flowering wallpaper.

The Shayōkan is definitely the high point of a side trip to the Tsugaru Peninsula, even if you can only drop in for a cup of coffee in their first-floor lobby. To spend the night, you should make reservations, far in advance for the summer months. Prices are on the low side for ryokan, but quite a jump from youth hostel cheap.

The Shayōkan is a 10-minute walk west of Kanagi Station; anyone and everyone in town can steer you in the direction of the home of the guy who put their otherwise obscure little town on the map.

For true Dazai fans and for those killing time till the next train, the Kanagi Historical and Cultural Museum is an intersting quick stop before leaving town. It's situated in a small kura-style modern building on the main road through the city to the northwest of the Shayōkan and a 2-minute walk south of Ashino Kōen Station. One room of the small building is devoted to the hometown boy who made good, and the others, to local artifacts—including old work clothes laboriously hand-stitched over nearly the whole garment surface in the Tsugaru district's kogin style.

If all you want from the Tsugaru Peninsula is a night at the Shayōkan, you'll need to take a short detour from the route between Hirosaki and Aomori City, Tsugaru's capitals old and new. From either city take a bus to the tongue-twister town of Goshogawara and then a small private electric line or another bus 30 minutes further north to Kanagi. Goshogawara also is on JNR's Gonō Line, connecting with Hirosaki via a train change in Kawabe.

If you happen to mention to a Japanese friend that you've been to Goshogawara, the chuckle you get won't necessarily be from your pronunciation. Saying "Goshogawara" in some circles is like saying "Podunk" to someone from New York or Chicago. Even people from nearby Hirosaki and Aomori City make fun of the Goshogawara hicks. In contrast to the Japanese view, however, the foreigner will find the blocks and blocks of glass storefronts along the busy main street boringly modern—and certainly unbefitting of a hick-town reputation.

THERE IS MORE to the Tsugaru Peninsula than Dazai's hometown, so, if you can spare the time, take a longer look around. If you head northwest you'll end up at Cape Tappi at the very tip of northwestern Honshu, a community that makes Goshogawara look like Broadway by comparison.

Tappi is only 23 kilometers from Hokkaido's Shirakami Promontory. By 1985 you should be able to reach this part of the next island without getting off the train from Aomori, when the 54-kilometer-long Seikan Undersea Tunnel is expected to be ready for commercial traffic. To get an idea of the immensity of this undertaking, you should realize that the world's next longest tunnel, an overland tunnel linking Italy and Switzerland, is only 19 kilometers long, just over a third the length of the Seikan and not even as long as its undersea portion.

Three shifts of men had to blast through hard rock up to 240 meters below the surface of the Tsugaru Straits and 100 meters below the sea floor to complete the mammoth project. This dangerous and labor-intensive operation has attracted hardy workers from other parts of Japan who relocated their families to the tiny nearby fishing village of Mimmaya. From the lighthouse above the cape you can see their high-rise apartment buildings standing in isolation in the hills beyond the shore-hugging village. The scene's incongruity with that of the weather-beaten fishing village seems to reflect the sense of intrusion the tunnel families must have felt at being thrust into such an insular little community.

The dangers of undersea tunnel construction have created an attitude of extreme caution in the workmen. They take no unnecessary chances, and that even includes any potentially evil omens that could come about from women's visiting the construction site. But the women who sell souvenirs at the lighthouse tourist facilities don't seem particularly offended by this primitive sexism —perhaps because the men who must spend eight hours every day digging through rock deep under the sea are their husbands.

To reach Cape Tappi from Kanagi, take a bus to Imabetsu on the northern coast and then another for Mimmaya and Tappi. From Aomori you can go as far as Mimmaya on JNR's Tsugaru Line, the same line that will soon continue on to Hokkaido. Once at the cape you can walk along the rocky shore for a short distance (the monument that greets you is in honor of—who else—Dazai) or you can head up a steep hillside before the main road ends to reach a lookout point near the lighthouse.

A bus or car ride in this neighborhood is character-building, as one must struggle to control audible gasps. The full-sized buses squeeze themselves along the narrow, winding coastal highway, which somehow squeezes through tiny fishing villages that are themselves miraculously squeezed between the sea and the cliffs rising sharply above the shoreline. And as compact as everything (but the bus and oncoming trucks) seems to be, the townspeople will nevertheless be out in force, standing in the road chatting with neighbors, playing catch in the only available open space (the road), or loading boxes of freshly caught fish into trucks (parked in the road). If you're driving, expect something or someone to be in the road around each curve; most of the time you'll be right.

Unfortunately, both the train from Aomori and the bus from Kanagi cut out the prettiest part of the peninsula's coastline between Imabetsu and Kanita to the southeast. Rugged-shore enthusiasts may want to cover this area by car or bus. The Horozuki Kaigan's sea-carved cliffs lie below the large parking lots and tourist stands selling dried wakame (a variety of seaweed) along the highway just east of Imabetsu. Paths lead down to the beach where you can camp or picnic.

As the highway bends southward, on most days you'll get a clear view of the famous white cliffs of the Shimokita Peninsula to the east. This might be your only glimpse of Shimokita's Hotokegaura cliffs because the area is very difficult to reach by land. After Kanita, the scenery quickly deteriorates into suburban big city as you near Aomori.

YOU MAY FEEL at this point that you have definitely covered the Tsugaru Peninsula, but, alas, you've missed the entire western shore. You may not be overly impressed by this fact, but this same shore was an extremely welcome sight to four crewmen of an American merchant ship that ran aground two kilometers off Shariki in 1889.

Try to visit Shariki's lonely, unkempt memorial to the less fortunate crewmembers of the Cheeseborough who drowned before local fishermen, braving rough seas in their small boats, could reach them.

The Cheeseborough (you may see it written as Chisblow, one of the hazards of putting a Western word into phonetic Japanese and then transliterating it back into Roman letters) was on its way to New York after loading up with sulfur at Hakodate on Hokkaido, until high seas and strong winds got the best of it. The mayor of tiny Shariki wasn't quite sure what to do with the four stranded foreigners pulled out of his coastal waters so he dispatched two runners in a sleet storm to report the incident to the prefectural government in Aomori City, sixty-five kilometers away. A local newspaper then ran a campaign for donations to help the sailors get back to the United States, thus solving—at least temporarily— the problem of the foreigners roaming the Tsugaru Peninsula.

Japanese and American military members stationed in the prefecture now compete in an annual relay race over the course covered by the two Shariki runners as a continuing memorial to the victims of the shipwreck and the friendship of the two nations.

The Cheeseborough Memorial is a difficult destination using public transportation, but if you have a car and want to visit Tsugaru's west coast, turn north off Highway 101 between Ajigasawa and Goshogawara, following the road signs for Shariki. The road follows the inland side of a windbreak separating wide, sandy Shichirinagahama (7–League-Long Beach) and a sparsely populated area in which tons of melons are grown in large fields of sandy soil. You may want to stop in the coastal village of Kizukuri, which is known for the prehistoric Jōmon-period relics found nearby which are now preserved in its new Kamegaoka Musuem.

To find the memorial, turn towards the coast at a sign for Takayama Inari Shrine. The monument is just before the shrine, beside a high lookout platform. After paying your respects, be sure to go next door for a pleasant surprise—the Takayama Inari Shrine is one of the nicest in the prefecture.

The prosperous new shrine is well supported by the locals since it is dedicated to a sea god in whose territory much of the peninsula's population seeks a living. The elaborate complex includes a well-landscaped lily pond and an interesting outdoor display of tiny altars dedicated to the fox god, each one unique, beyond an archway of sixty-four brightly painted torii. All this just when you think you've ventured about as far back into the back country as it'll go!

If you haven't yet been, it would make sense to continue along the coast at this point to Cape Tappi, but, unfortunately, the rugged topography of the peninsula has eliminated this option. You can, however, cross over to Kanagi on local roads.

The Takayama Inari Shrine and, to a much greater degree, the Seikan Undersea Tunnel epitomize the fact that, even in its most remote northern reaches, Tōhoku remains Japan's back country only in a historical sense and is indeed catching up with the rest of the nation.

The Western Coast

MENTION A DESIRE to explore Aomori's western coast on your way in or out of the prefecture and the northerner, with an inferiority complex from generations of living in Japan's back country, will reply, "But no one goes there. There's nothing to see."

On the other hand, the tourist bureau handouts boast of the area's "succession of sheer precipices" with "an exact resemblance to the Grand Canyon of Colorado."

As is typical of most extremes, the truth about Aomori's west coast lies somewhere in between. A side trip along JNR's coast-hugging Gonō Line or its constant companion, Highway 101, from Kawabe in the north to Akita Prefecture's Higashi Noshiro in the south will be a detour into the beauty of nature at her most serene—a diversion you just might welcome at this point in your journey.

Western Aomori's beaches of grass, sand, and rock gently ease themselves into the placid Sea of Japan, in stark contrast to the prefecture's rugged Pacific shore. And, although you definitely won't see anything that even vaguely resembles the Grand Canyon, you'll be glad you made the trek through beautiful Jūniko Forest for a look at the somewhat overrated Nihon Canyon.

Jūniko means twelve lakes, but there are actually thirty-three postcard-perfect ponds scattered among the quiet forests of this seldomvisited section of Tsugaru Quasi-National Park. A night at a ryokan overlooking one of these tranquil ponds and you'll good-naturedly overlook Nihon Canyon's obvious inadequacies.

"Unspoiled" is still an accurate description of Aomori's west coast even though the tour buses are gradually discovering the area's natural attractions. So if lovely deserted beaches and clear ponds hidden by tall trees appeal to you, don't wait too long to experience this part of the back country.

From Hirosaki, you can pick up the Gonō Line at its origin by taking the Ōu Main Line a few stops north to Kawabe or you can take a bus around the southern base of majestic Mount Iwaki to Ajigasawa, perhaps with a short stop at the Nikkō-style Iwaki Shrine along the way.

From Aomori City or Kanagi on the Tsugaru Peninsula, you can pick up the Gonō Line at Goshogawara, where Route 101 also begins.

By taking this Goshogawara route, you'll be traveling "behind" Mount Iwaki through countryside spared the destructive forces of the Second World War, an area therefore still rich in rural scenes of an earlier Japan. As you pass one lovely farm compound after another, take a picture or two of the scene. It won't look the same in five or ten years after the TV-generation grandkids inherit (and waste no time in modernizing) the wonderful old homesteads. This is what all Japanese countryside used to look like before pre-fabricated siding.

Once you hit the coast you'll be passing a string of fishing villages separated by a nearly unbroken line of the day's squid harvest drying along the busy highway—in a mixture of fresh ocean breeze and foul truck fumes! As the big Hino diesels speed by, try not to think of the shredded dried squid that tastes so good with a bottle of Kirin or Sapporo beer.

About 10 kilometers south of Ajigasawa is Senjōjiki (1,000 Tatami Mat Rock). The broad rock "platform" jutting out into the calm sea was used by feudal lords for picnics and meetings after it was formed by a an earthquake in 1793. It's a nice place for drivers to stretch legs and take advantage of tourist facilities but, feudal lords' preferences notwithstanding, there are much prettier picnic spots further down the coast. Simiarly, few train travelers would consider a two-hour layover here till the next train time well spent. If you do want to see this strange rock table, however, tiny Senjōjiki Station is just across the highway.

The Japanese seem to have a penchant for naming rocks and this leg of coastline is no exception. You'll have no trouble picking out Helmet Rock preceding Senjōjiki, but Lion Rock and Eagle Rock (it's a wing only) which follow are more challenging to spot. This is the most rugged section of the peaceful coast.

Once the shoreline's appearance begins to soften, you'll find several official campgrounds as well as lots of deserted beaches on which to create your own. Pull-offs leading to the prettiest spots are identified by rustic brown wooden signs with white lettering which appear every so often along the highway.

The entire 25-kilometer span between Senjōjiki and Jūniko is so lovely it's impossible to declare any one spot as "the" place to explore. But if you're on the train and want to spend a few hours walking the beautiful beaches, consider a stopover along the four-station stretch between Todoroki and Fukaura. Each station is only about 3 kilometers from the next—a pleasant walk if you know when the next train is coming and you haven't violated Rule of the Road Number One by carrying more than one small travel bag.

An alternative is to use the overgrown fishing village of Fukaura as a central jumping off point for a walk on the beach. The town has a small youth hostel. From the station, a short taxi ride or a 25-minute walk northward will take you to Yukiai, a grassy plateau extending into the sea like a big misshapen thumb. Actually, Yukiai is much prettier than any thumb could ever be, almost as visually pleasing, in fact, as the vistas it offers in all directions.

A 25-minute walk south from the station will take you to

JNR's Okazakinohama Campground, another pretty hike on the beach. But plan on coming back to Fukaura Station because the next station to the south is a long, long walk.

While waiting for the train at Fukaura, you may want to visit Enkaku-ji, a dignified old temple about 20 minutes on foot from the station. If you're driving, turn off the highway at the sign for Nakayama, and then make a right turn over the bridge.

Enkaku-ji was founded in the ninth century by Southerners sent up north to conquer the Ezo. The temple owns a statue of the eleven-faced Kannon supposedly made by Shōtoku Taishi (who stares up at us during those brief interludes in which we possess 10,000-yen notes) and a 600-year-old miniature shrine which is a national treasure.

But the highlight of the small temple's collection of religious art is an elaborately embroidered scene depicting the death of the Buddha, made early in this century. The single-color embroidery was made to comfort the souls of victims of the Russo-Japanese War—from the hair of 84,000 human donors! The temple's artist-priest took five years to finish the work and then spent another two years embroidering two smaller scenes with the leftover hair. Only long winters in a sleepy little fishing village in snow country could produce such patience!

Back on the road again, you'll pass more gentle green coastline and will have to work at not becoming numb to the ever-present beauty of it all.

The small town of Iwasaki is the gateway to Jūniko Park, although tiny Jūniko Station opens for business during the tourist season. Buses run to the inland park from the two stations five or six times a day. Guests of Jūniko's Suemaru Ryokan[1] can call the ryokan for transportation. Snuggled against the first of Jūniko's thirty-three ponds, Suemaru is the least shabby and best situated

1. Suemaru Ryokan, Matsukami, Iwasaki-mura, Nishi Tsugaru-gun, Aomori-ken 038–21; tel. (01737) 7-2226
末丸旅館　〒038-21 青森県西津軽郡岩崎村字松神

of Jūniko's three modest ryokan. Reservations for one of their few guset rooms is necessary from mid-July through October.

Jūniko's haphazard arrangement of ponds scattered throughout the forest was caused by an earthquake-generated landslide that occurred 500 years ago. Trees that drowned long ago when newly formed depressions filled with water are still visible in the clear ponds as are huge trout and carp which enjoy the protection of strategically posted No Fishing signs.

A few of the ponds have been "developed" for tourists and offer such accoutrements of civilization as places to eat and sleep, to buy souvenirs, and to rent rowboats by the half hour. They are poor indications of what lies beyond the pavement along the broad, graveled hiking trail.

From here on, it's one beautiful little pond after another appearing unexpectedly as the trail winds through the forest. Except for the well-maintained trail, the park probably looks to you much as it did in the early years of this century when the Meiji-era traveling poet Keigetsu Ōmachi described Jūniko as the most beautiful spot on the western coast of Tōhoku. There is a monument alongside one of the ponds dedicated to this man who did much to familiarize the rest of Japan with the natural beauty of the back country.

The most outstanding of Jūniko's quiet ponds is Aoike (Blue Pond). It is hidden deep in a mossy "hole" and has the clearest and bluest water imaginable. Unfortunately, the park's developers chose to place the area's only public WC right beside the natural tree-root steps leading down to the pond. The man-made structure may not add much in the way of atmosphere, but it does clearly identify Aoike's otherwise undetectable entrance!

As you pond-hop, don't try to count up to thirty-three, because the trail covers only the northern half of the park. The wide main trail makes a big circle back to the pavement, but there are a few well-kept narrow paths crossing the circle at various points. The last half of the main trail is long and pondless; therefore, a better use of your feet would be either to turn around after Aoike or to continue around the next few curves until a small path appears on the right. This winding and scenic little sub-trail goes past two more postcard-pretty ponds before connecting with the main trail about halfway between Aoike and the rowboats. Even taking time to enjoy the uniqueness of each peaceful little pond along this abbreviated route, you can cover the best of Jūniko in two hours from the beginning of the gravel trail.

A large underutilized campground is about an hour's hike into the park.

Please, please don't leave Jūniko without a glimpse of the Nihon Canyon! You can view it from a lookout on a hillside near Suemaru Ryokan. Walk past the putrid WC in the parking lot across from the ryokan and begin an easy climb up the hill on a good trail. If you'd rather skip the 30-minute hike, though, you can watch for the modest white cliff visible from the access road into the park. That is the Nihon Canyon, apparently named by an overly enthusiastic promoter who'd never been to the Grand. But what a wonderful area to be lured into by false advertising!

Back on the coast, you need only travel another 10 kilometers to officially become a tourist of Akita Prefecture. More pretty beaches dotted with strange rock formations will follow, especially around Takinoma Station.

Soon you'll cross the broad Yoneshiro River in the busy port city of Noshiro. Two stops later, at Higashi Noshiro, the Gonō Line rejoins the Ōu Main Line on which you can either head south through Akita Prefecture or east to connect with the Hanawa Line at Ōdate to reach Iwate Prefecture's capital city of Morioka.

But if you came north to hit Tōhoku's big three August festivals, don't rush through Noshiro too quickly. Noshiro, Akita's second largest city, does some colorful celebrating of its own on the evenings of the 6th and 7th. The Nebunagashi Festival shares its origin with Aomori's gigantic Nebuta, but Noshiro's lighted floats are huge castles rather than monsters and the celebrating itself is a bit more civilized. The floats are paraded downtown on the first night and their castle tops are floated down the river on the second.

Even if you're not wandering around Tōhoku during the August rush, you may want to use this medium-sized city as a convenient stopover along your way. Noshiro is a pleasant, modern town serving the local lumber industry with transportation facilities for its famous Akita sugi, or cryptomeria. The port was used by Yamato conquerors as long as 1,300 years ago, but two huge earthquakes left it unusable until modern technology recently worked its wonders.

A pleasant place to spend the night is nearby Noshiro Onsen, a hot springs community only a 15-minute bus ride north of Noshiro Station. The seaside onsen was discovered just 20 years ago by a surprised oil company drilling for a slightly more viscous fluid. There is a beachfront campground near the onsen. There's nothing really outstanding about Noshiro Onsen except its convenience to both the calm sandy beach and the city's friendly modern downtown.

If you're on your way to the traffic congestion and crowds of Akita City to the south, you'll need all that tranquility gathered from your detour through the beaches and forests of Aomori's west coast.

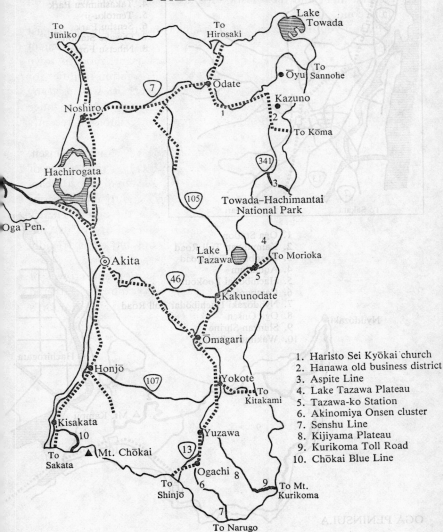

AKITA PREFECTURE

To Jūniko

To Hirosaki

Lake Towada

To Sannohe

⑦

Ōdate

Ōyu

To Kōma

Kazuno

1

2

Noshiro

341

Hachirogata

3

Towada–Hachimantai National Park

105

Oga Pen.

4

Akita

Lake Tazawa

To Morioka

46

5

Kakunodate

Ōmagari

Honjō

Yokote

To Kitakami

107

Yuzawa

Kisakata

10

Mt. Chōkai

13

Ogachi

8

To Sakata

6

9

To Mt. Kurikoma

To Shinjō

7

To Narugo

1. Haristo Sei Kyōkai church
2. Hanawa old business district
3. Aspite Line
4. Lake Tazawa Plateau
5. Tazawa-ko Station
6. Akinomiya Onsen cluster
7. Senshu Line
8. Kijiyama Plateau
9. Kurikoma Toll Road
10. Chōkai Blue Line

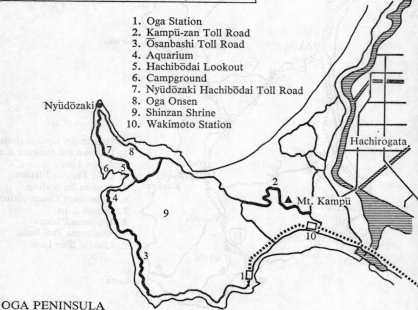

AKITA CITY AREA

1. Akita Station
2. Nara house
3. Prefectural museum
4. Takashimizu Park
5. Tentoku-ji
6. Senshu Park
7. Oiwake Station
8. Nibetsu Forest

To Sakata To Ōmagari

1. Oga Station
2. Kampū-zan Toll Road
3. Ōsanbashi Toll Road
4. Aquarium
5. Hachibōdai Lookout
6. Campground
7. Nyūdōzaki Hachibōdai Toll Road
8. Oga Onsen
9. Shinzan Shrine
10. Wakimoto Station

Nyūdōzaki

Hachirogata

Mt. Kampū

OGA PENINSULA

Introducing Akita

AKITA STANDS OUT from Japan's other forty-five prefectures for its magnificent forests of sugi, the stately Japanese cryptomerias; for its fuki, a rhubarb-like plant that grows to unbelievable size in Akita; for its Akita bijin, or beautiful fair-skinned women; and for the Kantō Festival, one of Tōhoku's "Big Three" August festivals.

"In my country, I don't need an umbrella. When it rains, I just find the right size fuki," goes an old Akita folk song. Fuki grows elsewhere in Japan, but only in Akita does it grow so big. The stems of an Akita fuki can be 180 centimeters long and two centimeters thick; a leaf can grow to 110 centimeters in diameter, a more than adequate umbrella in any storm.

The fuki plant may look like rhubarb, but there is no similarity in taste. The Japanese preserve the stems of fuki in sugar and use them in sweet pickles, yōkan (sweet-bean jelly) and other confections. Fuki stems can also be boiled as a strong-tasting vegetable. Fuki-no-to, its buds, are one of the first signs of spring in the cold back country. Sometimes the yellow-green buds pop out of the warming ground even before all the snow has melted.

Akita bijin are not only beautiful, but also cultured and hard-working. Their fair skin is much admired by the Japanese. Such fine qualities are said to come from a combination of their native

Akita heritage and from the prefecture's frequent contact with the cultural centers of Kyoto and Osaka during the feudal period. You can look forward to running into more than one contemporary Akita bijin as you explore the prefecture and you can also pay homage to these Akita beauties when you visit Lake Tazawa, the home of the legendary Akita bijin, Takko Hime.

Akita is perhaps best known today for its capital city's summertime Kantō Festival. Men balancing huge *kantō*, or bamboo poles illuminated with paper lanterns, parade through Akita City after dark. Crowds lining the parade route gasp in awe as the heavy poles sway above them, symbols of full stalks of Akita rice soon to be harvested.

In Akita's prehistory, its Stone Age residents laid circles of rocks akin to Stonehenge in distinct patterns. No one is sure why the stone circles were built, but you can ponder the mystery when you visit the small northern Akita town of Ōyu (covered in Iwate's Hachimantai section) to see the Ōyu Stone Circle on its outskirts.

Later, in eighth-century Akita, Yamato invaders from the south built an immense walled fortress to protect the territory they had just won from the Ezo. The Chinese-style complex is now completely surrounded by Akita City, a modern industrial center with some 300,000 residents.

Then, nine centuries later, the Satake clan came to Akita and taught the backward territory to exploit its natural advantages, setting the groundwork for Akita's present agricultural and industrial prosperity. You can get a feeling for life as a Satake samurai in Kakunodate Town's preserved samurai residential neighborhood. The site of their main castle is now a wooded park in Akita City. Here the Akita Prefectural Art Museum houses one of Japan's finest Western art collections.

Akita's natural attractions include Lake Tazawa, Japan's deepest lake, and the former Hachirōgata Lagoon, once the country's second largest body of water and now a reclaimed plain with a large-scale experiment in modern agriculture still in progress. Akita shares the volcanic mountains of Hachimantai with Iwate, Chōkai with Yamagata, and Kurikoma with both Iwate and Miyagi; it shares the famous caldera lake of Towada with Aomori. But its beautiful Oga Peninsula is shared only with the Sea of Japan—and with the thousands of visitors who come each year to enjoy its coastal scenery.

The brevity of the Akita section is by no means an indication of limited offerings. Since some of Akita's attractions are on routes leading into or out of other prefectures and since others span these prefectural borders, parts of Akita have ended up in other sections. You'll find Akita's northern coast and Lake Towada in Aomori, Hachimantai and northeastern Akita in Iwate, and its southern coast and Mt. Chōkai in Yamagata. You can, however, rectify this injustice to a lovely prefecture. As you visit these places that Akita shares with its neighbors, be sure to think to yourself, "Akita is a truly beautiful prefecture." It truly is.

The Oga Peninsula

MAYBE IT'S OGA'S unique position as one of Honshu's two major
projections into the Sea of Japan that draws so many tourists
to the foot-shaped peninsula. Or maybe it's Oga's beautiful
seascapes as seen from roads precariously carved into steep
mountainsides that fall dramatically into the sea. It's also likely
that Oga's real attraction is in its escape to nature, since the
peninsula is only thirty kilometers northwest of the industrial fumes
and traffic congestion of Akita Prefecture's busy capital city.
And a few visitors must come in hopes of spotting a namahage,
Oga's famous hairy and horned monsters who roam the peninsula in winter, seeking to purge it of lazy idlers.

Namamiko is the local word for a blotch on the skin caused
by sitting too long by the fire, and hage means to strip off. As
their name implies, namahage make it their business to discourage
anyone from being lazy enough to acquire a tell-tale blotch.

You can see the namahage in action on New Year's Eve when
they burst into local households shouting, "Are there any lazy
children here to be eaten up?" The fearsome monsters terrify
the kids and bring back childhood memories for the amused
elders. After their startling entrance, the namahage become
almost tame. They bow before the family altar, partake in the
sakè and mochi offered by the master of the house, wish their

host a successful harvest or a good catch in the new year, and then run, screaming their threatening chant, into the next household where a lazy child or even a lazy daughter-in-law may reside.

If you miss them on New Year's Eve, try the Namahage Fire Festival, held from February 13th through 15th at the Shinzan Shrine in the mountains near the middle of the peninsula. At other times, you can see souvenir photos and namahage dolls depicting the ugly creatures that the Akita winter brings to life.

Oga's first five namaghage came from China long, long ago. A Japanese man brought them to Oga by boat and made them work very hard. Their first break from this drudgery came on January 15th, at which time they stormed into the little village of Monzen and proceeded to raise hell and to help themselves to Monzen's young women.

The distraught villagers then made a pact with the creatures. If the namahage would leave the village women and property alone, the villagers would donate one young girl a year to them —but only if the namahage could perform a very difficult feat. They had to lay 1,000 stone steps up a hillside leading from the village to the present site of Akagami Shrine's Gosha-dō. All the steps had to be in place before the first rooster crowed on the following day.

To the villagers' surprise, it was not yet daylight when the lusting beasts had 999 steps in place. But a quick-thinking man saved the day by letting out with a rooster-like crow just before the last step was in place. The namahage left in defeat and never bothered the fishermen and farmers of Monzen again—except to harass the lazy on New Year's Eve. You can climb the namahages' 999 stone steps if you stop in Monzen on your tour around the peninsula.

OGA'S MAIN ATTRACTIONS, besides its namahage population, include the large and very modern Oga Suizokukan prefectural aquarium on Toga Bay, two mountaintop lookouts, and, of course, its beautiful coastal scenery. A quick trip around the peninsula will satisfy your curiosity about Tōhoku's outstretched foot in the Sea of Japan, and the peninsula's plentiful accommodations provide alternatives to a night in Akita City.

On the way to Oga, you may become equally curious about the strange flat, treeless, houseless and nearly unbroken rice fields separating both Highway 7 and the Ōu Main Line from the distant mountains of the peninsula.

This is Hachirōgata, once Japan's second largest body of water and later a destination for a group of modern-day pioneers. The massive project of filling in the saltwater lagoon began in 1957. Nine years later, the land was dry enough for recruits from all over Japan to begin new lives on the treeless, cropless and ever-so-flat virgin plain. In another two years, the pioneers had their first rice seedlings in the reclaimed ground.

Hachirōgata, now surrounded by a freshwater channel which empties into the sea between Akita and Oga City, was intended as a giant experiment to determine whether nontraditional modern farming methods and living arrangements would work in Japan, a country which has been doing such things in more or less the same way for centuries. So the Hachirōgata pioneers left their family farms and local villages to work the new land's vast rice fields, fields designed for efficient, large-scale equipment. They settled in its single community, Ōgata, in which every resident was a newcomer and no one was burdened or helped along by long-established roles or traditions. Japan's current rice surplus has eliminated much of the nation's enthusiasm to find a "better way" and has disillusioned many of the pioneers who came in search of a more prosperous life. Nevertheless, the experiment continues.

There's not a lot to see in Hachirōgata. In fact, its unvaried flatness is an offense to the traveler's eye, by now used to a succession of Tōhoku mountains, forests, lakes, and coastlines.

But as you pass the large fields of the Hachirōgata pioneers or look down on them from Oga's Kampū-zan Lookout, knowing their story makes it possible to empathize with the dreams of a better life that led them from their traditional farms to the stark plains of Hachirōgata.

Directly west of Hachirōgata is the Oga Peninsula. It thrusts itself a full twenty kilometers into the sea, and the famous green mountains that comprise its western coast extend fifteen kilometers from north to south.

Oga Onsen, a sizable resort on the northwest coast of the peninsula has lots of modern hotels, a youth hostel, and the Kokuminshukusha Oga.[1] The Monzen-sō kokuminshukusha[2] and the Chōraku-ji Youth Hostel are in the fishing village of Monzen, where Oga's calm southern coastline begins to turn northward toward the mountains. A campground is on Toga Bay, between Monzen and Oga Onsen.

Limited express trains on the Ōu Main Line whiz past Hachirōgata, destined for Akita Station, where the short Oga Line originates. The local line heads back to Oga Station near the peninsula's southeastern heel. From Oga Station, regular city buses and several sightseeing buses leave daily for the peninsula's most popular attractions. You can also reach these sites via express or sightseeing buses which leave from Akita Station, the former at frequent intervals and the latter several times a day, with varying courses.

If you're coming from Aomori Prefecture by car on Highway 7, you don't have to go all the way to Akita City to reach Oga. A local road which intersects with Highway 7 just north of Hachi-

1. Kokuminshukusha Oga, Yumoto, Kitaura, Oga-shi, Akita-ken 010–06; tel. (0185) 33–3181.
   国民宿舎男鹿　〒010–16 秋田県男鹿市北浦湯本
2. Monzen-sō, Monzen, Funagawa-kō, Oga-shi, Akita-ken 010–05; tel. (0185) 27–2221.
   国民宿舎門前荘　〒010–05 秋田県男鹿市船川港門前

rōgata runs between the former lagoon and the peninsula. The Kampū-zan Toll Road extends from this road into the center of the peninsula, taking visitors to the mountaintop Kampū-zan Lookout for an overview of the peninsula, the sea and the man-made plain. The view is interesting on a clear day, but the lookout's three-story revolving tower may be too much of a contrast to the peninsula's natural scenes for some tastes. Many sightseeing and regular buses from Akita City and Oga Station also stop at Kampū-zan Lookout, from which they head either northwest toward Oga Onsen or southwest toward Monzen.

If you want to skip the revolving view, the local road from Highway 7 also connects with Oga's southern perimeter road just past Wakimoto Station. This perimeter road winds westward through some fishing villages along a quietly pretty coastline until it comes to Monzen at the southwest corner of the peninsula. The namahages' 999 stone steps begin here at the gate of Chōraku-ji temple and lead to the Akagami Shrine's Goshado, five 300-year-old small, wooden buildings. The altar of the middle shrine is an Important Cultural Treasure.

Monzen's harbor is the starting point for the tour boats to the big prefectural aquarium at Toga Bay. If you want to see the peninsula's famous mountains rising sharply from the water without having to climb them by car or bus, take one of the four hour-long boat tours that leave for Toga Bay daily from late April through late October. Boats originating at Toga Bay either go back to Monzen or cruise about halfway down the mountainous coast and then back to the bay.

By land, the scenic Ōsanbashi Toll Road heads north from Monzen to the aquarium, where it becomes a climbing local road that intersects with Oga's third toll road, the Nyūdōzaki Hachibodai Toll Road. This road appropriately heads both southeast to Hachibodai Lookout and northwest to Cape Nyūdō. From either destination, you can then circle around to the busy

Oga Onsen, where many visitors choose to spend the night.

The Hachibōdai Lookout offers a panorama of the sea and of three mountainside lakes, Ichi-, Ni-, and San-nomegata. The lakes are actually water-filled depressions formed when the mountain burped volcanic gases but did not actually erupt. Unlike a crater lake, this type of volcanic body of water has no underground water source and is characterized by its smooth gas-bubble-formed shape. Evenly rounded Toga Bay was formed by the same process. Japan's only other such lakes are in Kagoshima in southern Kyushu.

If you head in the opposite direction on the toll road, you'll come to Oga's big toe, Cape Nyūdō. Taking advantage of the peninsula's tourist trade, the cape features a huge parking lot, a string of souvenir stands, and sometimes a "real" namahage who will pose for your camera. More aesthetically appealing are the cape's strange-shaped rock formations below your high perch. These rocks are the source of the fresh sazae (turbo) and abalone sold at the stands.

Once you reach Oga Onsen, the sightseeing part of your visit to the peninsula is about over. From here the northern local roads go through green foothills and small villages, taking you further and further from the beautiful Oga coastline.

Before you leave Oga, though, you might want to try hatahata, a fish which comes close to the northern Akita shore in late November and early December to lay eggs. Historically, the people of this region wait each year with great anticipation for the arrival of the spawning fish, especially when a poor harvest has left winter food supplies low. Hata-hata have always come in such numbers and have such a delicate flavor that the usually frugal farmers and fishermen could afford to gorge themselves on the fish.

Even today in the new land of plenty no one on the Oga Peninsula would think of ushering in the new year without eating hata-hata-zushi. To make this local delicacy, the head and tail of the fish are removed and the fish is pickled in salt to soften the bones. A few days later, the pickled fish is mixed with cooked rice, carrots, and turnips. In another few days the concoction is ready to eat, although it will keep for much longer.

Another product of the northern Akita sea is shottsuru, a liquid byproduct of pickling fish in salt. Like Southeast Asians, the locals use this strong, salty, fish-based liquid in place of soy sauce. Many restaurants in Akita City feature shottsuru kaiyaki, a stew of white fish, green onions, tofu, greens, and shottsuru served in a big scallop shell.

Take one last deep breath of fresh sea air as you leave the shores of Oga, for you'll soon be passing through the industrial section of the capital city of Akita. But once you get beyond the smokestacks and bumper-to-bumper truck traffic, you're on your way to discovering the big city's more attractive side.

Akita City

IT'S MUCH EASIER to tolerate the Akita seaside industrial park's byproducts of fumes and traffic when you realize how important such industry is to both the back-country prefecture and to the nation. Akita refines thirty percent of Japan's relatively minuscule natural oil depoists as the country's number two producer behind Niigata. Akita's busy refineries are joined on this stretch of industrial oceanfront between Oga and the city by producers of chemicals, paper, and fertilizer.

Lying beyond Akita's factories, though, are elements of the city's other roles as the prefecture's cultural, educational, and political center. Akita is a back-country city with a touch of class. Its Hirano Art Collection is one of Japan's finest, the displays at its modern prefectural museum are unusually well done, and the city's broad willow-lined main street comes into the national limelight each August during the Kantō Lantern Festival, the third of Tōhoku's Big Three summer festivals. Two former castle sites spanning the city's 1,200-year history add greenery and seasonal color to the busy metropolis of 300,000, and enthusiastic college students seem to be everywhere, eager to offer a friendly hand to the foreign visitor.

Akita Airport joins Highway 7 and JNR's Ōu and Uetsu Main Lines in serving the city. Like most cities, Akita has a selection of reasonably priced business hotels, but alternatives to a night in the city can be found on the Oga Peninsula to the northwest and at a campground in the Nibetsu Public Forest to the northeast.

The Akita Prefectural Museum is about 15 kilometers north of the central city in a former farming village the city has now encompassed. It is on a local road heading east off Highway 7 just beyond the turnoff for Oga; it's also a short walk from Oiwake Station, a local stop on the Ōu Main Line. Nearby the 10-year-old museum is a 220-year-old neighbor, the Old Nara Family House, which is also open to the public. Although the modern museum and the old house are a distance from the center of the city, they are worth seeing, especially if you are driving into the city from the nearby Oga Peninsula.

The modern museum building is spread across nicely land-scaped grounds which include a Japanese garden. Akita's pre-history, history, cultural treasures, and folkcrafts are skillfully displayed and are accompanied by an English-language brochure.

A 10-minute uphill walk through a winding residential area takes you from the spacious museum grounds to the compact home of the past nine generations of the Nara Family. The family originally came from Nara Prefecture and for several generations its heads had been village chiefs before their neighborhood became part of suburban Akita City. The current Mr. Nara, a lifelong bachelor, donated his family home to the prefecture, and today the Old Nara Family House is, like Tōno's Chiba House, one of Japan's most important restored minka.

The unusual U-shaped thatched-roof house has a dignified elegance in spite of its large earthen-floored stable and kitchen area in one leg of the U. Unlike the Chiba House, this minka feels more real than restored, and its quiet warmth encourages the visitor to leisurely wander through and reverently touch each age-smoothed wooden pillar.

Akita City has been a capital of some sort for over 1,200 years, since the first Akita Castle was built in 734 by Yamato warriors who were sent north to conquer the indigenous Ezo. Nothing remains of the Chinese-style castle fortress today, but historical records reveal that this northernmost outpost of eighth-century civilized Japan was a huge complex covering over 640,000 square kilometers. A document from the year 878 records a revolt by the Ezo which cost the Akita Castle the loss of 190 buildings and 1,500 horses. Like Beijing's Forbidden City, Akita Castle was divided into an inner castle and an outer castle, both surrounded by earth fences.

Schools occupy much of the ancient castle site, but one corner is now Takashimizu Park, a peaceful wooded park with cherries, pines, and cedars surrounding a small natural spring and the well-kept grounds of the Gokoku Shrine. It is a 20-minute bus ride from Akita Station to the Gokoku Jinja-mae Bus Stop.

Centuries after the first Akita Castle was reduced to ruins, the Satake family of the province of Mito, on the Pacific Coast above present-day Tokyo, came to Akita, built a new castle (this one conveniently located near Akita Station), and began to transform the backward, forested territory into a prosperous agricultural region.

In 1604, the Satakes built their Kubota Castle from which they ruled the area for eight generations, until the Meiji Restoration did away with the clan system. During this period, the Satake family had land cleared to grow rice; developed Akita's still thriving sugi (cryptomeria) lumber industry; started people producing silk, cotton, and sakè; and made a fortune mining the territory's stores of silver. For the summertime amusement of the common people, the Satakes popularized and expanded the Kantō Lantern Festival tradition, originally a small-scale ceremony of prayers for a successful rice harvest. During the late Edo period, the Satakes were the only back-country clan to support the return of the emperor to power. It took courage to go against the five neighboring clans who sided with the Tokugawa Shogunate, but the Satake lord's reward was minimal. He was given only a very small part in the new government, and his castle was soon destroyed.

Today the site of Kubota Castle is called Senshū Park, only 700 meters northwest of Akita Station. It is a wooded park sprinkled with public buildings including a library, an auditorium, the city art museum, and the prefectural art museum. The latter building, a two-storied copper-roof structure, is particularly noteworthy because the famous Hirano Collection occupies its second floor. This collection includes the works of such Western artists as Rubens, Goya, Picasso and van Gogh as well as the noted Japanese painter of Western-style oils, Tsuguji Fujita.

Fujita is perhaps best known for his paintings of pale, slender, long-faced Western women. He also painted the largest canvas of this century (3.6 × 20.5 m), depicting scenes from the four seasons of Akita. This gigantic work is also part of the museum's collection. He painted it in 1937 in the middle of Japan's war years in an earth-walled kura, or storehouse. The completed painting was so large that a wall of the kura had to be destroyed to remove it.

A final historical attraction of note in the city is the Satake family temple, Tentoku-ji. Its present structures date from 1708. The temple consists of four buildings connected by stepping stones and houses a collection of treasures and portraits of the Satakes. Heiwa Kōen (Peace Park), with its white peace tower, is located behind the temple. The quiet wooded temple is reached in a 20-minute bus ride from Akita Station to the Tentoku-ji-mae Bus Stop.

Northeast of the city on the slopes of Taihei-zan, the Nibetsu Public Forest was developed to meet the recreational needs of the city people and to preserve the natural forest lying dangerously close to the big city. Antelope and black bear roam unhindered here among the tall sugi and buna (beech) trees. For human entertainment, the park has a campground, nature trails through the trees and past scenic gorges, and the Nibetsu Public Forest Museum. The forest museum is Japan's first; it features stuffed versions of the area's wildlife, a mingei collection, and displays dedicated to the prefecture's famous sugi trees. The Nibetsu Bus Stop is 80 minutes from Akita Station.

Most Japanese, however, think not of fuki, oil wells, art, or even sugi when they hear the name Akita City. Instead their first thoughts are of Akita's famous Kantō Festival. Kantō is held the same week as Aomori City's Nebuta and Sendai's Tanabata. Thus, many Japanese out on Tōhoku's festival circuit during the first week of August include Akita City in their plans.

KANTŌ'S AFTER-DARK lantern-balancing parade is indeed deserving of its popularity. Not as obnoxiously crowded as Tanabata nor as obnoxiously noisy as Nebuta, Kantō has a slightly more subdued excitement all its own. On the nights of August 5th, 6th, and 7th, over 160 men and boys thrill the crowds lining downtown Akita's main street by balancing sixty-kilogram and ten-meter-high bamboo poles strung with lighted lanterns on their shoulders, hips, palms, foreheads and even in their mouths to the sound of traditional drum and flute music.

Each participant takes a turn balancing long swaying poles supporting nine horizontal cross poles, from which hang about forty-six paper lanterns. The heavy, illuminated poles sway back and forth menacingly over the crowds as the men struggle to keep them upright while moving them from one part of their bodies to another to elicit even more admiration from the enthusiastic spectators.

The parade line of swaying kantō poles resembles giant, heavily-laden rice stalks, like those in the surrounding rice fields almost ready to be harvested. And just as the kantō poles will soon be dismantled for another year, so too will the full rice plants be harvested—and so too will Akita's short summer be over. If you're out braving the crowds of the back country's most famous week, Akita's Kantō Festival shouldn't be missed.

Less inviting than Tōhoku's cool Augusts are its downright cold Januaries. Nevertheless, each January 17th Akita residents are out in force for another colorful parade down its snowy streets. The Bonden Festival is a religious ceremony, but, like many in Japan, it is more merry than solemn. This daytime parade features a procession of huge bonden, or colorfully decorated four-meter-high giant purification wands, on their way to Miyoshi Shrine. Each bonden is borne by a group of ten to thirty singing and dancing worshippers who blow conch-shell horns and jostle their way through the streets in an effort to get their bonden to the shrine first and to prevent other groups from doing the same. For a day, Akita residents ignore the cold, snow, and wintertime gloom to join friends, neighbors, and visitors in cheering on the bonden as they head for the shrine.

THOSE VISITORS TO AKITA who appreciate craftsmanship might also be interested in two of Akita's finer local arts. Akita Hachijō is the product of the 200-year-old art of dyeing kimono material with natural yellow dye from the root of the wild rose. Modern examples of this traditional fabric can be seen in the city's better kimono shops.

The craft of making jewelry and art objects decorated in patterns of very thin silver wire is called ginsenzaiku. This delicate craft originated with the gold artisans the Satakes brought from Mito. It flourished in Akita with the development of the prefecture's silver mines.

The cherry bark products you may notice in Akita City craft and souvenir shops come not from the big city, but from Kakunodate, a charming small town between Akita City and Lake Tazawa, Japan's deepest lake. You can visit both Kakunodate and the lake by heading through southeastern Akita Prefecture on your way south to or Yamagata.

Kakunodate and Lake Tazawa

As you head south from Akita City, you're faced with a decision. Do you want to remain close to the Sea of Japan on the Uetsu Main Line or Highway 7 in order to explore Yamagata Prefecture's Shonai district? Or do you want to follow the Ōu Main Line or Highway 13 through southeastern Akita to Yamagata City? If you choose the latter route, you won't be far from the preserved samurai houses of Kakunodate or from Lake Tazawa, Japan's deepest lake.

The Ōu Main Line has a major stop at the city of Ōmagari, about 50 kilometers southeast of Akita City. From here, the Tazawa-ko Line begins heading east to Iwate's Morioka, passing through Kakunodate and Tazawa-ko stations. The most direct car route to Kakunodate and the lake is Highway 46, which leaves Highway 13 in the middle of pretty rolling mountains about halfway between Akita City and Ōmagari. You can also reach this part of the prefecture from Lake Towada and Hachimantai via Highway 341.

In former times, Ōmagari was a prosperous rice trading port along the route western Tōhoku daimyo took on their annual trips to Edo. Today the city is better known as the home of the biggest fireworks festival in northern Japan. During the fourth weekend of August each year, fireworks makers from all over Japan come to Ōmagari for a grand-scale competition, the main winners of which are, of course, the entralled spectators.

You might want to detour through the countryside west of the city to find the Naraoka Pottery kiln in the tiny hamlet of Minami-Naraoka. Train travelers can take a bus to Minami-Naraoka from Ōmagari Station. By car, you have to stay on Highway 13 for another 18 kilometers past the Highway 46 junction until a narrow, paved country road leaves the highway heading south towards the village of Nangai and Highway 105. Minami-Naraoka is about halfway between the two highways. This little road passes many humble farms as well as a few rare and impressive Edo-period fenced homesteads of rural village chiefs.

Indistinguishable from its neighboring old-style rural houses, the 120-year-old Naraoka kiln of the Komatsu family is about halfway through Minami-Naraoka hamlet. The fifth generation Mr. Komatsu is still producing the rust-colored and ash-glazed utilitarian pots and dishes of his ancestors as well as more contemporary decorative pieces. You no doubt will have to seek help in finding the right old house, so ask for Komatsu Kōichirō of Minami-Naraoka, Nangai-mura; his telephone number is (018773) 18. Even if you aren't that interested in pottery, a visit to the Naraoka kiln is a nice excuse to get off the main highways and wander the back roads of this typical back-country rural area.

THE TOWN OF KAKUNODATE is a slice of Akita's feudal past alive and well for Showa-era travelers to experience. Surrounded on three sides by mountains and on the south by the Semboku Plain, Kakunodate was selected as an ideal location for a secondary castle by the Satake clan in 1620. The castle once stood on Kojō-san, the hill at the north end of the town and typical Edo-period neighborhoods delineated by the classes and trades of their residents once lined Kakunodate's narrow, winding streets.

Although twentieth-century buildings have, for the most part, replaced those built when the castle still loomed over the town, the basic layout of Kakunodate remains the same. For the visitor, the most interesting part of town is Uchi-machi, its still distinct former samurai residential district. The neighborhood is a 15-minute walk northwest of the station. Today, Uchi-machi's homesteads retain many of the gardens and tall weeping cherry trees, some of the houses, and much of the flavor of its feudal days. In spite of the presence of a few modern facades on the district's new tourist-oriented facilities, to walk along Uchi-machi's fence-lined streets, peeking into the mossy, shaded gardens of the old homesteads, is to experience life in a back-country castle town of 200 years ago.

If you want to prolong your journey into Akita's feudal past after wandering through Uchi-machi, plan to spend the night (at ryokan prices) at the Ishikawa Ryokan.[1] The Ishikawa family has been offering its hospitality and meals of local delicacies for ten generations.

You may still see posters proudly displayed in town of a historical drama made for television several years ago. That was the winter when an NHK film crew used Uchi-machi as the setting for an Edo-period drama. The crew had to wait for a good snowfall (not a long wait in Tōhoku) to conceal Uchi-machi's twentieth-century curbs and pavement.

Three Uchi-machi families have opened their samurai ancestors' homes to the visiting public for small entrance fees. You can see the Aoyagi family's 220-year-old house and garden on Uchi-machi's main street and then walk down the street to the Iwahashi family's restored samurai house. Be sure to note the Iwahashi's huge oak tree on the south side of their garden. The Matsumoto family's house is one block west of the main street.

Along with its paved streets, Uchi-machi's other twentieth-

1. Ishikawa Ryokan, Iwase-machi, Kakunodate-machi, Semboku-gun, Akita-ken 014–03; tel. (01875) 4–2030.
石川旅館　〒014-03 秋田県仙北郡角館町岩瀬町

century additions are a handful of craft shops featuring the cherry bark craft, or kabazaiku, for which the town is nationally famed, and the Kakunodate Denshōkan, the town's modern, red brick historical museum.

The painstaking process of kabazaiku involves scraping and smoothing cherry bark and then using it to cover useful or decorative items such as tea canisters, snack plates, letter boxes, and even small pieces of furniture. The craft is demonstrated in the museum, where the skill is also taught, and in several of the shops.

Kakunodate's kabazaiku began in the late Edo period, when Japan's dying clan system could no longer support all the members of its growing samurai class. The town's local Satake lord noticed the smoothed cherry-bark tobacco pouches carried by travelers from the northern part of the prefecture, and he urged his lower-ranking samurai to take up the craft to supplement their dwindling incomes. Later, the ranks of cherry bark craftspeople swelled when the Meiji Restoration put the entire samurai class out of work; it soon became the former castle town's most popular industry. Today the output of local craftspeople is found in mingei shops and department stores all over Japan. But the best selection is, of course, in the workshops and sales outlets of Uchimachi.

Although the new Denshōkan museum was built with Western-style white columns and archways, it is hidden behind a brick fence and thus doesn't clash too harshly with its Edo-period neighbors. Inside are displays of old treasures of the Satake clan and outstanding examples of local crafts.

One of these crafts is Shiroiwa-yaki, a heavy utilitarian pottery glazed in dull browns and creams. When an earthquake destroyed the kiln thirty years ago, the pottery ceased operation after 130 years of making unconsciously beautiful large pots for pickling vegetables, making miso, and storing water and foodstuffs. You can appreciate the remaining pieces of Shiroiwa in this and other

Tōhoku museums, and, if you're alert, you may also spot a stray Shiroiwa pot for sale in a Tōhoku antique shop.

The Denshōkan's gift shop has a large selection of local crafts and foods including inexpensive and lightweight cherry bark tea scoops. However, kabazaiku products do get expensive, a fact which becomes understandable when you observe the time-consuming process of turning the rough strips of bark into finished products. Another interesting local craft is called itayazaiku, the carving of packs of identical wooden foxes carved from a single young maple branch. If you buy the whole pack, the foxes will fit together like pie wedges to reform the original branch.

Kakunodate can be called Akita's cherry capital for more reasons than the magic local craftspeople perform with the tree's bark. You probably noticed the huge weeping cherry trees lining the streets of Uchi-machi. They were brought as cuttings from Kyoto by the local Satake lord, who was adopted into the family from the imperial household. Many of these trees are now 280 years old, and over 150 of them are National Natural Treasures. They form breathtaking cascades of pink when in bloom in early May.

More cherries were planted fifty years ago when the town's Hinokinai River had its banks built up and reinforced with tons of white concrete to control flooding. To lessen the harshness of the concrete, to honor the birth of Japan's crown prince that year, and to carry on Kakunodate's cherry tree tradition, a two-kilometer-long line of trees was planted along the river bank. Each May people from all over Tōhoku come to Kakunodate to walk through this brilliant riverside tunnel of pink.

LAKE TAZAWA is Japan's deepest lake, and its forested shores are a short ride by car or train from Kakunodate's cherry trees and samurai houses. You can approach Lake Tazawa from either the west or the east. The route for taking in rustic scenes of rural Akita is along Highway 105 and the tiny Kakunodate Line. Two access roads lead from the highway through wooded hills to the lake. By train, Matsuba Station is Lake Tazawa's western gateway. The Matsuba Youth Hostel is a 5-minute walk from the station.

The more popular access to the lake is from the east, via Highways 46 and 341. From this direction, Lake Tazawa is a 15-minute bus ride from the Tazawa-ko Line's Tazawa-ko Station.

The 423-meter-deep lake is surrounded by low, forested hills. A 20-kilometer-long paved road cuts through the hillsides to circle the round caldera lake; over half of this road is toll.

You can get down from your hillside perch to touch the water in only a few spots, all of which have been built up with tourist facilities. The main tourist center is on a sand beach on the lake's eastern shore. There is a cluster of hotels, a youth hostel, a hillside campground, and a small folk museum near the access road on this side of the lake; a pretty lakeside shrine near the Matsuba access road on the northwest; and near the other western access is a modern hotel and the much-photographed bronze statue of Takko Hime, a legendary Akita beauty who is now a dragon living in the depths of the lake.

Lake Tazawa is mainly a resort for vacationing families who sunbathe on the sand, row boats near the shore, take tour-boat rides across the lake, bike along the perimeter road, and frequent the lake's restaurants and souvenir stands.

If you want to avoid spending the night in this resort-type atmosphere, you can allot less than half a day to Lake Tazawa and still see it all. A drive around the lake takes only 40 minutes.

Besides the previously mentioned developments, there are almost no spots in the curving road wide enough to park a car without blocking traffic.

Lake Tazawa's most outstanding feature is the clarity of its water. It reaches its maximum depth quickly offshore, since its bottom is shaped more like a frypan with a ledge around it than like a wok. A freshwater source comes up from the deep bottom, a fact scientists say prevents the lake from freezing over in the cold Akita winters. Others, however, attribute this phenomenon to the wintertime goings-on at the bottom of the lake—the passionate lovemaking of the beautiful Takko Hime and her husband, Hachirōtarō.

Both Takko Hime and Hachirōtarō were once human. Hachirōtarō was a young man who very innocently caught a fish in a mountain stream. After he ate it, he got so thirsty that he had to drink water from a rapids for thirty-three days, and, as a result, he became a huge water dragon.

Since he couldn't very well return home in this condition, he dammed up a stream and made himself a lake to live in, a lake we now call Towada. His bad luck continued, however, and he was chased away from his new lake by a sorcerer. He headed south and made himself a new home, the lagoon of Hachirōgata.

Meanwhile, in a small Akita village, a very beautiful girl named Takko Hime had one great wish—to stay beautiful forever. She went to the top of a mountain to pray for 100 days, that her wish might come true. On the last day of her vigil, a voice told her to find some water to drink and her wish would be granted. She did as she was told, and immediately she also became a water dragon, violent storms began, and Lake Tazawa was formed before her eyes.

Both the sorcerer of Towada and the dragon of Hachirōgata fell in love with Lake Tazawa's beautiful dragon, and they fought each other for her love. Hachirōtarō, this time victorious, married the beautiful Takko Hime. So every year between the autumnal and vernal equinoxes, Hachirōtarō leaves his home in Hachirōgata—cramped quarters now that most of the lagoon has been reclaimed—to join his bride in the depths of Lake Tazawa. During his absences, Hachirōgata always freezes, but due to the heat of the lovers' passion, Tazawa-ko has never frozen over.

On July 20th and 21st each year, two huge dragon floats are carried into the shallow waters near Lake Tazawa's shoreline by groups of local men who festively create a reenactment of the union of the two water creatures who now winter in marital bliss somewhere in the 423 meters below the surface of Japan's deepest lake.

As romantic as this legend is, you may prefer to think of Takko Hime as she was before her transformation—the epitome of the incomparable Akita bijin, or beauty. In 1968 a bronze statue of Takko Hime standing in a demure, ethereal pose was erected on a pedestal in the shallow waters on the west side of the lake. Since then, the statue of Takko Hime the beautiful human stands serenely above the surface of Lake Tazawa, while Takko Hime the dragon and her mate keep its depths churning.

The prettiest developed site on the lake is the Mizanoishi Shrine on its northwestern shore. The old shrine has a Miyajima-like torii close to the water and a peaceful grassy lakefront. Mizanoishi, meaning royal sitting stone, was named for the time in 1648 when the second Satake lord sat on a large rock here to view the lake. If it's early evening, you may want to follow his example, because the sun setting behind the hills across the lake is indeed beautiful.

If you end your circle of the lake near its eastern access, you may be interested in the accommodations and recreational facilities of the Tazawa-ko Kōgen (Lake Tazawa plateau) on the slopes of nearby Mount Komaga. The plateau is on a local road about 10 kilometers northeast of Lake Tazawa. Buses from Tazawa-ko Station also come this way.

The Komakusa-sō kokuminshukusha[2] is near a sports complex and ski slope. Another six kilometers up the mountain is Nyūtō Onsen and the Tazawa-ko Kōgen Kokumin Kyūka Mura vacation village,[3] which has a large campground and the Nyūtō San-sō lodge. The most interesting onsen of the Nyūtō group is Kuroyu Onsen, a small complex of old thatched-roof buildings and outdoor baths. From Lake Tazawa and vicinity, you can continue on the Taza-

2. Komakusa-sō, Komagatake, Obonai, Tazawa-ko-machi, Senboku-gun, Akita-ken 014–12; tel. (01874) 3–0531.
駒草荘　〒014-12 秋田県仙北郡田沢湖町生保内駒ヶ岳
3. Tazawa-ko Kōgen Kokumin Kyūka Mura, Komagatake, Tazawa-ko-machi, Senboku-gun, Akita-ken 014–12; tel. (01874) 3–1141.
田沢湖高原国民休暇村　〒014-12 秋田県仙北郡田沢湖町駒ヶ岳

wa-ko Line or Highway 46 to Morioka, go north on Highway 341 towards Hachimantai, or make your way back to Ōmagari to continue through southeastern Akita Prefecture.

IF YOU HAPPEN TO BE on your way out of Akita through its southeastern corner in the dead of winter, specifically on February 15th, 16th, or 17th, consider stopping in the city of Yokote, 24 kilometers south of Ōmagari, to take in its two overlapping winter festivals. You can spend the night at the Kamataya Youth Hostel, a 5-minute walk from the station, or at the Sakura-sō kokuminshukusha[4] in the town of Ōmori, 10 kilometers west of Yokote on a local road.

Yokote's Kamakura Festival, which takes place on February 15th and 16th, hasn't a thing to do with the Minamoto clan's twelfth-century capital. Kamakura in this case is the Japanese equivalent of the Eskimo's igloo. City residents shape and hollow out these two-meter-high mounds of packed snow, place a mat on the packed-snow floor, a small altar on one side, and a brazier in the center. Then their children enter the kamakura, give offerings to the water god who is enshrined in the small altar, and warm themselves by broiling mochi over the brazier and drinking amazakè, a thick, sweet, sakè-based drink with a slight odor of fermentation, a delicate taste, and almost no alcohol content.

The kamakura tradition was already in place by the time the Satakes came to Akita and made Yokote a minor castle town. At one time, a serious shortage of drinking water called for a unified effort by the villagers to attract the attention of the ancient water god; this was the first Kamakura Festival. Nowadays, Yokote's kamakura village is set up every year in Yokote Park, a 15-minute walk from the station.

The Bonden Festival takes place on February 16th and 17th.

4. Sakura-sō, 165 Mochimukai, Ōmori-machi, Hiraka-gun, Akita-ken 013–05; tel. (018226) 2301.
さくら荘　〒013–05　秋田県平鹿郡大森町字持向 165

Much like Akita City's bonden celebrants, merry groups of Yokote bonden bearers noisily jostle their way to the Asahi Okayama Shrine, two kilometers south of the city.

From Yokote you can continue south on the Ōu Main Line or Highway 13 to Yamagata or head east for Iwate's Kitakami via the Kitakami Line or Highway 107.

If you've chosen to head south and its more seasonable traveling weather than that of Kamakura/Bonden time, you might want to detour through the Kurikoma Quasi-National Park. You do this by getting off the train or highway 30 kilometers south of Yokote in the city of Yuzawa, itself worth a short visit if it's time for one of its August festivals.

Yuzawa, like Kakunodate and Yokote, was a lesser castle town of the Satakes. And like Kakunodate's, its castle became the new home for Kyoto royalty. Yuzawa eased its Kyoto princess's homesickness not with cherry trees but by adding huge illuminated square lanterns painted with traditional ukiyo-e scenes to the city's Tanabata celebration. You can see Yuzawa's giant lanterns among its more typical Tanabata streamers decorating the streets every August 6th and 7th during its Tanabata E-dōrō Festival.

During the Edo period, Yuzawa, like Ōmagari, was on the route taken by daimyo traveling to the capital. Two hundred years ago, the going got pretty rough beyond Yuzawa as the entourages faced crossing the Ōu mountains which separated the Satake and Datè clan territories. Each August 23rd and 24th, you can get an idea of how such a procession appeared as it passed through the city when a "daimyo procession" of costumed young boys makes its way to Atago Park, 2 kilometers south of Yuzawa Station.

Highway 108 is a new road linking Akita and Miyagi that follows the route of these Edo-period processions. The highway begins 13 kilometers south of Yuzawa at Ogachi-machi and ends in Miyagi's delightful onsen community of Narugo (see that section). To travel this daimyo trail, known as the Senshū Line, by bus, be sure to make your connection at Ogachi's Yoko-hori Station.

Sixteen kilometers south of Ogachi on the Senshū Line is the Akinomiya Onsen Cluster—four onsen, a campground, and the Akinomiya San-sō kokuminshukusha.[5] One of these onsen, Yunomata, has an outdoor bath carved out of a huge rock.

But the daimyo route bypassed the area now known as the Kurikoma Quasi-National Park. So if the big mountain is your chosen destination, you must transfer at Yuzawa to a local road that heads across the northern flanks of the 1,628-meter-high volcanic peak. If you enjoyed Aomori Prefecture's spooky, barren Mount Osore and the Oirase's walking path past the rapids, plan to make several stops in the Kijiyama Kōgen pla-teau area, about 30 kilometers from Yuzawa on this road. The Kijiyama area is one of Tōhoku's kokeshi making centers.

On a side road heading west from the plateau is a campground; a hotel; the Doroyu (Muddy Water) Onsen, with outdoor baths of murky natural hot-spring water that is reputedly good for skin ailments and rheumatism; and the barren, sulfuric hill called Kawarage Jigoku-zan. Since the year 807, Kawarage Jigoku-zan. (Hell Mountain) has been considered a part of the spirit world like Osore-zan.

About 3 kilometers south of this turnoff back on the main road is the Oyasu Gorge, with its 8-kilometer-long walking path along the river and an onsen of the same name. One kilometer north of the Oyasu Onsen along this path, hot water and steam gush at one spot from the rocky riverbank. When the river is high in spring and fall, its water mixes with the hot water to form a pleasant warm-water swimming hole.

5. Akinomiya San-sō, Denjō, Akinomiya, Ogachi-machi, Ogachi-gun, Akita-ken 019–03; tel. (01835) 6–2146.
秋の宮山荘　〒019-03 秋田県雄勝郡雄勝町秋の宮殿上

Mount Kurikoma itself lies to the southeast of Kijiyama Kōgen at the point where the three prefecutres of Akita, Iwate, and Miyagi converge. Six kilometers beyond Oyasu Onsen, the road from Yuzawa turns into a toll road that cuts through Kurikoma's northern slopes to Iwate's Sugawa Onsen, the most popular starting point for climbing the mountain. The 1,100-meter-high onsen has a few ryokan, a hotel, and a campground. It is reached by bus ride in 2 hours from Yuzawa Station and from the opposite direction in 2 hours and 20 minutes from Iwate's Ichinoseki City, which is on the Tōhoku Expressway and the Tōhoku Main Line.

Whatever your last view of Akita—Tazawa-ko's deep, clear waters, Naraoka's earthy pottery, Yokote's winter snow huts, Yuzawa's summer lanterns, Akinomiya's big rock bath, or Kawarage Jigoku-zan's barren slopes—you'll no doubt be leaving the prefecture feeling glad you decided to pass through this side of the back country.

YAMAGATA
PREFECTURE

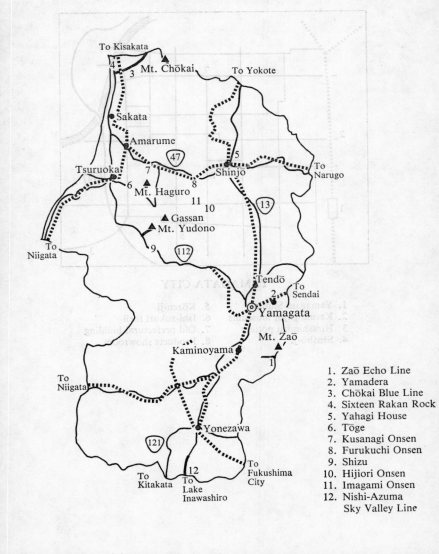

To Kisakata
Mt. Chōkai
To Yokote
Sakata
Amarume
47
Shinjō
To Narugo
Tsuruoka
Mt. Haguro
Gassan
Mt. Yudono
To Niigata
112
13
Tendō
To Sendai
Yamagata
Mt. Zaō
Kaminoyama
To Niigata
Yonezawa
121
To Kitakata
To Lake Inawashiro
To Fukushima City

1. Zaō Echo Line
2. Yamadera
3. Chōkai Blue Line
4. Sixteen Rakan Rock
5. Yahagi House
6. Tōge
7. Kusanagi Onsen
8. Furukuchi Onsen
9. Shizu
10. Hijiori Onsen
11. Imagami Onsen
12. Nishi-Azuma
    Sky Valley Line

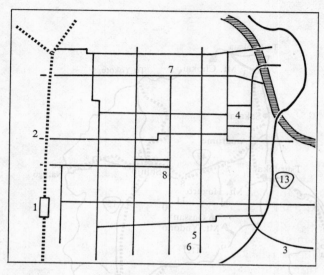

YAMAGATA CITY

1. Yamagata Station
2. Kasumigajō, museums
3. Hirashimizu pottery
4. Senshō-ji
5. Kōzen-ji
6. Ishi-zukuri torii
7. Old prefectural building
8. Products showroom

Introducing Yamagata

YAMAGATA MEANS mountain-form, an appropriate name for a prefecture bordered on all sides by mountains except for a strip on the northwest that falls into the Sea of Japan. Yamagata's mountains are meccas for sightseers, climbers, and skiers—and historically for the yamabushi, members of a strange religious sect who worshiped the three peaks of an inland range called Dewa Sanzan and who lived in these mountains throughout Yamagata's terrible winters to make themselves pure and holy. Today their followers, and the curious, still visit the sacred mountains, but they usually choose the more inviting weather of Yamagata's short, cool summers.

Between the mountains of Yamagata are the basins and the plains. Here are the big cities and the country towns. And this is where Yamagata farmers grow their famous rice, eighty percent of all Japan's cherries, more persimmons and pears than in any other prefecture, and benibana, or safflowers, once the essential ingredient in Japanese cosmetics and dyes. Wooden chips for shōgi, the traditional chesslike game, sea chests of heavy wood and elaborate ironwork, straw and yarn back pads called bandori, and baby-sitter baskets called izumeko, are also part of the heritage of these populated areas between the mountains.

273

Yamagata is where in 1690 Japan's most famous haiku poet, Bashō, wrote his two best-loved poems, one about the surging Mogami River that runs through the prefecture and the other about a peaceful hillside of temple buildings called Yamadera, or mountain temple.

Today you can follow Bashō's route through the prefecture as some Japanese tourists do or create your own itinerary. You can visit the Sea of Japan's Shōnai district with its beautiful beaches, delightful castle town of Tsuruoka, and busy port of Sakata; the temples and shrines of the yamabushi in Dewa Sanzan; the inland capital city of Yamagata, which has a rural pottery village in its city limits and a festival honoring the safflower during Tōhoku's big festival week in August; and, finally, the mountains of Zaō, in winter dotted with huge snow monsters and thousand of skiers.

> From far Hot Springs Hills
> All the way to Windy Beach—
> How cool the evening view!

> The river Mogami
> Has drowned the hot, summer sun
> And sunk it in the sea!

These are the words Bashō used to sum up his visit to Yamagata. His journey was from east to west and then along the Sea of Japan, mainly on foot but at times on horseback or by boat. Today you can use the highways and train lines crisscrossing the prefecture on your mission, which, much like Bashō's centuries ago, is simply getting to know the back country's mountain-form prefecture.

The Shōnai District

AFTER AKITA CITY, the Ōu Main Line begins to turn inland once again toward Fukushima City to complete the elongated circle through Tōhoku that it forms with the Tōhoku Main Line. But if you've fallen in love with the peaceful Sea of Japan, you may not be quite ready to leave it; and there are several good reasons not to.

In addition to the pretty coastline yet to come along the Akita–Yamagata border, majestic Mount Chōkai hasn't yet loomed into view. Nor have you seen the Yamagata Prefecture cities of Sakata and Tsuruoka with interesting bits of their back-country castle-town pasts on display. And, finally, you haven't yet been to the mountaintop home of the yamabushi, a trio of peaks worshiped by an unusual religious sect of mountain men.

Furthermore, the good news is that JNR's Uetsu Main Line connecting the capital cities of Akita and Niigata, Highway 7 from Aomori to Niigata, and Highway 112 from Tsuruoka to Yamagata City make these spots easy and logical stopovers as you leave the back country for the other Japan to the south.

South of Akita City, the highway does a somewhat better job of hugging the coast than does the train, but both touch the shore at Kisakata, the northernmost point of the poet Bashō's journey to the far provinces. Here he wrote one of his most beautiful prose descriptions, about the peaceful lagoon of Kisa-kata. He wrote of its beautiful Matsushima-like islets but then qualified his simile: "While Matsushima had a gay, laughing beauty, Kisakata's face was full of bitterness and rue. There was a sense of the desolate loneliness and sorrow of a tormented soul."

The poet's sensitivity must have given him insight into the future of the lovely little lagoon, because today it is no more. In 1804 a huge earthquake lifted the sea floor, and Bashō's beautiful pine-clad islets are now in the middle of rice paddies. So, unfortunately, if you're following the poet's course, you will not be able to share his Kisakata at all. Maybe the lagoon's "tormented soul" has at last found peace as fertile farmland.

There is a youth hostel in Kisakata if you want to spend some time lamenting the fickleness of nature.

Just south of Kisakata is the Chōkai Quasi-National Park, which is really a towering Fuji-like volcanic peak rising steeply from nearly the edge of the sea. Enough room remains between the mountain and the sea, however, to bring you to a decision point. The train and the highway squeak between the two, but there is also the Chōkai Blue Line, a U-shaped toll road from Akita's Kamihama to Yamagata's Fukura that detours from Highway 7 across the mountain and back.

On a bright clear day in midsummer you may want to choose this mountain course because the 2,200-meter-high summit of Chōkai offers an outstanding view of the Sea of Japan from Akita's Oga Peninsula in the north to Niigata's Sado Island in the south. Tōhoku's other Fujis, Mount Iwaki to the north and Mount Iwate to the east, are also visible.

Although conical in appearance, Chōkai has twin peaks from separate eruptions. After 150 years of silence, the dormant volcano surprised residents in 1974 with a shower. The high snow-country mountain has isolated patches of snow on its slopes even in late summer, and the skiing season lasts well into spring. Accommodations along the toll road include a campground and the Taihei-zan-sō kokuminshukusha.[1]

To further complicate your decision-making process, note that the shoreline between Kisakata and Fukura—which the tollroad bypasses—is a magnificent blend of rocky coves, pine trees, and sand beaches with the dark tile roofs of small villages sandwiched between the transportation arteries above and the lovely shore below.

Fukura is where the toll road rejoins the highway just north of Fukura Station. The town offers camping in the pine trees along the beach as well as a seaside youth hostel and a kokuminshukusha, the Torimi-sō.[2] This particularly lovely stretch of beach is also the site of an unusual man-improved rock formation jutting out into the sea.

The Jūroku Rakan Iwa (Sixteen Disciples Rock) is still partially visible on a promontory just north of the toll-road intersection. In 1864 the priest of the local Zen temple began carving twenty-two religious statues on the rocky sea-eroded shoreline to protect local fishermen from the rough waves that complicated their work. He carved a large Buddha in the center and two lesser Buddhas on either side. Then he surrounded them with sixteen disciples and four animals. Over the past 120 years the waves he sought to control have taken a heavy toll on the carvings, but you can visit what the sea has left. Perhaps the ravaged sculptures did take some of the abuse meant for Fukura fishing boats over the years.

Unless you're heading south to Niigata to catch a train to Tokyo from there, the beach at Fukura will be your last glimpse of the Sea of Japan this trip, since both train and road turn inland

1. Taihei-zan-sō, Chōkai-san, Fukura, Yusa-chō, Akumi-gun, Yamagata-ken 999–85; tel. (02342) 3–4911.
大平山荘　〒996-85 山形県飽海郡遊佐町吹浦鳥海山
2. Torimi-sō, Nishihama, Fukura, Yusa-chō, Akumi-gun, Yamagata-ken 999–83; tel. (02347) 7–2240.
とりみ荘　〒999-83 山形県飽海郡遊佐町吹浦西浜

to pass through the Shōnai Plain. As anyone traveling through the area when it isn't covered in snow can readily tell, Shōnai is rice country, the prefecture's most notable producer of the famous Yamagata rice. The nearby Shōnai Dunes are one of Japan's largest melon and tulip growing centers. But of greater interest to the visitor are the two former castle towns of the Sakai clan of Shōnai—Sakata and Tsuruoka.

SAKATA MEANS sakè fields, and, although the city is still turning Shōnai rice into sakè, Yamagata's second largest city is better known today for its modern industrial complex and bustling international port. Sakata has little of its former castle-town charm left, but the few remaining patches of old Sakata are worth at least a few hours of your time.

Thirty-six samurai escaping the wrath of the shogun Yoritomo in the early days of the thirteenth century settled at the spot where the Mogami River joined the Sea of Japan. Yoritomo's troops had invaded the territory of the Fujiwara family of Hiraizumi, seeking revenge for the clan's protecting of Yoshitsune from his brother's very unbrotherly intentions (see Iwate's Hiraizumi section). The refugee samurai came to Sakata first of all to save their heads and secondly to find a new way to make a living. They wisely chose to exploit the natural attributes of their new home and went into the sea-transport business. The seaport at the river's mouth also bordered the Shōnai Plain, and for the next 700 years Sakata prospered as the center for distribution of Shōnai rice to distant Edo and Osaka population centers via the Sea of Japan and Lake Biwa near Kyoto. Today Shōnai rice still travels through Sakata; however, as an international port, Sakata also handles much more, such as lumber from Russia. In fact, any stray foreigners wandering the streets of Sakata may be taken for Russian sailors, which may be a pleasant change for European travelers who are tired of being taken for Americans. Even the city's tourist brochure welcomes visitors in Russian as well as English—but all the useful information is in Japanese.

If you have come to the city for just an hour or two, the Homma Art Museum is the place to go, but not necessarily for its art. Go to see the 170-year-old former imperial guest house set in a lovely old garden. It comes with your admission to the modern concrete art museum that now takes up one of the garden's corners.

Sketches of Japanese history frequently describe the strictly class-conscious society of feudal Japan—the samurai, farmers, craftspeople and, at the very bottom, merchants. As the feudal period wound down, however, there was a mingling of these classes based on economic necessity; the skill-less samurai and local rulers got hungry, while some of the lowly but clever merchants got rich. Such was the case in Sakata in the late Edo period.

The Hommas of Sakata had been merchants in the port city since the seventeenth century, trading mostly in medicine, china, and rice and using the profits to accumulate vast areas of Shōnai's fertile land. The family business soon accounted for over half of the city's tax revenue. In addition, the lowly Homma merchants were able to donate to shrines and charities as well as as to put money into improving local farming techniques. They even made loans above and beyond their taxes to the ruling Sakai clan as well as to the Uesugi clan in neighboring Yonezawa. Later, they bought the guns and bullets the Sakai clan used to resist the Meiji Restoration forces. By the third generation, the Hommas had been given a samurai name and the right to carry swords.

Of greater significance to us today are the two beautiful houses, both still standing, the Hommas built for their back-country lord to entertain visiting dignitaries from Edo in proper style. The Homma-ke Hontei, the Homma Family Main House, is a massive structure built in 1768 to house visiting government inspectors. Although you can't go inside today, you can see the exterior by taking a 10-minute bus ride from the station toward Hamahata-chō.

Forty-five years after they built the main house, the Hommas built a second house for the Sakai family. This one was a more modest two-story wooden house overlooking a beautiful garden. The Hommas had intended it as a make-work project for unemployed dock workers one winter and then for the Sakai family's own use. But the house was to become a guest house for Tokugawa shogunate officials and, after the restoration, for representatives of the imperial government and other dignitaries. The Taishō emperor stayed there in 1925.

The Hommas donated it to the city as an art musuem in 1948, and today any one of us can walk through the old building to admire its rich woodwork; Edo period screens, hanging scrolls, and ceramics; view of the garden; and place in history. The new art museum, an imposing structure with a vast sloping roof, was built twenty years later and now houses part of the Homma family art collection. The museum complex is only a 5-minute walk to the right as you leave the station. It is across the street from a new Pizza Hut, whose unexpected presence is further evidence that you should be exploring the back country now, before it becomes indistinguishable from the rest of modern Japan.

The Hommas, by the way, are still a Sakata trading company. Once Japan's biggest landowners, with 2,700 peasants growing rice in their fields, they lost most of their land to the tenants through Occupation land reforms; they then turned to the warehousing end of Sakata's rice industry.

If you have time to explore more of the city, see the old Homma main house and the nearby Sakata City Bussan-kan, the City Products Showroom. Here you can see a complete selection of local products before selecting a treasure or a souvenir. In the former category is sturdy wooden furniture made with craftsmanship handed down from the makers of Sakata funa-dansu, beautiful ships' safes made of heavy wood and nearly covered in metal-work. Today the finest examples of old funa-dansu are in Tōhoku museums such as the Chidō Museum in Tsuruoka and the Keiko-kan in Aomori City; a few are sold at very high prices.

More practical as souvenirs than furniture and yet also part of the Sakata tradition are such items as locally brewed sakè made, of course, from Shōnai rice; unique strawberry-sized eggplants pickled in mustard; painted clay dolls called kawara ningyo, and dolls bundled in baskets called izumeko ningyo. Relatively in-expensive at Sakata and Tsuruoka antique shops and much nicer than the newer souvenir versions are antique kawara ningyo, which were colorfully painted with natural dyes and displayed on Girls' Day in Shōnai homes until just after World War II. The izumeko ningyo also represent an old custom. Tōhoku farm families once wrapped their babies securely in layers of cloth and bedding and bundled them into big thick baskets called izumeko originally used to keep the heat in cooked rice. In this way the babies were kept both warm and safely immobile while the rest of the family attended to their farming duties. This straw basket baby-sitter was used in other parts of Tōhoku as well; in the Nambu region of eastern Aomori and Iwate it is known as ejiko.

If you are still wandering in the city, visit the row of eleven 100-year-old thick-walled rice warehouses still in use today. The Sankyosōko are across the river beyond the Homma main house. Hiyoriyama Kōen, a hillside park overlooking the harbor, is also popular with residents and visitors. The view includes the oldest wooden lighthouse in Japan, the entire harbor area, and the Mogami River as it feeds into the Sea of Japan. Also in the park is a monument to Bashō, who spent nine days in town a few centuries ago. Finally, if you've hit Sakata in winter, be sure to pay a visit to some fellow travelers. Over 1,300 Siberian swans winter at the mouth of the Mogami every year from November to March by the Dewa Bridge. As you shiver in the icy winds com-ing off the Sea of Japan, it might warm you a bit to note that these large graceful birds are here to enjoy the Japanese snow country's "mild" winter. (See Aomori's Along Mutsu Bay section for more on the visiting swans.)

You may be wondering about the squat-looking little island you spotted on the way down from Fukura or from your high perch at Hiyoriyama Kōen park. It's name is Tobishima, and it is 38 kilometers out to sea. Its 1,100 residents maintain a connection with the mainland via a daily ferry from Sakata. If this out-of-the-way island appeals to the adventurer in you, you can visit—but you won't be its first tourist. Surprisingly, the 200-household island has eighteen minshuku, ten ryokan, and a youth hostel.

The 2.3-square-kilometer island's main attractions are its seascape and its very remoteness. And if Tobishima isn't remote enough, a boat will take you to Oshakujima, a pillar-like rock formation 1.5 kilometers to the west of the island, unload you for a day of swimming and fishing, and pick you up later.

Tobishima has been inhabited since Jōmon times and is known for its umineko, migratory black-winged seagulls, who come for the summer with their aggravating meow-like screech. The wild flowers of Tobishima Kansō and the Ogami Shrine sea cave are also local attractions. If you make it to the cave shrine on the island's north coast, note its "dragon scales," or mineral deposits formed by drops of water seeping through cracks in the rock that are worshiped by the islanders. Until recently this sacred place was off limits to women; today female residents still will not come to Ogami Shrine, but women visitors are welcome.

Ferries leave Sakata's Higashi Futō (East Pier) at 8 a.m. and 1:40 p.m. from mid-July to mid-August and at 9:20 a.m. the rest of the year.

AFTER SEEING WHAT you can of Sakata and perhaps Tobishima, you must tear yourself from the Sea of Japan to head inland to one of Tōhoku's most delightful towns for wandering winding streets and soaking up the warm feelings of old Japan. Although nearly as populous as Sakata, Tsuruoka gives off a completely different aura. Like Sakata it has a few relics of its castle-town days to visit, but, in this case, you need some time to walk the city to discover and enjoy what lies in between the tourist spots.

To find old Tsuruoka, you have to get beyond the bland, new part of town around the station. Thrusting its multistoried modern head far above neighboring residences along narrow winding lanes and old-fashioned basket, fish, and vegetable shops is the comfortable business hotel, the Sannō Plaza.[3] By going deeper into old Tsuruoka (and your pockets) you can stay at the charming Tsuruoka Hotel,[4] which is really a lovely old-fashioned ryokan. And a youth hostel is also in the city.

Other than the old downtown through which a small river peacefully winds, Kyoto-style, and the old residential areas where homes are hidden behind high fences and heavily planted gardens, you'll find the sights of Tsuruoka conveniently concentrated around the old castle grounds now called Tsuruoka Jōshi Kōen, or Tsuru-oka Castle Park, a 30-minute walk from the station. The station is on the northern edge of the city, and the park is to the southwest. But like many castle towns that still retain much of their original flavor, Tsuruoka's backtracking and winding streets, designed to confuse the enemy invaders, still succeed with present-day visitors. Thus, you'll probably have to stop for directions a few times—and discover the people of Tsuruoka warm and attentive, appreciative of the rare foreigner who has thought enough of their city to come.

The castle no longer stands, another victim of Meiji-era anti-feudalism, but the wooded castle site has several other buildings

3. Hotel Sannō Plaza, 6–8, Sannō-machi, Tsuruoka-shi, Yamagata-ken 997; tel. (0235) 22–6501.
山王プラザ 〒997 山形県鶴岡市山王町 6–8
4. Tsuruoka Hotel, 1–18, Hon-chō 2-chome, Tsuruoka-shi, Yamagata-ken 997; tel. (0235) 22–1135.
鶴岡ホテル 〒997 山形県鶴岡市本町二丁目 1–18

and some sections of the moat remaining. A nicely aged shrine now stands where the main castle keep was, and a tiny local-history museum with old maps and documents is nearby. Along the south moat is the Taishōkan, a 1916 example of Taishō-era architecture still in use as an office building. Although the sturdy old building looks classic to us, it was an extremely modern structure for the back country when it was built to honor the new emperor.

Just to the southeast of the park is the Chidōkan, a National Historic Property, not to be confused with the Chidō Hakubutsukan, the museum complex to the west of the park. The Chidōkan used to be a sprawling campus for the young sons of Shōnai samurai who from age nine learned archery, martial arts, and horsemanship as well as scholarly subjects here. Today only a few of the 180-year-old school buildings remain.

The Chidō Hakubutsukan contains the most interesting of Tsuruoka's preserved history. Its collection of local artifacts and crafts are housed in a group of old buildings, museum pieces themselves. You'll want to allot a few hours to wandering through this compact but absorbing collection of the Shōnai district's history.

The museum is on the site of the Sakai retirement residence immediately west of the park, just beyond the tennis courts. The old house and garden remain, along with the Sakai family treasures, which are on display in the house. The remaining buildings were constructed for the museum or moved here to become part of Tsuruoka's preserved history. The two western-style buildings are from the Meiji era's nationwide Westernization zeal; one was a police station, and the other a government office building. The Meiji emperor visited the latter building, which today is an Important Cultural Treasure of Japan.

Another such treasure is the three-storied thatched-roof farmhouse, the Shibuya Family House. It was built in 1822 in the little farming community of Tamugimata near Dewa Sanzan and moved to the Chidō Hakubutsukan in 1965.

The Tamugimata villagers built their houses big, three or four stories high, to accommodate the many religious pilgrims who passed through on their way to the sacred mountains. But when the Meiji reforms necessitated a clear separation of shrines and temples, the worshipers of Dewa Sanzan had a rough time practicing their religion, which included elements of both Shintoism and Buddhism. So the little village lost most of its pilgrim business and turned to making charcoal and raising silkworms. Their now-empty upper floors were nearly perfect for the silkworm business except that they needed more light than their sloping thatched roofs let in. Thus, a small window was cut in the thatch called a taka happo, which is now a unique characteristic of Shōnai rural minka, homes the Shibuya House represents for the city folk who would normally never make it out to tiny Tamugimata.

The museum's treasure house is indeed just that, with a wonderful assortment of crafts, old furnishings, and implements out of Shōnai's past. Inside are two floors of funa-dansu, pottery, wooden tubs for making pickles and miso, lacquerware, old shop signs, and the like.

Here you'll also see a collection of bandori, strange-looking flat straw and yarn rounds with dangling cords and straps. These traditional back pads were worn by Shōnai people as protective padding between them and their loads. They range in design from spartan to elaborately decorated, the latter being the iwai, or congratulatory, bandori that the Shōnai bride used when she bore her trousseau to her new home. Traditionally, the iwai bandori was a wedding gift from her new husband, handmade by him for his bride. Bandori means flying squirrel in the local dialect, which is what someone wearing one must have looked like, with the wide cross piece above the round pad sticking out beyond both shoulders.

After touring the museum, pick any side street heading towards the river to the east and you'll end up downtown. Along one of these streets is the Maria-en Tenshu-dō, a 1892 Catholic church designed by a French missionary. Its gate, however, is pure Japanese, in Edo-period style, the site having belonged to a retainer of the Sakai clan.

Throughout this former samurai neighborhood, called Baba-chō, you'll find traces of Tsuruoka's feudal days. Even downtown offers much more of the old Tsuruoka than the new. Here you'll find a scattering of antique shops and, if you're lucky, a rare funa-dansu or black lacquered Shōnai tansu with its characteristic naturally rusted brown hardware. These shops also have good selections of the more affordable and portable antique kawara ningyo.

Near the Sannō Plaza Hotel is the Togashi Rōsoku-ten, a 300-year-old candle shop still in business for the relatively few customers who still appreciate—and are willing to pay for—the labor-intensive art of handmade candles. The Sakai lord used to bring these hand-painted candles as gifts for the shogun on his regular trips to Edo. Once, when the candles arrived broken and no candle maker in Edo could repair them properly, the Tsuruoka candle craftsman was sent for. He became the number-one candle maker in Japan and was given the right to wear the Sakai family crest.

The candles are made by hand-dipping the papered wick in wax again and again to form concentric layers. Finally a secret-formula liquid is used so the wax will accept paint, and the candles are decorated with traditional designs, some on solid red, gold, or silver backgrounds. You can watch the process at the shop located between the hotel and the large shrine on the main road leading to the station.

If you are heading for Niigata after Tsuruoka, both the highway and the Uetsu Main Line will take you back out to the coast for a scenic ride south and out of the back country. You probably won't notice your passing from Tōhoku into Niigata Prefecture, but at one time you would have had to pass through the Nezugaseki barrier, one of the three man-made entrances to the back country in existence since ancient times. The other two Michinoku barriers were at Shirakawa in the mountains north of Nikkō and at Nakoso along the Pacific coast.

At Nezu there used to be a fence stretching from the water to the top of a nearby hill where guards stood watch in a tower designed to control the comings and goings of visitors to the back country. Today you'll pass through the Nezugaseki barrier without ceremony, except perhaps for a flicker of regret at having to leave so soon.

But for those who aren't yet ready to say sayonara to Tōhoku, there's lots left to see—beginning with the mountain home of the yamabushi, Dewa Sanzan.

Dewa Sanzan
And The Mogami River

DEWA SANZAN—the three neighboring peaks of Haguro, Gassan, and Yudono—have been worshipped since ancient times by members of an ascetic sect which combines elements of Buddhism, Taoism, Shintoistic primitive mountain worship, mysticism, and shamanism. Popularly known as yamabushi, mountain ascetics, few if any of them still inhabit the frigid slopes of the sacred mountains full time. But their mountainside of religious buildings among tall trees remains, attracting pilgrimages by present-day followers and other curious visitors.

Modern pilgrims still put on traditional yamabushi garb to make the difficult pilgrimage on foot up Mount Haguro and back down, then to the mountaintop shrines of Gassan and Yudono. Tourists can follow this tradition or make use of modern toll roads going up the mountains.

On Haguro-san are found almost all of the religious buildings of the yamabushi and nowadays even all the images of the deities of all three peaks, since it is the only mountain accessible to worshipers all year round. Its buildings, spread over the mountainside, are collectively known as Dewa Sanzan Shrine even though many of them are Buddhist temples and the religion of Dewa Sanzan's yamabushi is considered a subsect of Buddhism's Shugen-dō sect.

Shugen-dō's Haguro subsect was founded by an imperial crown prince, Prince Hōshi, who, during the early seventh century, gave up his title to become a monk. He took the name of Kōkai and traveled all over Japan. While on a beach in Dewa Province, which today includes Akita and Yamagata, he saw a big black bird with three legs who led him first to Mount Haguro (which means black wings) and then to the other two holy peaks. Kōkai stayed in Dewa Sanzan teaching his unusual brand of Buddhism until he died at ninety-on. He is buried at the top of Haguro-san, the only imperial grave site in Tōhoku.

Kōkai's mountain ascetics believed that living in the depths of the snow-country mountains, meditating, sleeping out of doors, and other such sacrifices of bodily comfort would make them pure and holy. They would practice their mysticism in neighboring villages where they would sometimes draw their swords in search of "donations" to keep the sect going. Besides their swords, the mountain ascetics were also known for carrying large conch-shell horns and wearing distinctive clothing.

Bashō visited the yamabushi on his journey, and, although he would not reveal the secret yamabushi rites he saw on the mountains, he did describe their "cloisters stand[ing] row upon row, where mountain ascetics diligently practiced these disciplines. The good emanating from this holy hill is most wonderful and awe-inspring. It is a truly marvelous place and will surely prosper forever."

This time the poet's predictions were a little off. The number of cloisters in Tōge Hamlet at the foot of Mount Haguro has dwindled from a record of 360 to 35, as the number of yamabushi followers decreases over time. Partly at fault for this decline in popularity were Meiji-era reforms that required clear separation of Japan's two major religions, making it difficult for a hybrid such as the yamabushi practiced to continue unchallenged. Additionally, the hardships of the yamabushi life style on the snowy mountainsides of Dewa Sanzan has stiff competition from the alternatives available to Japanese young men today. The habitat of the mountain warriors, however, still offers the visitor an interesting stopover between the Shōnai district and the capital city of Yamagata, both for its historical and religious significance and for its mountain scenery and recreation opportunities.

Religious pilgrims begin with Mount Haguro, and so should the tourist who finds the yamabushi world of interest. Buses from Tsuruoka Station go through the town of Haguro and up the two-kilometer-long Haguro-san Driveway toll road to the main part of the religious complex. The Haguro Kokumin Kyūka Mura,[1] with a lodge, camping facilities, and skiing and nature trails, is near the toll-road entrance.

But there's a more interesting—if more exhausting—way to see Haguro-san. The bus passes the traditional entrance to the mountain at Tōge, where the pilgrims get off to walk the 2,446 stone steps through the tall cedar trees to the summit. To help you decide whether to join them, here is what you'll find along the path: from the road you'll see the largest torii in Tōhoku, a cement job twenty meters high and fifteen across. Also in Tōge are the Ezokan, a small museum displaying the area's prehistoric past, and the Ōgon-dō Pavilion, an Important Cultural Treasure housing six statues of Jizō and thought to have been built by Yoritomo to celebrate his victory after he conquered the back country in 1193.

Through the torii is the zuishinmon, a modest thatched-roof temple gate that marks the beginning of the sacred precinct of Dewa Sanzan Shrine. Long ago, pilgrims would strip and bathe in the small stream you'll pass over to purify themselves before

1. Haguro Kokumin Kyūka Mura, Tōge, Haguro-machi, Higashitagawa-gun, Yamagata-ken 997–02; tel. (023562) 4270.
羽黒国民休暇村　〒997-02 山形県東田川郡羽黒町手向

going any further into the sacred grounds. Further on, the huge tree to the left of the path is Ojiichan (Grandfather) Sugi, a 1,000-year-old, forty-two-meter-high National Natural Treasure that stands alone since its mate, Obaachan (Grandmother) Sugi, was destroyed in a typhoon. Before the path starts to climb, you'll see the five-storied pagoda that is a 600-year-old National Treasure. It is a replacement for the original, which was built in 980.

From the pagoda on, you'll be doing some real uphill legwork as the stone steps climb through 300- to 600-year-old cryptomerias whose shade makes the path almost tunnel-like. Eventually, to your relief, the Gassai-den will come into view. This is the main temple, which houses the three gods of Dewa Sanzan. Here you'll rejoin those who stayed on the bus and, between deep breaths, you can fill them in on what they missed along the 2,446 stone steps.

Because the Gassai-den houses the deities from each of the three sacred peaks it has three separate plaques bearing the names of the gods under its two-meter-thick thatched roof. The pond in front is sacred and is the home of the dragon gods. Traditionally, pilgrims offered mirrors to this pond and so far over 500 old metal mirrors have been fished out. The best of the batch are displayed in the Dewa Sanzan History Museum on the temple grounds.

The temple bell is also very special. Its thatched-roof tower is the second oldest structure on the mountain, and the bell itself, cast in 1275, is an Important Cultural Treasure. It was a gift from the Kamakura shogunate to the sacred mountain in solemn gratitude to the dragon gods of Haguro-san for their sinking of the invading Mongolian fleet of Kublai Khan.

The grave of Kōkai, the imperial prince who founded the temple, is nearby. As a royal gravesite, it is administered by the Imperial Household Agency.

After visiting the deities of Haguro-san, pilgrims traditionally take another path across three leagues of grass, three leagues of forest, and three leagues of rocks to the summit of Gassan. Although Gassan's deity is now in the Gassai-den, modern believers still want to visit the modest shrine atop the mountain. If you're sticking with them, note that some now take a bus from Haguro-san to Gassan's eighth station, located in a marshy area called Midagahara. Midagahara is 1,400 meters up the 1,900-meter-high mountain, and you still have a 2-hour hike to the top, where a fantastic view of the surrounding countryside and the Sea of Japan awaits you.

From Gassan's summit it's a 9-kilometer hike to Yudono-san's shrine. You may have trouble finding it if you aren't forewarned that the deity of Yudono-san lives not in a building but in a hot-water cascade. A very small building and a signpost mark the holy falls. Pilgrims take off their shoes and climb down to the rock hit by the holy water to offer their prayers. If you're skipping the hiking itinerary but the sacred falls sounds interesting, the 2.6-kilometer-long Yudono-san Driveway toll road will get you very close. The toll road is off Highway 112, which connects Tsuruoka and Yamagata City.

Most visitors to Dewa Sanzan today are more interested in their own bodily pleasures than in the ascetic ways of the yamabushi, and for them Dewa Sanzan's biggest attraction is the Gassan Ski Resort that opens once the fiercest winter weather subsides in April and continues through July. Accommodations for skiers and summer sightseers are available in the tiny hamlet of Shizu at a campground, in minshuku, or at the nearby Gassan-sō kokumin-shukusha.[2] The ski area is also along Highway 112.

THE MOGAMI RIVER will be next on your itinerary if you chose to see the yamabushi territory of Haguro-san but eliminated the hike across the mountains to Gassan and Yudono-san, for you're in a good location for a tour of the mighty Mogami, the 250-kilo-

2. Gassan-sō, Shizu, Nishikawa-machi, Nishitagawa-gun, Yamagata-ken 990–09; tel. (02377) 5–2117.
　月山荘　〒990–09　山形県西田川郡西川町志津

meter-long river which winds through the prefecture to the Sea of Japan. The river is historically significant as a transportation artery through the territory and has been known for centuries for the difficulty of navigating its rapids and strong currents, a problem now eased by modern technology.

The most beautiful stretch of the Mogami is north of Haguro-san along Highway 47 and the Rikuu West Line which runs from Amarume to Shinjō where it connects with the Ōu Main Line for Yamagata City. You can see the river from the train or highway or, for a firsthand look, from a sasabune, or long flat-bottomed boat, guided by a folk-song-singing navigator who appears to have stepped right out of your image of what an old-time backcountry boatman should be.

Bashō took the river boat tour, enjoying the feeling of "thick mountains hanging over us on either side." Here he wrote one of his most famous haiku, making the Mogami a national celebrity.

> Gathering as it goes
> All the rains of June, how swiftly
> The Mogami River flows!

As the poet says, the scenery here is one of steep, wooded canyon walls rising sharply on both sides of the wide, now tamer, Mogami. It is indeed a beautiful sight.

You can take a bus from Haguro-san to Kasanagi Onsen, famous for its fresh water crabs and the 120-meter-high Shiraito no taki, a waterfall Bashō described as "white threads (falling) through spaces in the greenery." From May to September, sasabune river boats leaving from the onsen take tourists along the Mogami River several times a day to Furukuchi, 8 kilometers away. From Furukuchi it's a 25-minute bus ride to Shinjō on the Ōu Main Line.

If you have time, you might want visit the Shinjō area before heading south to Yamagata City. Several old-fashioned onsen and a restored eighteenth-century farmhouse can be found nearby.

The castle town itself has run into hard times in the past. It was prosperous until the Edo period when it suffered from famine in 1755. Later, the castle and half the town were burned during resistance to the Meiji Restoration. One survivor of such hardships was the Yahagi family house. Built in the mid-eighteenth century, the thatched-roof farm house has been moved to the Hagino Kōminkan civic center in the Izumida section of town, about 4 kilometers north of the station. It is an Important Cultural Property of Japan.

Finally, Shinjō is the gateway to two remote onsen between itself and Dewa Sanzan. The Hijiori Onsen faces a section of rapids on a branch of the Mogami near the foothills of the sacred mountains. It has been attracting visitors since it was founded in 1390 by a yamabushi. Hijiori's old-fashioned thatched-roof inns have only recently been joined by a modern ryokan, but the quiet, out-of-the-way atmosphere of the old-style onsen continues. The onsen is a 75-minute bus ride from Shinjō Station.

Reaching the even more remote Imagami Onsen entails a bus ride to Kadokawa and then a 12-kilometer-long walk. But the isolated onsen deserves mention because the strange mysticism of Dewa Sanzan has spilled over into its foothills at Imagami. This is a nembutsu, or prayer, onsen founded in 1724 by a hunter who saw the Buddha in the water's steam and realized the sinful ways of his occupation. He then undertook the less brutal line of work of an onsen keeper at the location of his vision.

Pilgrims who come here to pray do so—while bathing—to images conveniently located at a tubside altar. Such soak-and-pray sessions are serious worshiping for those who come. The onsen is open only from July to September.

Both Highway 13 and the Ōu Main Line will take you southward following the course of the Mogami to Yamagata City, 60 kilometers from Shinjō and eons away from the mountain warriors of Dewa Sanzan.

Yamagata City and Yamadera

YAMAGATA'S CAPITAL and largest city is in the middle of the mountain-formed prefecture in a basin that fills with snow in winter. It has all the amenities of a back-country metropolis, is a convenient transportation center, and hosts the prefecture's educational and cultural institutions—the university, the prefectural museum, the prefectural art museum, and the Hanagasa Festival, Tōhoku's fourth largest August festival.

But the two most interesting spots in the big city are its own unusual city museum and the old rural pottery village, within its city limits, that has somehow managed to retain the country potter atmosphere that gives Japanese pottery purchases significance beyond their earthy beauty.

The Ōu Main Line comes through the city on its way south to Fukushima and north to Akita, and the Senzan Line connects it with Miyagi's Sendai as does Highway 48 via the sprawling onsen town of Tendō. Even if you aren't planning to travel the Yamagata-Sendai route, if you've come as far as Yamagata City you must visit the old hillside temple complex of Yamadera, only 13 kilometers away by bus or train.

Coming into Yamagata City from Shinjō, you'll pass through the city of Tendō, a former castle town with a newly developed onsen section and a small mingei museum, both near the station.

As you pass through, you'll be going by the source of nearly all the shōgi chips produced in Japan. Shōgi is a chesslike game played by moving wooden chips across a board. Tendō gained this unusual distinction out of necessity. Towards the end of the Tokugawa Period, times were hard, the safflower crop, their main source of income, wasn't selling well, and, due to a lack of tax revenue from his struggling subjects, the Tendō lord had to reduce the salaries of his samurai by fifty percent. To save the hungry samurai, a craftsman from Yonezawa was brought in to teach them a new skill—the art of making shōgi chips.

You can buy a set of shōgi chips as your souvenir of Yamagata from most omiyage shops in the Yamagata City/Yamadera area.

Yamagata City itself has the usual cluster of business hotels around the station, but you can "do" the city in less than a day. A good tourist map of the city is displayed at the bus station adjoining the JNR station.

A short walk across the tracks to the north of the station is a park called Kasumigajō Kōen, once the site of the Mogami clan's castle. The Tokugawa Shogunate abolished the Mogami supremacy over the district and then appointed a succession of nonresident daimyō to rule the area from Kasumi Castle. Today the people of Yamagata have taken over the wooded site for their recreation facilities and museums, and only a few sections of the moat and retaining walls remain.

Getting a glimpse of Yamagata's past is a convenient one-stop effort for the traveler because not only are the prefectural and city museums in the park, but there is also a modern prefectural art museum just outside the castle grounds in a complex of equally modern government buildings.

The Yamagata Prefectural Museum is much like the other prefectural museums of Tōhoku. Exhibits of the prefecture's geology, plants, and animals lead into the archeological and folk customs and crafts sections which are of greater interest to the foreign visitor. In the latter category are a reconstructed farmhouse scene and a display from the days when the Mogami River was alive with rice and safflower traders making their way through the rapids to the Sea of Japan at Sakata. Yamagata City was a popular stop in those days both for pilgrims to Dewa Sanzan and for Tōhoku daimyo passing through on their way to Edo.

Just behind this architecturally bland modern building is the Saiseikan, a fascinating Meiji-era prefectural hospital which is now the city museum. It's a strange-looking Western-style building, built in 1878 as a tiered circle around an atrium with a central tower, giving it a wedding cake appearance. It was saved from destruction by the city fathers in 1965 when progress demanded the land the old building occupied. The building was moved piece by piece out of the way of modern Japan and reconstructed at its present location among the trees of Yamagata's feudal days. The reconstruction itself is carefully documented in the museum's second floor with examples of original hinges, nails, and even pieces of plaster on display.

The circular building was a medical school as well as a hospital. Two years after it was established, an Austrian doctor, Albrecht Von Loretz, came to Yamagata to teach Western medicine. Drawings, photos, texts, and medical equipment of Yamagata medicine's early Westernization fill much of the museum. The building itself, however, now an Important Cultural Treasure of Japan, is the main attraction.

Outside the park's main entrance, you can pick out the Yamagata Prefectural Art Museum by the fountains in front of the low modern building. The emphasis inside is on the modern, too, with many Western-style sculptures and paintings on display. But there are also some old hanging scrolls, pieces of folk art, and a graphic depiction of Bashō's journey north by the well-known artist and poet Yosano Buson.

Lacking the charm of the Saiseikan but making up for it in size, the huge, new prefectural hospital across the street from the art museum is a good place to pick up a taxi for the pottery village of Hirashimizu. You could also go back to the station for a bus destined for Odachi, Nishi Zaō or Iwanami, get off the bus at Hirashimizu, and walk ten minutes uphill until you come to the rural pottery village just off the big city's busy bypass.

The Hirashimizus had been an important samurai family in the Mogami clan since the Nara period who later became leaders of the small village which bears their name. On the way to the potters' farmhouses you'll see a plaque beside a 1,000-year-old holly tree that was planted by the original family members who settled here.

Spread along a tree-lined stream at the foot of Mount Chitose, Hirashimizu has the feeling of being much, much further from the bypass traffic of modern Japan than it actually is. Among the prosperous-looking, old fashioned, but not necessarily old, farmhouses and narrow winding and climbing roads are five potters whom you can find by following their signs or asking at small stores.

The pottery at the Seiryūgama is the finest in town. It has been exhibited in America and Europe and was awarded a grand prize at the Brussels World Expo of 1958. Less elegant, and more fun and affordable, is Nanaemon Pottery's extensive collection spread across the main room of their big farmhouse up the hill from Seiryūgama.

Back in the city proper there are a few other places of interest tucked here and there between Yamagata's modern buildings. Two kilometers west of the station is the Senshō-ji temple where you can pay your respects at the grave of Komahime, the 16-year-old daughter of a Mogami lord who was given to Shogun Toyotomi Hidetsugu in the sixteenth century to become another of his many mistresses. When the shogun was overthrown in a family power struggle, Hidetsugu's teenage present, Komahime, was executed along with the rest of his immediate family.

On the same side of town are the stately Meiji-era former prefectural office building northeast of the temple and the Yamagata-ken Bussankan, the prefectural products showroom, between Senshō-ji and the station.

Southwest of the station is a stone torii from the Heian period, the Ishizukuri Myōjin Torii. In the same general direction, in Teppō-machi, you can also see the Kōzen-ji temple's early Edo-style garden and its burial site of the Mogami lord Yoshimitsu. His remains were moved here when the Mogami clan lost power.

If you've come to Tōhoku during the hectic festival season of the first week of August, as so many of Tōhoku's visitors do to catch the Big Three festivals in Sendai, Aomori, and Akita, you can catch Number Four as well. For those who can stand more merry-making crowds, Yamagata City's Hanagasa Festival is held on the evenings of August 6th, 7th, and 8th each year. The city's main street fills with 10,000 dancers from all over the prefecture dancing and singing the famous Hanagasa Odori and wearing large straw hats called hanagasa, or flower hats, because of the safflowers which decorate them.

The festival was originally intended to thank the gods for the year's safflower crop, safflowers being at one time the most important export of the prefecture because of their use in making dyes and coloring cosmetics. Today the Hanagasa Festival is a giant celebration of summer and of the prefecture's heritage.

Now put on your walking shoes and catch a train or a bus for the mountain temple of Yamadera.

IN 860, YAMADERA, a branch of Enryaku-ji temple of Mount Hiei in Kyoto was opened on a hillside just northeast of present-day Yamagata City. The Hōjusan Risshaku-ji, more commonly called simply Yamadera (Mountain Temple), is a complex of buildings spread over the wooded slopes of Mount Hōju. Even if you don't make it all the way to the top of the hill's tree-lined gravel path, a visit to Yamadera will give you the good feeling of sharing the same pleasures of nature which attracted the first pilgrims to the hillside 1,100 years ago.

Yamadera is only 13 kilometers from Yamagata, a stop on the JNR's Senzan Line. There are accommodations in the village at the foot of the hill and there is a campground 4.5 kilometers southeast of Yamadera Station in Oku Yamadera. From Oku Yamadera a series of hiking trails begin through wooded gorges and cliffs, rock formations, and waterfalls along a river to the Futakuchi Onsen 15 kilometers away in Miyagi Prefecture.

You may at first find it difficult to share with Bashō "the profound tranquility and beauty of the place" as you walk from the station into a town that is one big tourist facility. You have to cross the river, turn to the right and walk past several blocks of nearly identical souvenir shops before coming to the entrance to the temple grounds. Standing out from the crowd of shops is a basket shop near the temple entrance which stocks the bamboo and straw articles once in daily use by back-country people but now attracttive to folkcraft collectors and the sentimental. The forked bamboo noodle scoops sold here make unique, inexpensive, and lightweight souvenirs.

Just after entering the temple grounds, you'll come to the Konponchū-dō, the temple building which houses the eternal light of Buddhism, a flame originally transported from Mount Hiei that has been constantly burning for over 1,000 years. The building itself was restored in 1358 and then again in 1963, but its unfinished wood has aged nicely over the past twenty years. Its image was carved by Jikaku Daishi, the temple's founder. The temple and its very special contents are Important National Treasures.

After passing the small Heian-style treasure house and a statue of Bashō, your serious climbing begins along the cryptomeria-lined stone steps leading to the summit, steps in some places broken, in some places nonexistent, and in some places so narrow that only one person can pass. The curving and climbing path is dotted with stone monuments, and you may run into an ancient woman selling soft drinks, miraculously appearing in a tiny clearing around a curve.

Although you may have to share your adventure with a steady stream of panting tourists and a few determined pilgrims in white, in Bashō's day the hillside was much quieter. Here in the late afternoon stillness he wrote his most famous haiku, one that nearly every Japanese can readily quote:

> In this hush profound,
> Into the very rocks it seeps—
> The cicada sound.

The Niōmon, the gate leading to the temple complex on the summit, is the largest structure on the hill. When it comes into view, you'll know you're almost there. The main temple is just ahead—but still uphill. Off to the left beyond the gate is the Godai-dō which offers a view of the valley below. And at the top is the Kaisan-dō where the temple's founder is entombed, and the first location of the sacred flame in the Konponchū-dō so many stone steps below. A huge stone lantern at the Okunoin marks the summit; it is one of the three largest such lanterns in Japan.

For those who consider this hillside hike child's play, there are side paths going across the hill near the top where you can walk along rocks holding onto a metal chain. Some say the view of the surrounding countryside is worth it. The descent, of course, is much easier and, like Bashō, you can stop to enjoy beautiful surroundings and listen for the sounds of nature.

Once you're safely on level ground again you have the choice of following the Senzan Line to Tōhoku's largest city, perhaps with a stop at Sakunami Onsen to ease your readjustment into bustling modern Japan (see Miyagi's Sendai section), or of heading back to Yamagata City to pick up the Ōu Main Line south so you won't miss Yamagata's famous Mount Zaō and the Uesugi clan castle town of Yonezawa.

Mount Zaō and Yonezawa

NEARLY EVERYONE in Japan has heard of the juhyō, the gigantic snowy "monsters" which inhabit the mountains of Zaō Quasi-National Park during the frosty months of January and February each year. Some people even visit this range of volcanic peaks on the Yamagata/Miyagi border just to gaze in awe at the strange and frightening forms the monsters take. But most others, totally wrapped up in their favorite wintertime activity, boldly whiz past the monsters with hardly a glance in their direction.

The latter group is made up of the over one million skiers who come to Zaō each winter to take advantage of the mountains' plethora of slopes, lifts, ropeways, and accommodations. They confidently share their winter playground with the giant but harmless creatures, knowing that the warm spring sun will soon turn the fearsome juhyō back into unintimidating alpine trees.

In the depths of winter on Mount Zaō, as the peaks of the park are collectively known, weather conditions are just right to coat the trees with iridescent layers of ice and snow, thereby creating the famous juhyō, literally the "silver thaw," of Zaō.

Once the snow melts and the mountains turn green, another breed of traveler comes to Zaō, on the Zaō Line, the Zaō Echo Line and the Zaō High Line toll roads to enjoy the mountain scenery—highlighted by the barren moonscape of Lake Okama—and to take advantage of the healthful and relaxing onsen waters which dot the slopes.

And long, long before the skiers, the monster gawkers, and the sightseers came to Zaō, as long ago as 873, religious pilgrims were coming here to what they called East Mountain to worship the mountain gods who lived there. But the gods weren't as hospitable as they could have been, and, in thoes days before roads, ropeways, and chairlifts, many people met with fatal accidents while climbing the slopes of Zaō.

In 1775 a large statue of Jizō, the guardian of dead spirits, was erected on the mountain to protect the souls of those who lost their lives on the mountain. You can visit this Jizō by using the highest ropeway to reach Mount Jizō and then walking for 15 minutes. (See Aomori's Shimokita Peninsula section for more on Jizō).

Modern visitors to Zaō often use Zaō Onsen as a convenient headquarters both for skiers and sightseers. It hosts two million tourists a year and in 1979 was the site of the Interski meeting of ski instructors of the world.

The onsen community is loaded with accommodations ranging from plush hotels to youth hostels. Three kokuminshukusha in the area are the Nishi Zaō San-so,[1] the Ryūzan-so,[2] and the Zaō Bōdai San-so.[3] A campground is located by Shiginoyachi Pond.

Zaō Onsen is a 45-minute bus ride from Yamagata City. The

1. Nishi Zaō San-so, Tsuchizaka, Yamagata-shi, Yamagata-ken 990; tel. (023632) 0525.
   西蔵王山荘　〒990　山形県山形市土坂
2. Ryūzan-so, Kawa-mae, Zaō Onsen, Yamagata-shi, Yamagata-ken 990–23; tel. (023694) 9457.
   竜山荘　〒990-23　山形県山形市蔵王温泉川前
3. Zaō Bōdai San-so, Zaō Bōdai, Kaminoyama-shi, Yamagata-ken 999–31; tel. (023679) 2121.
   蔵王坊平山荘　〒999-31　山形県上山市蔵王坊平

Ōu Main Line gets closest to the mountains at Kaminoyama City, also an onsen town. The 6.5 kilometer Zaō Line which connects the two onsen communities stays open all year.

If you're getting off the train in Kaminoyama to catch a bus for Zaō, you may want to make a short stop at the Kaisen-dō Museum, only a 5-minute walk from the station. The private museum has collection of Ming and Ching dynasty lacquerware and Japanese swords on exhibit.

From the Miyagi side of the mountains, the 26-kilometer-long Zaō Echo Line connects with the Tōhoku Expressway city of Murata, except when the toll road closes while winter runs its course from November to April. There are also ski slopes on this side of the quasi-national park.

About halfway through the Echo Line, the 2.5-kilometer-long Zaō High Line climbs a hill so visitors can have a look into the water-filled crater, Lake Okama. In sharp contrast to the whiteness of its barren surroundings, Lake Okama is an eerie green, a green in which subtle color changes occur several times daily. If you're driving through the Zaō mountains, a first-hand look at this often photographed scene is well worth a short stop.

If you're seeking both snow monsters and moonscapes from a trip through Zaō Quasi-National Park, you'll just have to come twice, once for Zaō in green and again for Zaō in white. On one of these visits you may pass through the city of Yonezawa, Yamagata's southern gateway, located just before the prefecture blends into neighboring Fukushima in the mountainous northern reaches of the Bandai–Asahi National Park.

YONEZAWA IS the last major stop before the Ōu Main Line terminates at Fukushima City. The former headquarters of the Uesugi clan, rulers of southern Yamagata for 250 years, is now a sizable city producing textiles and beef for modern Japan. Yonezawa has the dubious distinction of being the first site of rayon production in Japan. For some of you it may also have another dubious distinction—it is your last back-country experience before you catch the Tōhoku Shinkansen heading back to Tokyo.

For others, Yonezawa may mark the beginning of an exploration of the green mountains of the Bandai–Asahi National Park to the south. The Sky Valley Line toll road connects the city with the park that lies between Yonezawa and Aizu-Wakamatsu, Fukushima Prefecture's largest city.

The city of Yonezawa offers the visitor wanderings through the temples and shrines of the Uesugi clan and several nearby ski resorts.

Only parts of the moat and foundation remain where Yonezawa's castle once stood. The grounds are now Matsugasaki Park, a 10-minute bus ride west of the station along Highway 121 which bisects the city. The castle first belonged to the Datè clan of Miyagi Prefecture from 1238 until the Uesugi clan took it over 400 years later.

Today the park honors the second family to rule the area. The Uesugi Shrine now stands on the castle site, and next to it is the Uesugi Keishōden museum, a treasure house of historical materials and art treasures dating from the time of the Uesugi's most famous member, Kenshin. Uesugi Kenshin is known throughout Japan for his dramatic battle with Takeda Shingen, the Lord of Kai, in the sixteenth century.

If, like many Japanese, you are a Kenshin admirer, you can also visit the Uesugi Family Mausoleum northwest of the park and across the river. The bus to Onogawa Onsen passes by; get off at Gobyō-mae. Other Uesugi rulers are also buried here, those of even numbered generations on the right and the odd generations on the left. Kenshin's memorial is the large one in the center of the odds. His remains were moved here from the castle grounds in 1876.

Those with time to wander the area may want to visit two

old gardens south of Matsugasaki Park. The Old Uesugi Family Garden is less than a kilometer to the south. Further away and across the river is the highly praised garden of the Risen-ji temple.

If Christianity's struggle to take hold in Japan interests you, you'll also want to visit the Kita-Yamabara Martyrs' Site, a 12-minute bus ride northwest of the station. Take the bus for Akayu and get off at Kasuga 2-chome. Seventy-four Christians were decapitated here during the Tokugawa-era purge of Christianity from the land in the seventeenth century. The victims honored here are seventeen members of the Amakasu family and fifty-seven of their followers. Non-Christians of Yonezawa erected a Jizō statue at the site to protect the victims' souls; later local Christians added a statue of Christ on the cross and a German-made statue of the Virgin Mary.

Shoppers should note that local crafts are on display at the Kankō Bussankan, Tourist Products Showroom, near the park. Beyond the Uesugi Family Mausoleum along Highway 121 is the Yoneori Kankō Center where the local weaving called ori is on display.

Along with Yonezawa ori, a second local product also has a national reputation—Yonezawa beef. In addition to the usual steaks and sukiyaki, the tender beef is served East-meets-West style as sashimi, or paper-thin slices of raw beef, and as gyuniku misozuke, thin slices of beef marinated in miso and sometimes packaged to take home as a souvenir. Another local delicacy is koi, or carp, which Yonezawans have been eating raw, or deep-fried and in a sweet-and-sour sauce for 200 years. Sasano-itōbori, handcrafted wooden hawks, make nice nonedible souvenirs of Yonezawa. Tail feathers of paper-thin wood curls are their trademark.

If you come to town on May 3rd, you can really get into the spirit of the Yonezawa of feudal times. On this final day of the five-day annual Uesugi Festival, a kilometer-long procession of samurai on horseback parades through the streets. Many of the "samurai" are wearing their ancestors' armor and helmets to celebrate their personal links with Yonezawa history.

Several popular ski resorts can be found in the hills to the south of the city towards the Fukushima border. Along Highway 13 and the Ōu Main Line towards Fukushima City are the slopes of Yonezawa Ski Resort and the larger Kuriko International Ski Resort. And at the entrance to the Sky Valley toll road is the Tengendai International Ski Resort.

For travelers who like their mountains green instead of white, the Shirabu Kokuminkushusha[4] and a youth hostel located at Tengendai may be convenient springboards for a visit to the mountains, lakes, and ponds in the national park just beyond the toll road entrance.

THOSE LEAVING TŌHOKU from Fukushima City will no doubt feel a sense of regret that their back-country adventure is coming to an end, but also a sense of relief at the prospect of soon being back in the big city of Tokyo. In Tokyo, trains, subways, and buses run minutes rather than hours apart, everyone wants to practice their English, and you can stay in a first-class hotel and go out for French, Indian, Indonesian or whatever cuisine you feel like for dinner.

This is the Japan the back country is scurrying to catch up with. Tōhoku rightfully wants to share in the prosperity, comforts, conveniences, and opportunities which have already arrived in other parts of Japan. And the hardworking people of the back country, used to working harder for success in their harsh climate, will someday soon get theirs. Already the young of Tōhoku are speaking standard Japanese, bundling up for Tōhoku winters in ski jackets instead of traditional hanten quilted coats, and passing up their outstanding sushi shops for hamburgers

4. Shirabu Kokuminshukusha, Seki, Yonezawa-shi, Yamagata-ken 992–14; tel. (023855) 2207.
白布国民宿舎　〒992-14　山形県米沢市関

and fried chicken from various American-style fast-food chains.

Come back to the back country for another visit in another ten or twenty years and see how much it has gained on the rest of modern Japan—and be very, very glad you were able to experience Michinoku, Japan's back country, before it disappeared.

Japanese Historical Periods

Jōmon period c. 3,000–200 B.C.	Neolithic culture of hunters and fishermen; characterized by "cord-patterned" (jōmon) earthenware. Imperial dynasty founded by Jimmu (the great-great-great-grandson of the Sun Goddess) c. 660 B.C.
Yayoi period 200 B.C.–A.D. 250	Bronze culture introduced from the Asian mainland; beginning of agriculture, especially the cultivation of rice.
Tumulus period 250–552	Age of semi-legendary emperors of Yamato. The Yamato capital, or imperial residence, was moved upon each emperor's death, and tumuli were erected on the sites of abandoned capitals.
Asuka period 552–646	Buddhism first introduced (c. mid-sixth century); Shōtoku Taishi reformed and strengthened the growing Yamato state.
Nara period 646–794	Imperial residence established in Heijo, or Nara (710), the first permanent capital of Japan.
Heian period 794–1185	Imperial residence moved to Heian-kyō, or Kyoto (which remained the imperial capital until 1868); Yoshitsune defeated rival Tairas.
Kamakura period 1185–1336	Minamoto shogunate establishes military capital in Kamakura; Hōjō regency took over (1219); two Mongol invasions repelled.
Muromachi period 1336–1568	Ashikaga shogunate moved military capital to Kyoto.
Momoyama period 1568–1603	Period of civil strife; Oda Nobunaga and Toyotomi Hideyoshi rose as great leaders; Tokugawa Ieyasu emerged victorious in the struggle for supremacy.

310 · JAPANESE HISTORICAL PERIODS

Edo period 1603–1868	Tokugawa shogunat established legislative capital in Edo (Tokyo).
Meiji era 1868–1912	Restoration of emperor as ruler; imperial capital moved to Tokyo.
Taisho era 1912–26	Reign of current emperor's father.
Showa era 1926–present	Reign of Emperor Hirohito.

NOTE: You'll often run into the traditional Japanese dating system that is based on these historical periods and their subdivisions. For example, the year called Meiji 33 (the thirty-third year during which the emperor known as Meiji reigned) is 1900, and Shōwa 5 is 1930.

Principal Tōhoku Festivals

THE PEOPLE OF THE BACK COUNTRY love their festivals, or matsuri. Each community has several a year, often one or two in the spring, summer, or fall, and then another to break up the long, snowy winter. Some of these matsuri recreate ancient rites of primitive religions; other are much newer, some with commercial overtones. Some are even part of a circuit of traveling rent-a-festival operations which take their floats and concessions from town to town throughout the back country. Local citizens then individualize their festival with folk dancing groups and a few locally made floats.

With so many festivals throughout the district in communities of all sizes, this listing cannot be complete, so your chances of stumbling onto a local festival as you pass through a small town, especially during the festival month of August, are very good. And the townspeople will be especially glad you showed up just in time to share in their celebration.

JANUARY

1 Yamagata: Dewa Sanzan Shrine Festival
14 Miyagi: Sendai's Ōsaki Hachiman Shrine Dontosai Bonfire
17 Akita: Akita City's Miyoshi Shrine Bonden Festival
20 Iwate: Hiraizumi's torchlight Noh performances at Chūson-ji temple
midmonth Hadaka Mairi, naked festivals, held at local shrines throughout the district.

Young men in traditional fundoshi loincloths brave the cold and snow to test their endurance.

FEBRUARY

1–10 Iwate: Koiwai Ranch's Iwate Snow Festival
2nd week Aomori: Hirosaki's Snow Lantern Festival
13–15 Akita: Oga Peninsula's Shinzan Shrine Namahage Festival
15–16 Akita: Yokote's Kama-

kura (snow house) Festival

16–17   Akita: Yokote's Bonden Festival

15–17   Yamagata: Tsuruoka's Kuromori Kabuki performances

17–20   Aomori: Hachinohe's Emburi Festival (17th is best day)

March

10   Miyagi: Shiogama's Omikoshi (portable shrine) Festival

April

24–May 7   Aomori: Hirosaki's Sakura Matsuri (Cherry-Viewing Festival)

25   Miyagi: Shiogama Shrine's Hana Matsuri afternoon parade and evening fireworks

29–May 3   Yamagata: Yonezawa's Uesugi Shrine Festival

May

1–5   Iwate: Hiraizumi's Spring Fujiwara Matsuri (Noh performances, reenactment of Yoshitsune's flight on 3rd, and parade on 5th)

2–4   Iwate: Mizusawa's Komagata Horse Parade

3–5   Aomori: Towada City's Taiso Parade

3–7   Miyagi: Shiroishi's Kokeshi Festival

20   Yamagata: The Sannō Matsuri of Sakata's Hie Shrine

June

15   Iwate: Morioka's Chagu-chagu Horse Festival

July

3rd weekend   Aomori: Lake Towada Grand Opening

3rd weekend   Aomori: Misawa's Lake Ogawara Grand Opening

20–21   Akita: Lake Tazawa's festival

20–24   Aomori: Shimokita Peninsula's Osore-zan Itako Festival

23–24   Fukushima: Haranomachi's Sōma Nomaoi Wild Horse Festival

August

1   Aomori: Asamushi Onsen fireworks

1–7   Aomori: Hirosaki's Neputa

3–4   Miyagi: Ayukawa's Kujira (Whale) Festival fishing boat parade

3–7   Aomori: Aomori City's Nebuta (parades on 5th and 6th)

5   Miyagi: Shiogama's Port Festival decorated fishing boats parade

5–7   Akita: Akita City's Kantō Festival

1st Sunday   Fukushima: Hongō's Seto-ichi pottery market

6–7   Akita: Yuzawa's Tanabata E-doro Festival

6–7   Akita: Noshiro's Nebu Nagashi

6–8   Miyagi: Sendai's Tanabata

6–8 Yamagata: Yamagata City's Hanagasa

10 Miyagi: Iwadeyama's Masamunekō Sparrow's Dance Festival

11–16 Aomori: Towada City's Summer Festival

14 Iwate: torchlight Noh performances at Hiraizumi's Chūson-ji

14–16 Iwate: Morioka's Funakko Nagashi Obon Festival (floating lanterns on 16th)

15 Miyagi: Matsushima's Tōrō Nagashi (floating lanterns) Obon Festival

15 Aomori: Momoishi's evening fireworks

16 Iwate: Hiraizumi's Daimonji Okuribi hillside bonfire

18–20 Aomori: Noheji's Summer Festival

17–20 Aomori: Kuroishi's Summer Festival

21–23 Aomori: Hachinohe's Summer Festival

26–28 Aomori: Misawa's Summer Festival

last Sunday Akita: Omagari's national fireworks competition

(Obon, Buddhism's period when the spirits of deceased relatives return home takes place in mid-August in Tōhoku)

SEPTEMBER

7–9 Akita: Kakunodate's Shim-

mei Festival of colliding floats

7–9 Miyagi: Narugo's Kokeshi Festival

9–11 Aomori: Towada City's Autumn Festival

13–15 Fukushima: Shirakawa's Lantern Festival

14–16 Iwate: Morioka's Hachiman Shrine Festival

15–17 Aomori: Momoishi's Autumn Fsetival

22–24 Fukushima: Aizu-Wakamatsu's Byakko Festival

2nd or 3rd week (depending on lunar calendar) Aomori: Hirosaki's Mount Iwaki Oyamasankei

OCTOBER

4–5 Fukushima: Nihonmatsu's Lantern Festival

10 and 1st and 2nd Sundays Miyagi: Kinka-zan's deer-horn cutting

Mid-October–mid-November Aomori: Hirosaki's Chrysanthemum Festival

NOVEMBER

1–3 Iwate: Hiraizumi's Autumn Fujiwara Festival

DECEMBER

31-January 1 Akita: Oga Peninsula's Namahage Festival

English-Japanese Finding List

Abukuma Cavern　阿武隈洞
Adachigahara Onibaba Park
　安達ケ原鬼婆公園
airport (kūkō)　空港
Aizu History Museum　会津歴史館
Aizu-Hongō Yakimono Kaikan
　会津本郷焼物会館
Aizu Line　会津線
Aizu Minzoku Kan　会津民俗館
Aizu Sakè-brewing Museum　会津
　酒造博物館
Aizu Sakè-brewing History Museum
　会津酒造歴史館
Aizu-sō　会津荘
Aizu-Wakamatsu　会津若松
Aizu-Wakamatsu Green Hotel　会津
　若松グリーンホテル
Ajigasawa　鰺ケ沢
Akagami Shrine Gosha-dō　赤神
　神社五社堂
Akayu　赤湯
Akimoto, Lake　秋元湖
Akinomiya Onsen cluster　秋の宮
　温泉郷
Akinomiya San-sō　秋の宮山荘
Akita Airport　秋田空港
Akita Castle　秋田城
Akita City　秋田市

Akita City Art Museum　秋田市立
　美術館
Akita Prefecture　秋田県
Akita Prefectural Art Museum
　秋田県立美術館
Akiu Bungalow Village　秋保
　バンガロー村
Akiu Falls　秋保大滝
Akiu Onsen　秋保温泉
Amarume　余目
Anadōshi　穴通し
Anshō-ji temple　安勝寺
antique shop (kottō-ya)　骨董屋
Aoba Dōri　青葉通
Aobajō History Exhibit (Shiryō
　Tenjikan)　青葉城資料展示館
Aobayama　青葉山
Aoike pond　青池
Aone Onsen　青根温泉
Aoni Onsen　青荷温泉
Aoyagi Family House　青柳家住宅
Arakawa　荒川
Arakawa Plateau　荒川高原
Araya Barrier Station　新谷番所跡
art museum (bijutsukan)　美術館
Asadokoro Kaigan beach　浅所海岸
Asahi Okayama Shrine　旭岡山神社
Asamushi Onsen　浅虫温泉

Asaseishi River　浅瀬石川
Ashino Kōen Station　芦野公園駅
Ashinomaki Onsen　芦ノ牧温泉
Aspite Line　アスピーテライン
Atago Park　愛宕公園
Atago Shrine　愛宕神社
Ayaori Station　綾織駅
Ayukawa　鮎川

Babachō　馬場町
Bandai–Asahi National Park　磐梯
　朝日国立公園
Bandai–Azuma Lake Line　磐梯
　吾妻レークライン
Bandai–Azuma Sky Line　磐梯吾妻
　スカイライン
Bandai Gold Line　磐梯ゴールド
　ライン
Bandai Kōgen plateau　磐梯高原
Ban'etsu East Line　磐越東線
Ban'etsu West Line　磐越西線
Banji Iwa　磐司岩
bath house, public (kyōdō yokujō)
　共同浴場
beach (hama, kaigan)　浜，海岸
Benkei-dō　弁慶堂
boat, ferry　フェリー
boat, sightseeing (kankō-sen)
　観光船
Buke-yashiki　武家屋敷
business hotel　ビジネスホテル
bus stop　バス停留所
bus terminal　バスターミナル

castle (shiro, -jo)　城
Chiba Family Magariya　千葉家曲屋
Chidōkan　致道館
Chidō Museum　致道博物館
Chitose Kaigan beach　千歳海岸
Chōjasan Park　長者山公園
Chōja Shrine　長者神社
Chōkai, Mount　鳥海山
Chōkai Blue Line　鳥海ブルー
　ライン
Chōraku-ji temple　長楽寺

Chōraku-ji Youth Hostel　長楽寺
　ユースホテル
Chōshō-ji temple　長勝寺
Chosuichi-mae　貯水地前
Christian Martyrs' Monument
　キリシタン殉教碑
Chūō Dōri　中央通リ
Chūō Hirosaki Station　中央弘前駅
Chūson-ji temple　中尊寺
Chūson-ji Hondō　中尊寺本堂
city (shi)　市
Cobalt Line　コバルトライン
Cobalt-sō　コバルト荘
coffee shop (kissaten)　喫茶店

Deko-yashiki　デコ屋敷
department store (depāto)　デパート
Dewa Sanzan　出羽三山
Dewa Sanzan History Museum
　出羽三山歴史博物館
Doroyu Onsen　泥湯温泉

east (higashi)　東
Ebisu-ya　恵比須屋
Eboshi-sō　烏帽子荘
Enkaku-ji temple　円覚寺
Entsū-ji temple　円通寺
Entsū-ji Bodai-ji temple　円通寺
　菩提寺
Ezo-kan　蝦夷館

festival (matsuri)　祭
folkcraft shop (mingei-ten)　民芸店
folk museum (mingeikan)　民芸館
Fubō-kaku Kōgen Hotel　不忘閣
　高原ホテル
Fudai　普代
Fujimi Ryokan　富士見旅館
Fukagawa-chō　深川町
Fukaura　深浦
Fukiage Kōgen plateau　吹上高原
Fukura　吹浦
Fukurajima　福浦島
Fukusen-ji Kannon　福泉寺観音
Fukushima City　福島市

Fukushima Prefecture　福島県
Funakoshi Peninsula　船越半島
Furukawa　古川
Furuhata Ryokan　古畑旅館
Furukuchi　古口
Futakuchi Onsen　二口温泉

Ganjō-ji temple　願成寺
garden (-en)　園
Gassai-den　合祭殿
Gassan, Mount　月山
Gassan Ski Resort　月山スキー場
Gassan-sō　月山荘
gasoline station　ガソリンスタンド
Geibikei Gorge　猊鼻渓
Gembikei Gorge　厳美渓
Gobansho Tenbō Park　御番所展望
　公園
Gobyō-mae　御廟前
Godai-dō　五大堂
Gohyaku (500) Rakan　五百羅漢
Goishi Kaigan beach　碁石海岸
Gojū no tō　五重塔
Gokoku Jinja-mae　護国神社前
Gokoku Shrine　護国神社
Gonohe　五戸
Gonō Line　五能線
Gotō Monument　後藤伍長雪中
　行軍遭難者銅像
Goshikinuma　五色沼
Goshikinoma Iriguchi Bus Stop
　五色沼入口バス停
Goshugawara　五所川原
Gourd Line　ゴードライン

Hachibōdai Lookout　八望台
Hachiman-gū Shrine　八幡宮
Hachiman Jinja-mae　八幡神社前
Hachiman Mikaeri Tōge Bus Stop
　八幡見返り峠バス停
Hachiman-numa　八幡沼
Hachimantai　八幡平
Hachimantai Ski Resort　八幡平
　スキー場
Hachinohe　八戸

Hachinohe Historical and Folk
　Museum　八戸歴史民族館
Hachinohe Harbor　八戸港
Hachinohe Line　八戸線
Hachirōgata　八郎潟
Hagino Kōminkan　萩野公民館
Haguro, Mount　羽黒山
Haguro Kokumin Kyūka Mura
　羽黒国民休暇村
Haguro-san Driveway　羽黒山
　ドライブウェイ
Hakkōda Mountains　八甲田山
Hakkōda Ropeway　八甲田ロープ
　ウェイ
Hakubutsukan-mae　博物館前
Hamahata-chō　浜畑町
hamlet (buraku)　部落
Hanamaki　花巻
Hanamaki Airport　花巻空港
Hanamaki Onsen Prefectural Nat-
　ural Park　花巻温泉県立自然公園
Hanawa　花輪
Hanawa Line　花輪線
Hanayama　花山
Hanayama Gobansho　花山御番所
Hanayama Youth Travel Village
　花山青年旅行村
Hanzō　半造
Hara Takashi Museum　原敬記念館
Haranomachi　原町
harbor　港
Haristo Sei Kyōkai　ハリスト聖教会
Hasekura Tsunenaga Monument
　支倉常長石碑
Hashimoto Art Museum　橋本
　美術館
Hayachine, Mount　早池峰山
Heiwa Park　平和公園
Hibara, Lake　檜原湖
Hibara-sō　檜原荘
Hibarino　雲雀野
Higashi Futō　東埠頭
Higashi Hachimantai　東八幡平
Higashi Noshiro　東能代
Higashiyama Onsen　東山温泉

highway ハイウェイ
Hijiori Onsen 肘折温泉
Hinokinai River 檜内川
Hiraizumi 平泉
Hirano Collection 平野コレク
ション
Hirasawa 平沢
Hirashimizu 平清水
Hirosaki 弘前
Hirosaki Park 弘前公園
Hirose River 広瀬川
historical museum (rekishi hakubu-
tsukan) 歴史博物館
Hiyoriyama Park 日和山公園
Hōjin-no-ie 封人の家
Hōjusan Risshaku-ji temple 宝珠山
立石寺
Hokkaido 北海道
Hokubu Rikuchū Kaigan Toll Road
北部陸中海岸有料道路
Hokugen-kaku 北限閣
Homma Art Museum 本間美術館
Homma Family Main House
本間家本邸
Hongō 本郷
Hon-Hachinohe Station 本八戸駅
Hōon-ji temple 報恩寺
Hōrai-sō 蓬莱荘
Horinai Station 堀内駅
Horozuki Kaigan 袰月海岸
Hosokura Station 細倉駅
Hosoura Station 細浦駅
hotel ホテル
Hotel Kaibō-en ホテル海望苑
Hotel Kokumin Kenkō Shukusha
ホテル国民健康宿舎
Hotel New Yagen ホテルニュー
薬研
Hotokegaura Coastline 仏ケ浦
海岸
Hyakuzawa 百沢

Ibaraki Prefecture 茨木県
Ichibancho 一番町
Ichinohe 一戸

Ichinoseki 一の関
Ikarigaseki 碇ケ関
Imabetsu 今別
Imagami Onsen 今神温泉
Iimoriyama 飯盛山
Iimori Iriguchi Bus Stop 飯盛入口
バス停
Inawashiro, Lake 猪苗代湖
Irimizu Cavern 入水鍾乳洞
Ishigado 石ケ戸
Ishigami-chō 石上町
Ishikawa Ryokan 石川旅館
Ishikoshi 石越
Ishinomaki 石巻
Ishizukuri Myojin Torii 石造明神
鳥居
Itadome Onsen 板留温泉
Itozawa Station 糸沢駅
Iwadeyama 岩出山
Iwahashi Family House 岩橋家住宅
Iwaizaki 岩井崎
Iwaizumi 岩泉
Iwaki (Fukushima) いわき
Iwaki, Mount 岩木山
Iwaki Kaigan beach 磐木海岸
Iwaki Shrine 岩木神社
Iwaki Skyline 岩木スカイライン
Iwamatsu Ryokan 岩松旅館
Iwanami 岩波
Iwasaki 岩崎
Iwate, Mount 岩手山
Iwate-Funakoshi Station 岩手
船越駅
Iwate-Futsukamachi Station 岩手
二日町駅
Iwate Prefecture 岩手県
Iwate Prefectural Museum 岩手
県立博物館
Iwate-sanroku Kokumin Kyūka
Mura 岩手山麓国民休暇村
Iwayama 岩山
Izumida 泉田
Izumi Station 泉駅

Jinya Restaurant レストラン陣屋

Jizō, Mount 地蔵山
Jōban Line 常磐線
Jōban Hawaiian Center 常磐ハワイ
  センター
Jōban-Yunodake Panorama Line
  常磐湯ノ岳パノラマライン
Jōdogahama beach 浄土ケ浜
Jōdogahama Toll Road 浄土ケ浜
  有料道路
Jōetsu Line 上越線
Jōken-ji 常堅寺
Jōsen-ji Iriguchi Bus Stop 浄泉寺
  入口バス停留所
Jōsen-ji temple 浄泉寺
Jōshidai-mae 女子大前
Jōzen-ji Dōri 定禅寺通
Jūniko 十二湖
Jūichimen Kannon 十一面観音
Jūroku Rakan Iwa 十六羅漢岩

Kabushima 蕪島
Kadokawa 角川
Kaichū Park 海中公園
Kairaku-en garden 偕楽園
Kaisan-dō 開山堂
Kaiseikan 開成館
Kaiseizan Park 開成山公園
Kai Shōten 甲斐商店
Kajimachi kiln 鍛治町焼
Kakunodate 角館
Kakunodate Denshōkan 角館
  伝承館
Kamaishi 釜石
Kamaishi Dai Kannon 釜石大観音
Kamaishi Line 釜石線
Kamasaki Onsen 鎌先温泉
Kamasaki Point 鎌崎
Kamataya Youth Hostel 鎌田屋
  ユースホステル
Kamegaoka Museum 亀ケ岡考古館
Kaminohashi 上の橋
Kaminoyama 上の山
Kamiyanagi Bus Stop 上柳バス停
Kammata Station 神俣駅
Kampū-zan Lookout 寒風山展望台

Kampū-zan Toll Road 寒風山有料
  道路
Kanagi 金木
Kanagi Historical and Cultural
  Museum 金木歴史文化資料館
Kanita 蟹田
kankō bus 観光バス
kankō bussankan 観光物産館
Kankō-sen Hatchaku-jo Pier
  観光船発着所
kankō hotel 観光ホテル
Kanōzu Bansho 叶津番所
Kanrantei 観瀾亭
Kappa-buchi pool 河童渕
Karakuwa Peninsula 唐桑半島
Karakuwa-sō 唐桑荘
Kasaishi House, (old) 旧笠石家
Kashima Station 鹿島駅
Kashi Onsen 甲子温泉
Kashō-en 佳松園
Kasuga Ni-chōme 春日二丁目
Kasumigajō Park 霞ケ城公園
Katayama Jigoku 片山地獄
Kawabe 川部
Kawarage Jigoku-zan 川原毛
  地獄山
Kaya no Chaya 萱の茶屋
Kazuno 鹿角
Keikokan 稽古館
Kesen-numa 気仙沼
Kesen-numa Line 気仙沼線
Kesen-numa Ōshima Kokumin
  Kyūka Mura 気仙沼大島国民
  休暇村
Kijiyama Kōgen Plateau 木地山
  高原
Kinka-zan 金華山
Kinrōsha Ikoi no Mura Kurikoma
  勤労者いこいの村栗駒
Kinzoku Hakubutsukan-mae 金属
  博物館前
Kisakata 象潟
Kisen Hatchaku-jo Pier 汽船発着所
Kitakami 北上
Kitakata 喜多方

Kitakata Green Hotel 喜多方
グリーンホテル
Kitakawa Family Oshira-sama
House 北川オシラサマの家
Kitayama 北山
Kita-Yamabara Martyrs' Site
北山原殉教遺跡
Kita-Yamazaki Lookout Point
北山崎展望台
Kizukuri 木造
Koganeyama Shrine 黄金山神社
Kōgensha 光源社
Kogota 小牛田
Koiwai Ranch 小岩井牧場
Koiwai Station 小岩井駅
Koiwai Toll Road 小岩井有料道路
Kojō-san 古城山
Kokeshi Dōri こけし通り
Kokuji-yaki 小久慈焼
Kokumin Hoyō Center Senshin-sō
国民保養センター洗心荘
kokumin kyūka mura 国民休暇村
kokuminshukusha 国民宿舎
Kokuminshukusha Matsukawa Ura
国民宿舎松川浦
Kokuminshukusha Oga 国民宿舎
男鹿
Kokuminshukusha Towada 国民
宿舎とわだ
Kokuminshukusha Towada-ko
国民宿舎十和田湖
Komaga Peak 駒ケ岳
Komagata Shrine 駒形神社
Komaki Onsen 古牧温泉
Komakusa-sō 駒草荘
Komanoyu Onsen 駒の湯温泉
Kōma Station 好摩駅
Kominato Station 小湊駅
Kōminkan-mae 公民館前
Komoto 小本
Kōmyō-ji temple 光明寺
Kōnan Bus Station 弘南バス駅
Kōnan Testudō Line 弘南鉄道
Konjiki-dō 金色堂
Konpōnchu-dō 根本中堂

Korekawa 是川
Kōriyama 郡山
Kōriyama Bara-en 郡山バラ園
Kosode Kaigan beach 小袖海岸
Kōzen-ji temple 光禅寺
Kubota Castle 久保田城
Kuji 久慈
Kuji Line 久慈線
Kumano Shrine 熊野神社
Kunohe 九戸
Kurihara Dentetsu 栗原電鉄
Kuriko International Ski Resort
栗子国際スキー場
Kurikoma Quasi-National Park
栗駒国定公園
Kuroishi 黒石
Kuroishi Onsen Prefectural Natural
Park 黒石温泉郷県立自然公園
Kuromori Hill 黒森山
Kurosaki-sō 黒崎荘
Kuroyu Onsen 黒湯温泉
Kusanagi Onsen 草薙温泉
Kushibiki Hachiman Shrine 櫛引
八幡神社
Kyōdokan 郷土館
Kyōun-sō 狭雲荘
Kyōzō 経蔵
Kyūbunhama 給分浜

lake (mizuumi, -ko) 湖
Lu Hsün Monument 魯迅の碑

Mabechi River 馬渕川
Magata 曲田
Makado Onsen 馬門温泉
Manjū Fukashi 饅頭ふかし
Maria-en Tenshu-dō マリア園
天主堂
Marumitsu-mae Bus Stop 丸光前
バス停
Masuzawa Station 鱒沢駅
Matsuba Station 松葉駅
Matsuba Youth Hostel 松葉ユース
ホステル
Matsugasaki Park 松ヶ崎公園

Nanko Park 南湖公園
Nara Family House 奈良家住宅
Naraoka pottery 楢岡焼
Narugo 鳴子
Narugo Gorge 鳴子峡
Nasukashi Toll Road 那須甲子有料道路
Nasu Kokumin Kyūka Mura 那須国民休暇村
Nasu Onsen 那須温泉
national highway (kokudō) 国道
Natori Rapids 名取渓流
Natsudomari Peninsula 夏泊半島
Nebuta-no-sato ねぶたの里
Nehama Kaigan Campground 根浜海岸キャンプ場
Nenokuchi 子ノ口
Nezugaseki Barrier 鼠ケ関
Nibetsu Forest Museum 仁別森林博物館
Nibetsu Public Forest 仁別国民の森
Nihō-ji temple 如宝寺
Nihon Canyon 日本キャニオン
Nihon Kokeshi-kan 日本こけし館
Nihonmatsu 二本松
Niigata 新潟
Nikkawa Line 新川線
Nikko National Park 日光国立公園
Ninohe 二戸
Niōmon 仁王門
Nishi-Azuma Sky Valley Line 西吾妻スカイバレーライン
Nishine Interchange 西根インターチェンジ
Nishi-Towada-sō 西十和田荘
Nishi-Towada Youth Hostel 西十和田ユースホステル
Nishi-Wakamatsu Station 西若松駅
Nishi Zaō 西蔵王
Nishi-Zaō San-so 西蔵王山荘
Nitagai Bus Stop 似田貝バス停
Noguchi Hideyo Memorial Museum 野口英世記念館
Noda 野田

Noda-Tamagawa Station 野田玉川駅
Noheji 野辺地
Noh theater 能楽堂
north (kita) 北
Noshiro 能代
Noshiro Onsen 能代温泉
Nurukawa Onsen 温川温泉
Nuruyu 温湯
Nyūdō, Cape 入道埼
Nyūdōzaki Hachibōdai Toll Road 入道埼八望台有料道路
Nyūtō Onsen 乳頭温泉
Nyūtō San-sō lodge 乳頭山荘

Obuke Station 大更駅
Ochiai 落合
Odachi 小立
Ōdate 大館
Ōfunato 大船戸
Ōfunato Line 大船戸線
Oga 男鹿
Ogachi-machi 雄勝町
Ōgama 大窯
Ogami Shrine 遠賀美神社
Ogata 大潟
Ogawara, Lake 小川原湖
Ōgon-dō pavilion 黄金堂
Ohanabe, Mount 御鼻部山
Ohara Onsen 小原温泉
Ōhashi bridge 大橋
Ōhata 大畑
Ōhata Line 大畑線
Okazakinohama Camp 岡崎の浜キャンプ場
Ōhazama 大迫
Oirase River Valley 奥入瀬渓流
Oiwake Station 追分駅
Okama, Lake お金湖
Okatsu 雄勝
Okinajima 翁島
Okinajima-sō 翁島荘
Okiura bus stop 沖浦バス停
Oku-Aizu Folk Museum 奥会津民芸館

Oku-Nikkawa 奥新川
Okunoin 奥の院
Oku-Yagen 奥薬研
Oku-Yamadera 奥山寺
Ōmagari City 大曲市
Ōmazaki 大間埼
Ōmori Town 大森町
Ōminato Line 大湊線
Ōminato Naval Base 大湊海軍基地
Onagawa 女川
Onagawa Onsen 女川温泉
Onikōbe Lodge 鬼首ロツジ
Onikōbe Onsen Cluster 鬼首温泉郷
Onoe Town 尾上町
Onagawa, Lake 女川湖
On'naishōja 恩愛精舎
Onsen 温泉
Onsen Shrine 温泉神社
Ōnuma Lodge 大沼ロッジ
Ōsaki Hachiman Shrine 大崎八幡
神社
Osanai Bridge 長内橋
Ōsanbashi Toll Road 大桟橋
Oshakujima 御積島
Oshika Peninsula 牡鹿半島
Oshika Town Whaling Museum
牡鹿町立鯨博物館
Oshima (Matsushima) 雄島
Ōshima 大島
Oshitate Onsen 押立温泉
Osore-zan 恐山
Ōtaki Onsen 大滝温泉
Otamayabashi Bus Stop お霊屋橋
バス停
Ōtanabu 大田名部
Ōtanabu Port 大田名部港
Ōuchijuku 大内宿
Ōu Main Line 奥羽本線
Ōwani 大鰐
Oyaku-en 御薬園
Oyasu Onsen 小安温泉
Ōyu 大湯
Ōyu Stone Circle 大湯ストーン
サークル
Ōzuchi 大槌

Ōzuchi-so 大槌荘

park (kōen) 公園
peninsula (hantō) 半島
plateau (kōgen) 高原
pond (numa) 沼
port (Minato, -kō) 港
post office (yūbin kyoku) 郵便局
pottery shop 焼物店
prefecture (ken) 県
Puutaro- mura プータロ村

Rikuchū Hanawa Station 陸中
花輪駅
Rikuchū Kaigan National Park
陸中海岸国立公園
Rikuchū-Matsukawa Station 陸中
松川駅
Rikuchū Miyako Kokumin Kyūka
Mura 陸中宮古国民休暇村
Rikuchū Takada Station 陸中
高田駅
Rikuu East Line 陸羽東線
Rikuu West Line 陸羽西線
Rikuzen Hashikami Station 陸前
階上駅
Rikuzen Takada Station 陸前
高田駅
Ringo Park りんご公園
Rinnō-ji temple 輪王寺
Rinsen-ji temple 林泉寺
river (kawa) 川
road (michi) 道
Rokunohe 六戸
Rōsoku Iwa 蠟燭岩
ryokan 旅館
Ryūsen-dō cave 竜泉洞
Ryūsen-dō Youth Travel Village
竜泉洞青少年旅行村
Ryūzan-sō 竜山荘

Sabishiro beach 淋代海岸
Saginoyu 鷺の湯
Sai 佐井
Saigyodō Park 祭魚洞公園

Saiseikan　済生館
Saishō-in Pagoda　最勝院五重塔
Sakaida　堺田
Sakata　酒田
Sakata City Bussankan　酒田市物産館
Sakunami Onsen　作並温泉
Sakura Kaikan　さくら会館
Sakura-sō　さくら荘
Samè Station　鮫駅
Samuraihama Station　侍浜駅
Sanbiru Department Store　サンビル・デパート
Sankōzō　讃衡蔵
Sannohe　三戸
Sannō-kaku　山王閣
Sannō Plaza Hotel　山王プラザホテル
Sannō Station　山王駅
Sanriku　山陸
Sanjūsan Kannon　三十三観音
Sazae-dō　さざえ堂
Seibi-en garden　盛美園
Seigan-ji temple　誓願寺
Seikan Undersea Tunnel　青函海底トンネル
Seiryūgama　青竜釜
Sekiōzen-ji Bussharitō　石応禅寺仏舎利塔
Seki Sakè Factory　関酒造店
Sendai　仙台
Sendai City Museum　仙台市立博物館
Sendai Museum of History and Ethnology　仙台市歴史民俗資料館
Senjinzawa　千人沢
Senjōjiki　千畳敷
Sennin Tunnel　仙人トンネル
Senseki Line　仙石線
Senshō-ji temple　専称寺
Senshū Line　仙秋ライン
Senshū Park　千秋公園
Senzan Line　仙山線
Seto-machi Dōri　瀬戸町通リ
Shariki　車力

Shayōkan　斜陽館
Shichirinagahama beach　七里長浜海岸
Shichinohe　七戸
Shifuku-ji temple　資福寺
Shiginoyachi Pond　鴫ノ谷地沼
Shimanokoshi Port　島の越港
Shimofuro　下風呂
Shimokita Peninsula　下北半島
Shimokita Station　下北駅
Shimonohashi　下の橋
Shinzan Shrine　真山神社
Shiofuki Ana　潮吹穴
Shiogama　塩釜
Shioyazaki-sō　塩屋埼荘
Shingō　新郷
Shinjō　新庄
Shirabu Kokuminshukusha　白布国民宿舎
Shiraito-no-Taki　白糸の滝
Shirakawa　白河
Shirakawa Barrier　白河の関
Shiriyazaki　尻屋埼
Shiroishi　白石
Shiroyama Park　城山公園
Shizu Village　志津村
Shizukuishi　雫石
Shōnai　庄内
shopping area (shōten-gai)　商店街
shrine (jinja)　神社
ski slope/resort　スキー場
Sōma　相馬
south (minami)　南
souvenir shop　土産屋
station (eki)　駅
Suemaru Ryokan　末丸旅館
Sugawa Onsen　須川温泉
Sugaya Station　菅谷駅
Sugiyama　杉山
Suigun Line　水郡線
Suiren Numa　水蓮沼
Sukagawa Botan-en　須賀川牡丹園
Sukayu Onsen　酸ヶ湯温泉
Sunroad　サンロード
Suzuro Pastry Shop　お菓子処寿々炉

Towada Onsen Hotel 十和田温泉ホテル

Towada Science Museum 十和田科学博物館

town (machi) 町

Tōzō Ryokan 藤三旅館

train line (sen) 線

Tsubakiyama 椿山

Tsubo Stone つぼの石碑

Tsugaru Onoe Station 津軽尾上駅

Tsugaru Peninsula 津軽半島

Tsugaru Quasi-National Park 津軽国定公園

Tsugaru Straits 津軽海峡

Tsukinoura bay 月の浦

Tsukidate 月館

Tsurugajō castle 鶴ケ城

Tsurugamine Bus Stop 剣ケ峰バス停

Tsuruoka 鶴岡

Tsuruoka Hotel 鶴岡ホテル

Tsuruoka Jōshi Park 鶴岡城跡公園

Tsuta Onsen 蔦温泉

Tsutsujigaoka Park 榴ケ岡公園

Tsutsumi 堤

Tsutsumi pottery 堤焼

Tsuzuki Stone 続石

Uchi-machi 内町

Uesugi Family Garden, (Old) 旧上杉家庭園

Uesugi Family Mausoleum 上杉家御廟

Uesugi Keishōden museum 上杉稽照殿

Uesugi Shrine 上杉神社

Uetsu Main Line 羽越本線

Unedori Shrine 卯子酉神社

Unosumai Station 鵜の住居駅

Uoichiba fish market 魚市場

Ura Bandai Kokumin Kyūka Mura 裏磐梯国民休暇村

Ura Bandai Kokuminshukusha 裏磐梯国民宿舎

Ura Bandai Mingei-kan 裏磐梯民芸館

Usori, Lake 宇曽利湖

Utarube 宇樽部

village (mura) 村

Wainai 和井内

Wakaki Shoten 若喜商店

Wakayanagi 若柳

Wakimoto Station 脇本駅

Wakinosawa 脇野沢

Wappameshi Takino わっぱめし田季野

west (nishi) 西

Yagen Onsen 薬研温泉

Yahagi Family House 矢作家住宅

Yakeyama 焼山

Yamada 山田

Yamada Line 山田線

Yamadera 山寺

Yamagata City 山形市

Yamagata Prefecture 山形県

Yamagata Old Prefectural Office Building 旧山形県庁

Yamagata Prefectural Art Museum 山形県立美術館

Yamagata Prefectural Museum 山形県立博物館

Yamagata Prefectural Products Showroom 山形県物産館

Yamato Urushi Lacquerware History Museum やまとうるし歴史館

Yasumiya 休屋

Yatsumori 八森

Yawata Uma Manufacturing Company 八幡馬製造合資会社

Yokokawa Minshuku Village 横川民宿村

Yokohori Station 横堀駅

Yoko River Gorge 横川渓谷

Yokote 横手

Yoneori Kanko Center 米織観光センター

Yoneshiro River 米代川

Glossary-Index

Abukuma Cavern, Fukushima, 34
airports, 67, 114, 170, 253
Aizu-Wakamatsu, Fukushima, 39–47
Akita City, 253–58, Fig. 24
Aomori City, 193–200
Aoni Onsen, Aomori, 216
Asamushi Onsen, Aomori, 192

Bandai–Asahi National Park, 50, 57–59
Bashō, Matsuo: Japan's best known haiku poet, who wrote about his trip to Tōhoku in 1689, 3, 5, 6–7, Fig. 1; on Akita, 275–76; on Fukushima, 25; on Iwate, 102, 106, 108; on Miyagi, 81–82; on Yamagata, 274, 281, 289, 293, 300, 301
buses, local tourist (kankō bus); 12; Akita, 249; Aomori, 203; Fukushima, 37, 40, 47, 57-58, Iwate, 115; Miyagi, 73

campgrounds, 16, 18; Akita, 149, 240, 249, 256, 264, 266, 269; Aomori, 164, 173, 183, 184, 189, 203, 205, 213, 216, 231, 236, 237, 239; Fukushima, 30, 32, 34–35, 49, 54, 59; Iwate, 103, 123, 132,

148, 270; Miyagi, 68, 70, 91, 94; Rikuchū Kaigan, 138, 139, 140, 141, 142, 143; Yamagata, 277, 292, 300, 303
Chitose Kaigan, Iwate, 161
Chōkai Quasi-National Park, 276–77

Dewa Sanzan, Yamagata, 288–92

folkcrafts, see mingei
foods, local specialties: Akita, 243, 251–52; Aomori, 158, 166, 191–92, 200, 212, 225, 235; Fukushima, 47; Iwate, 122, 124; Yamagata, 273, 281, 306
Fukushima City, 37–38

Geibikei Gorge, Iwate, 111
Gembikei Gorge, Iwate, 103
Goishi Beach, Iwate, 138–39
Goshogawara, Aomori, 229
government-sponsored lodges, see kokuminshukusha

Hachimantai mountains, 146–49
Hachinohe, Aomori, 163–69
Hachirōgata, Akita, 248–49
Hakkōda mountains, 200–208, Fig. 18, 23

327

JAN BROWN first came to Japan in 1969 and lived in Tokyo for five years. Accompanying her husband, an Air Force officer, on his next assigments, she was able to return to Japan, this time staying in Misawa, Aomori Prefecture, in 1977. Since that time she has been a part-time instructor of business, management, marketing, and English at the Misawa Air Base campus of the University of Maryland. Keenly interested in all aspects of Japan, she has traveled extensively, especially throughout Tohoku; in fact, the notes taken during her many trips form the basis of this guidebook. Her collaborator, Yoko Sakakibara Kmetz, majored in English and now teaches Japanese for the University of Maryland. She has also translated a book by Alan Watts into Japanese.

The "weathermark" identifies this book as a production of John Weatherhill, Inc., publishers of fine books on Asia and the Pacific. Book design and typography: Miriam F. Yamaguchi and Stephen B. Comee. Layout of the monochrome illustrations: Yutaka Shimoji. Composition: Korea Textbook Co., Seoul. Printing of the text: Shōbundō, Tokyo. Platemaking and printing of monochrome illustrations: Kinmei, Tokyo. Binding: Okamoto Binderies, Tokyo. The text is set in Monotype Times New Roman.